CALCULATE LIKE A GRANDMASTER

Learn from the world-class attacking players

Danny Gormally

BATSFORD

First published in the United Kingdom in 2010 by

Batsford
Old West London Magistrates' Court
10 Southcombe Street
London
W14 0RA

An imprint of Anova Books Company Ltd

ISBN:9781906388690

A CIP catalogue record for this book is available from the British Library.
10 9 8 7 6 5 4 3 2 1

Reproduction by Spectrum Colour Ltd, Ipswich

Printed and bound by Bell & Bain Ltd, Glasgow

This book can be ordered direct from the publisher at the website:
www.anovabooks.com

Or try your local bookshop

Contents

Index of Games

Meaning of Symbols

+ Check

± White has a slight advantage

± White has a great advantage

+- White is winning

∓ Black has a slight advantage

∓ Black has a great advantage

-+ Black is winning

∞ unclear position

Introduction

I am often approached by people who ask me the question, "How do I study?" or "What must I do to improve my chess?" Interesting questions to which there is no easy reply. I normally fob them off by giving them the stock response, "I study master games, my own games etc.", whilst not really knowing the answer myself.

One of the first books that attracted my attention when I was first getting into chess was Alexander Kotov's classic *Think like a Grandmaster*. Here was a book that got down to the nitty gritty of how top players actually analyse and calculate in a way that had probably not been done before, or at least not very well. It introduced the 'tree of analysis' into the public chess domain, breaking down the thought processes that go into selecting each move.

It seems to me that such books, which delve into the methods that grandmasters use in identifying candidate moves, are surprisingly few and far between. Of course top players are not always keen to give away their secrets, the secrets of their success, for fear that by giving their methods away the general chess public will be more easily able to elevate themselves to their level – and thus the mythical 'golden key' (sorry I just made that up) to chess success remains hidden. Not that there really is a key, a system, to chess improvement. There is no easy solution to the problem of how to improve, such a question can only possibly be answered through hard work and application.

Therefore the analysis by grandmasters in chess magazines and publications tends to be watered down a little, with the notable exception in recent years of the Dvoretsky books, which stand out in both the quality of their analysis and their honesty. As a friend of mine once said, serious study of those books will add between 100 and 200 points to your Elo rating (incidentally, with this book I'm looking for 300).

One of the things that constantly surprises me is how even very strong chess players are so staid and complacent when it comes to subjecting their chess weaknesses to thorough scrutiny, trying to 'think outside the box' so to speak. What characterises the truly great players in any sport or competitive activity is a willingness to take risks, to take the hard road to achievement, to play without fear, so to speak. When a Roger Federer or a Tiger Woods makes a mistake, that mistake is magnified a million times, but it is precisely their willingness to take risks, to play without a safety net, that brought them to the pinnacle of their sport in the first place.

With this book I have firstly selected the games of Mikhail Tal, as I believe he paved the way for the new generation of attacking players, the Shirovs, the Morozevichs and of course Kasparov and Anand. And of course he ideally fits the criteria identified above, of competing without fear of failure. Laying scrutiny to these games will hopefully give you a closer insight into the workings of these great attacking geniuses. I believe that without thorough discipline in analysis and calculation it is impossible to fully utilise your chess potential. I hope this book can go some way towards achieving that discipline.

Chapter 1

Tal and the tree of plenty

Mikhail Tal was a breath of fresh air in the chess firmament of the late fifties and sixties. Until his arrival reinvigorated the chess scene, it was dominated by the likes of Botvinnik, whose scientific and rigorous approach took some of the passion out of the game, and Smyslov, whose mastery of the endgame had enabled him to defeat Botvinnik and become world champion, only to lose the title in a rematch.

Tal, from Riga in Latvia, succeeded in becoming the youngest player ever to hold the world chess crown, when he defeated Botvinnik in a famous match which sent shock waves around the chess world. A hardened drinker and smoker, he was to die an early death brought on by illness resulting from his unhealthy lifestyle, but he will always be remembered by chess fans for the dashing attacks and sacrificial flair that shone like a bright beacon through the drab, positional and materialistic chess of the Soviet era that was more attuned to getting results than entertaining the chess public.

Tal evoked memories of the days of Morphy, where players would attack without fear of losing, and it was considered ungentlemanly not to accept a sacrifice. Sweeping through the chess scene like a hurricane, grandmasters rooted in the iron discipline of Botvinnik were unable to contain his enormous flair for combinations, and his willingness to provoke a maelstrom of wild complications, and were simply swept away in a tide of chess imagination and brute force calculation. In this chapter I will attempt to discover some of the secrets behind Tal's extraordinary calculating abilities, although this will be no easy task, I hope to be able to work my way through the labyrinth of variations with the help of the aforementioned tree of analysis.

1

Y.Averbakh – M.Tal

USSR Championship,
Riga 1958

Modern Benoni Defence

1 d4 ♘f6 2 c4 e6 3 ♘c3 c5

The Modern Benoni – Tal's preferred choice of opening in his early career against 1 d4, although he also scored many potent wins with the King's Indian. Nowadays many Benoni players prefer to play the opening against the Queen's Indian move order, with 3 ♘f3, fearing the dreaded 'flick knife' attack, which White can launch with his knight on c3.

4 d5 exd5 5 cxd5 d6 6 e4 g6

7 ♗e2

7 f4 ♗g7 8 ♗b5+!? is the flick knife, a move order that isn't possible if White has already committed his knight to f3. No less a player than Garry Kasparov scored a famous win against John Nunn in this variation. Nowadays this move order tends to frighten Benoni players to death, so that they prefer to play a Nimzo Indian with 3...♗b4 in reply to 3 ♘c3.

Then 8...♗d7 (8...♘bd7 9 e5! dxe5 10 fxe5 ♘h5 11 e6 ♕h4+! 12 g3 ♘xg3 13 hxg3 ♕xh1 14 ♗e3 leads to unfathomable complications that would have been right up Tal's street; nowadays the last word on the variation is supposed to be 14...♗xc3+ 15 bxc3 a6 16 exd7+ ♗xd7 17 ♗xd7+ ♔xd7 18 ♕b3!± as Sokolov used to defeat Topalov. Or 8...♘fd7 9 a4 ♕h4+!? 10 g3 ♕e7) 9 a4. In general this variation only became popular after Tal's heyday, it would have been fascinating to see how he would have dealt with it in his prime. Not surprisingly, Averbakh chooses a more sedate variation. But it was very difficult to restrain Tal!

7...♗g7 8 ♘f3 0-0 9 0-0 ♖e8 10 ♕c2

10 ♘d2 is perhaps more highly regarded by theory; White intends to reinforce the centre with f3, rather than with pieces; play may continue 10...♘a6 11 f3 ♘c7 12 a4 b6 13 ♘c4 ♗a6 14 ♗g5 h6!? ∞ (14...♕d7?).

10...♘a6 11 ♗f4 ♘b4 12 ♕b1

12...♘xe4?!

"You gotta be kidding!" – ?!!!?? would be a more appropriate notation! It is easy to underestimate the psychological shock which Averbakh must have experienced on seeing this daring sacrifice. A remarkable conception, though, in this day and age of super strong computers that have the ability to refute any risky sacrifice, probably flawed. But in a practical sense Tal's adventurous spirit was richly rewarded! What is most remarkable is that it hasn't been repeated since! 12...♘h5 is the 'normal' but far more boring move! Then might follow 13 ♗g5 f6 14 ♗d2 f5∞.

13 ♘xe4 ♗f5 14 ♘fd2 ♘xd5

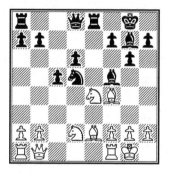

15 ♗xd6?

The critical position. Now let's consider what would have happened if Averbakh had made the more testing retreat. I think the conclusion we can draw from this dense tree of variations is probably the same that Averbakh came to in the game, that the sheer complexity of the lines after the critical reply 15 ♗g3! was overwhelming, which persuaded him to play the 'safe' reply 15 ♗xd6? – but this was a mistake! As we can see, 15 ♗xd6? led to his later defeat, whereas 15 ♗g3! would have kept the game unclear. He

would have been better off throwing himself into the morass of complications.

In fact there is, I believe, an inherent 'justice' in chess – that those who are brave and willing to dive headlong into the abyss, are favoured over those who err on the side of caution, always looking for the easy route. I believe that Tal intuitively felt that the sacrifice ♘xe4 was risky, but in a practical sense he would be able to out-think Averbakh, and in any case he didn't have to prove the soundness of the sacrifice, as Averbakh avoided the most criticial line. Such was the intimidation factor with Tal!

But the reader has a right to ask, how to go about calculating all this in a game? After all, it is one thing to be able to calculate and identify four or five candidate moves in a sedate position, but it is quite another to do the same thing in such a complicated one. Of course the reason we love chess so much is the beauty that lies in its complexity and that the human mind cannot master the game. It is only through practice and thorough study of such complex games that we can improve our calculating abilities and approach each game with confidence. After all, we will never have a perfect calculating brain, and mistakes and oversights will always be made, but in a competitive sense, it is only important to see more than your opponent, who is after all faced with the same problems of complexity himself!

Although I believe Tal's style would have scored very badly against computers, in a practical game, against flesh and blood opponents, with the ticking of the clock and the inherent tension involved, he didn't do too badly! So much of Tal's play was intuitive, and of course he was disposed towards sacrifices and attacking play. But he allied this to a razor-sharp calculating ability which meant that any 'refutation' (assuming there was one) of his play was by no means easy.

15 ♗g3!

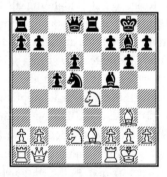

What would Tal have done now? In fact, at the point where he considered the sacrifice, he would have had to visualise this position and consider what moves he had available. Of course we have the luxury of being able to jump forward and just consider this position. Now we have to identify the candidate moves and 'build our tree' – the four

candidate moves we can easily identify are 15...♕e7, 15...♘b4, 15...♘f6, and the best one, 15...♗h6! Let's just imagine, for a moment, that Averbakh did indeed play the brave ♗g3, and put ourselves in Tal's shoes. How would he have gone about trying to prove the correctness of his sacrifice?

A) 15...♕e7 "looks natural, ganging up on the e-file, what does he do then?"

A1) 16 ♗xd6 ♗xe4 17 ♘xe4 (17 ♗xe7 ♗xb1 18 ♖axb1 ♖xe7 "and I'm clearly better") 17...♕xe4 18 ♕xe4 ♖xe4 19 ♗f3 ♖e6 (19...♖d4 20 ♗xc5 ♖d2 21 ♖ad1 "is irritating") 20 ♗xc5 ♘f6 21 ♗xb7 ♖b8 22 ♗f3 ♖xb2 23 ♗xa7 ♖a6 "just about burns out to equality";

A2) 16 ♗d3 instead, then 16...♘b4 17 ♗xd6 ♕e6 "is annoying for him, a lot of his pieces are hanging, I'm going to get some material back (on 17...♕d8 "he has the annoying 18 ♗b5"; and 17...♕d7 18 a3 ♘xd3 19 ♕xd3 "isn't convincing") 18 ♗xc5 ♘xd3 19 ♕xd3 ♗xe4 20 ♘xe4 ♕xe4 21 ♕xe4 ♖xe4 "only seems to offer equality, but Black might be be slightly better due to the pressure on the b-pawn."

A3) 16 ♗f3! "is annoying";

A3a) 16...♘f6 17 ♘xf6+ (17 ♖e1 d5 18 ♘xf6+ ♕xf6 19 ♕d1 ♕xb2 "I have a lot of pawns and I'm threatening to win the exchange, looks okay") 17...♕xf6 18 ♗e4

♕xb2 ("But not 18...♗xe4 because
of 19 ♘xe4 ♕xb2 20 ♕xb2 ♗xb2
21 ♘xd6 ♗xa1 22 ♘xe8 ♗d4
23 ♘c7 ♖c8 24 ♘b5 and I probably
don't have enough to hold this
endgame.");

A3a1) 19 ♗xf5 ♕xd2 (19...♕xa1
20 ♕xa1 ♗xa1 21 ♗d3 ♗e5 "and
with so many pawns I must be
happy.");

A3a2) 19 ♕xb2! ♗xb2 20 ♖ab1
"and if the b7 pawn wasn't dropping
I'd be happy, but unfortunately it is."
20...♗c3 (20...♗xe4 21 ♘xe4 ♖xe4
22 ♖xb2 "doesn't seem to be a lot of
fun either, although he still has a bit
of work to do after 22...b6 23 ♗xd6
♖d8±") 21 ♗xf5 ♗xd2 (21...gxf5
22 ♘c4±) 22 ♗d7 ("Maybe 22 ♗c2
is more sensible, I'm bound to lose
either the b7 pawn or the d pawn,
when it's an uphill struggle for
the draw.") 22...♖e7 23 ♖xb7 ♖d8
24 ♗c6 "and even here I can fight on
with 24...♖xb7 25 ♗xb7 c4 26 ♗d5
♖c8! and the c-pawn should devour
one of his bishops" 27 ♗e4 d5!
"That's a nice trick" 28 ♗c2
(28 ♗xd5 c3) 28...d4 29 ♖d1 c3;

A3b) 16...♗h6 17 ♕d1! "Hmmm,
I'm not getting anywhere."

B) 15...♘b4 "is an interesting
idea, I'm threatening ...d5. Can
White escape?" 16 a3! "Unfortunately
he can" ("He won't play 16 ♗d3 as
it loses to 16...♘xd3 17 ♕xd3 d5.")
16...♘c6 17 ♗d3 "and it doesn't
look like I have sufficient
compensation, so I can dismiss
♘b4."

C) 15...♗h6!

"This is much more like it!" and
this is the move that I believe that
Tal would have played. Now the tree
diverges into another branch; White
now has no less than six(!) credible
candidate moves: 16 ♗c4, 16 ♗d3,
16 ♕d3, 16 f4, 16 ♕d1 and finally
16 ♗b5.

C1) 16 ♗c4 ♘b4! 17 ♗xf7+
(17 ♗b5 "That's another interesting
try. So many bishop moves!"
17...♖e6 "and he doesn't seem to
have solved the problem of the pin";
17 f4 d5! gets the piece back with
interest.) 17...♔xf7 18 ♘xd6+ ♕xd6
19 ♕xf5+ (19 ♗xd6 ♗xb1 20 ♘xb1
"Now I have a killing shot"

20...♘c2) 19...gxf5 20 ♗xd6 ♗xd2 "and I'm winning";

C2) 16 ♗d3 ♘b4! "Again forced, otherwise the whole idea is stupid, but now he has a serious problem as I'm threatening ...♘xd3 and ...d5. 17 ♗b5 ♖e6 transposes to the above variation. So ♗d3 doesn't seem to solve his problems."

C3) 16 ♕d3

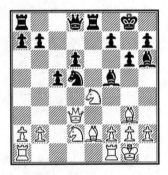

"Trying to get out of the pin by brute force. As we can see in many variations, the root cause of many of White's problems is the passive nature of the queen on b1."

C3a) 16...♘b4 17 ♕f3 d5 18 ♘d6 ♗xd2 19 ♘xf5 (19 ♘xe8 ♕xe8 "looks good for me, his queen looks funny and again I have two pawns for the exchange") 19...gxf5 20 ♕xf5 ♕g5 "and Black is certainly not worse, so we can conclude that ♕d3 is not really dangerous";

C3b) 16...♘f6!? 17 ♗h4 g5! 18 ♕xd6 ♗xe4! "looks good for me, even if I'm walking a fine line, but when am I not?";

C3c) 16...♗xd2? 17 ♕xd5 ♗xe4 18 ♕xd2 "won't do";

C4) 16 f4

"The most ambitious. He's trying to hold as much material as possible even if f4 looks like a horrible move from the positional point of view. Okay, what alternatives do I have then? ♘f6, ♘b4, ♗g7, ♕e7 and ♘e3, hmmm... let's analyse."

C4a) 16...♘f6 17 ♗d3! "doesn't seem much different from a similar variation, ♘f6 is too passive";

C4b) 16...♘b4 17 a3 d5 18 axb4 dxe4 19 ♘c4 ♕d4+ 20 ♔h1 cxb4 "is a bit messy, hmmm, hard to assess but I guess a piece is a piece after 21 ♖d1";

C4c) 16...♗g7 "looks a bit slow, can I really afford to waste time like this?" 17 ♔h1 (17 ♗d3 ♘b4! "and I'm mixing it up") 17...♘e3 18 ♖f3 ♗d4 "transposes to that other variation, does he have anything better? possibly not";

C4d) 16...♕e7 17 ♗f3 (17 ♗d3 ♘b4! "and I can't see a good reply for him, I'm threatening too much action.") 17...♘xf4 (17...♘e3 18 ♖e1 d5 19 ♖xe3 dxe4 20 ♗xe4 ♗g7 21 ♗f2 ♗d4 22 ♖e2 "and I don't see anything convincing for me here." But maybe 17...♗xf4 "and I'm rocking, three pawns for the piece and quite active.") 18 ♕d1 ♖ad8 "Okay, ♕e7 looks like a good reply to f4";

C4e) 16...♘e3?! "worth a look!"

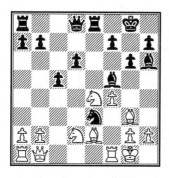

17 ♖f3

C4e1) 17...♘xg2 18 ♔xg2 d5 19 ♗d3 "This is too much, White is on top";

C4e2) 17...♗g7;

C4e3) 17...♗g7! "a nice switchback" 18 ♔h1 (18 ♖xe3 ♗d4 19 ♕d3 d5) 18...♗d4

C4e31) 19 ♗b5 d5? (19...♖e6! keeps up the pressure.) 20 ♗xe8 ♕xe8 21 ♖xe3 ♗xe3 22 ♘f6+ "Oops";

C4e32) 19 ♗d3

C4e321) 19...c4!? "Keep the tricks coming." 20 ♖xe3 ♗xe3 21 ♘xc4

♗xe4 (21...♗d4 22 ♘exd6 ♗xd3 23 ♕xd3 "also looks worryingly strong for White") 22 ♗xe4 d5 23 ♘xe3 ♖xe4 (23...dxe4 "doesn't look totally clear, although the dark squares around my king may come back to haunt me.") 24 ♕d3 "and White is on top";

C4e322) 19...♗g4

C4e3221) 20 ♖xe3 ♗xe3 21 ♘c4 ♗d4 "This may well be best play, I have two pawns and a rook for two pieces but he's immediately winning one back..." 22 ♘cxd6 ♖e6 (22...♖f8 "may be safer.") 23 h3! ♗h5 24 f5!;

C4e3222) 20 ♖f2 ♘f5! 21 ♖f1 d5 22 ♘f2 ♘xg3+ 23 hxg3 ♗e2 24 ♗xe2 ♖xe2 "and I'm winning";

C4e4) 17...d5?! 18 ♖xe3 dxe4 "and he's survived the first wave, but his pieces are very passive and I'm immediately threatening his knight, and if

C4e41) 19 ♘xe4 then 19...♗g7! "is a powerful reply." 20 ♗f2 ♗d4 21 ♗d3 ♗xe3 22 ♗xe3 ♗xe4 23 ♗xe4 ♕e7 "a nice variation!";

C4e42) but 19 ♕c1 "looks annoying." 19...♗g7 20 ♔h1 ♗d4 21 ♘b3 or just simply 21 ♖b3 b6 "but do I have enough for the piece? I doubt it, but it's not completely clear.");

C5) 16 ♕d1 ♗xe4 17 ♘xe4 ♖xe4 18 ♗f3 ♖d4 "looks quite simple";

C6) 16 ♗b5 "an interesting shot."

C6a) 16...♖e6 17 ♗c4! "is very perplexing, I don't want to run into a pin myself";

C6b) 16...♖e7 "I could try this move, though it looks risky."

C6b1) 17 ♗xd6!? ♕xd6? (17...♖e6! 18 ♗xc5 ♗xd2 "looks good.") 18 ♘xd6 ♗xb1 19 ♘xb1;

C6b2) 17 ♗c4! "That move again. Mucho irritato." 17...♘b4! "The only move, but a strong one." (17...♘b6 is nothing, he has 18 ♗d3) 18 ♗h4 (18 a3 ♗xd2 19 axb4 ♗xe4 "is good for me"; 18 ♗xd6 ♖d7! "and all my pieces are co-ordinating, whilst many of his are hanging." 19 ♗xc5 ♗xd2) 18...♗xd2! 19 ♗xe7 ♕xe7 "is similar to that other variation, I have two pawns for the exchange and I'm doing very well";

C6b3) 17 ♗h4 ♗xd2 18 ♗xe7 ♕xe7 19 ♕d1 ♗xe4 (19...♗h6 "trying to keep the two bishops" 20 ♘xc5 ♘c7! "is another nice trick") 20 ♕xd2 ♘c7 "and I've got two pawns for the exchange, hmmm, doesn't look too bad, so ♖e7 is okay";

C6c) 16...♗xd2 17 ♗xe8 ♕xe8 18 ♘xd6 (18 f3 "is meek, I already have two pawns for the exchange.") 18...♗xb1 19 ♘xe8 "now it's important to find the right move"

C6c1) 19...♗xa2 20 ♖xa2 ♖xe8 21 ♖xa7 "looks bad";

C6c2) 19...♗d3? 20 ♖fd1 "doesn't help" (20 ♘c7);

C6c3) 19...♗c2! "I've got to keep the two bishops to have a chance to make something of my queenside pawns" 20 ♘d6 (20 ♘c7 ♖d8 "looks less clear, my bishops are controlling the white rooks.") 20...b6 21 ♘c4 ♗h6 22 ♖fe1 "and it would appear that I am worse, but I have some holding chances";

D) 15...♘f6

"looks tempting, but I can quickly dismiss it on account of 16 ♗d3! (16 ♘xf6+ ♕xf6 17 ♗d3 ♕xb2 18 ♗xf5 ♕xd2 "looks a bit messy, hmmm, not so bad.") 16...♘xe4 17 ♗xe4 ♗xe4 18 ♘xe4 "and I don't seem to have enough, for example 18...♗xb2 19 ♕xb2 ♖xe4 20 ♕xb7 "and I have only two pawns, hmmm."

15...♘f6!

Now Black is on top, and White cannot hold on to the extra material.

16 ♗f3

16 ♗xc5 ♘xe4∓.

16...♘xe4   17   ♘xe4   ♗xe4 18 ♗xe4 ♕xd6 19 ♕c2 ♖e7

Black is simply a pawn up, and for a player of Tal's class, the technical task isn't particularly difficult.

20 ♗f3 ♖ae8 21 ♖ad1 ♗d4!

The bishop is very powerfully placed on d4, where it aims at the f2 pawn. White is already objectively lost.

22 a4

22 g3 b6 23 ♔g2 h5 24 h4 would have been a better try at defence, but you suspect that Tal would have broken through eventually after 24...♖e5.

22...b6 23 b3 ♖e5 24 ♖d2 h5 25 ♖e2 ♖xe2 26 ♗xe2 h4!

Further increasing his influence on the dark squares and making it impossible for White to play g3.

27 ♔h1 ♕f4 28 g3 ♕f6 29 ♕d1

29 ♔g2 ♕c6+ 30 ♗f3 h3+!

29...♖d8

29...♗xf2? 30 ♔g2 ♖d8 (30...h3+ 31 ♔xh3 ♕d4) 31 ♕c2 ♕c6+? (31...h3+ 32 ♔xh3 ♕d4) 32 ♗f3 h3+ 33 ♔xf2.

30 ♗g4 ♗xf2 31 ♕e2 ♖d2!

Of course, Tal would never miss a tactical shot that hastens the winning process.

32 ♕e8+

32 ♕xd2 ♕c6+ 33 ♗f3 ♕xf3 mate; while 32 ♕e4 hxg3 33 hxg3 ♕h8+ 34 ♔g2 ♗g1+! 35 ♗e2 (35 ♔f3 ♕c3+ 36 ♔f4 ♖d4) 35...♕h2+ 36 ♔f3 ♕h5+ 37 ♕g4 ♕d5+ is a nice winning line.

32...♔g7 33 gxh4 ♕d4!

Centralisation, always!

34 ♗h3

34 ♗f3 ♕d3.

34...♕d3

35 ♗g2?

35 ♕e5+! was a much better try. The last moves give the impression they may have been played in a time scramble. 35...♔h7 Now White has a choice between four candidate moves. 36 ♕f4, 36 ♕f6, 36 ♕c7 and 36 ♕e7. All pretty similar queen moves, huh, likely to be little difference between them? Wrong! Let's look at each move in turn.

(i) 36 ♕f4

(ii) 36 ♕f6 ♕e4+ 37 ♗g2 ♕xg2+ 38 ♔xg2 ♗xh4+ -+;

(iii) 36 ♕c7 ♕xb3 37 ♕f4 ♕d5+ -+;

(iv) 36 ♕e7 ♕d5+ 37 ♗g2 ♕xg2+ 38 ♔xg2 ♗xh4+ 39 ♔h3 ♗xe7 40 ♖xf7+ ♔h6 41 ♖xe7 a5 42 ♖e3 ♖d4∓; 36 ♕f6) 36...♕d5+ (36...♕xh3 37 ♕xf7+ ♔h6 38 ♕f8+ ♔h5 39 ♕h8+ ♔g4 40 ♕c8+ ♔xh4 41 ♕h8+ ♔g4 42 ♕c8+ is a miraculous draw) 37 ♗g2 ♕xg2+! 38 ♔xg2 ♗e3+ 39 ♔h3 ♗xf4 40 ♖xf4 ♔g7 looks winning for Black, but at least would have offered some possibilities to go wrong.

35...♖d1

Now it's all over.

0-1

So what have we learnt from this game? After all, the variations following 15 ♗g3 are extremely complex, and the tree of analysis gets very dense very quickly. How to prune it down? For example, after 15 ♗g3, if we remember Black had four credible replies to that move. But some investigation will help us to pare it down to the main branch, that move being 15...♗h6. Simply by the process of elimination a strong player will be able to eliminate the other replies and concentrate on 15...♗h6, therefore with some analysis he can play that move.

Of course it is logical that once the player realises 15...♗h6 is the best move, he should play it immediately, and leave his opponent to ponder which of the six candidate moves he should play in the game. Then he can utilise his opponent's time by considering a reply to each candidate move. I'm not sure how deeply Tal saw into the positions after 15...♗h6 when he played the sacrifice ...♘xe4 in the first place, but it's quite possible that he simply assessed the positions as unclear, and regarded it as a practical choice. One that paid off!

The above 'conversation with Tal' may seem to the reader somewhat bizarre, but I want to convey to the reader the possibility of internal verbalisation during the game, that by putting your thoughts into words you add clearer meaning to your inner game logic.

I also recommend writing down afterwards the thoughts that you had during the game, so that the memory of the thoughts that you had at the time isn't lost – possibly including a graph of the calculations and variations that you analysed – all this is useful to build a more accurate picture of your strengths and weaknesses at this part of the game. Another useful and simple thing to do is to write down the time spent on each move – so that you know how much time you used on critical decisions. For example English grandmaster Jon Speelman seemed quite unhappy when I mistakenly took his score sheet, on which he had written the time he had spent on each move – and of course, as is usual for my clumsy nature, I managed to lose it all together. Sorry Jon!

But really, it's difficult to communicate how important calculation is. While a player may be obsessed with the ability to calculate long and lengthy variations, as this seems much more of an achievement, it's also a mistake. It's far more important to get the basics right. Calculate four or five candidate moves at a time. Look

for strange, funny moves that don't appear obvious at first glance. Get the first couple of moves correct. Once you have mastered the basics, then you can move on to the more demanding stuff of calculating lengthy variations.

2

E.Chukaev – M.Tal

USSR Championship, Semi-Finals, Tbilisi 1956

King's Indian Defence

1 d4 ♘f6 2 c4 g6 3 ♘c3 ♗g7 4 e4 d6 5 ♗e2 0-0 6 ♗g5

The Averbakh variation – of course named after Tal's last vanquished opponent!

6...c5!

The exclamation mark is more for the style of the move than whether it is objectively stronger than the main alternative 6...♘a6 7 ♕d2 e5 8 d5 ♕e8. But this is a more solid choice – Tal remains faithful to his aggressive style!

7 d5 e6 8 ♕d2

8 ♘f3 is the other main move, Black can reply 8...exd5 9 cxd5 h6 10 ♗h4 g5 11 ♗g3 ♘h5 12 ♘d2 ♘xg3 13 hxg3 ♘d7!? as Fischer once played with success.

8...exd5 9 exd5

9 cxd5 ♘a6 would transpose into a sort of Benoni position, in which, as we have already seen, Tal felt most comfortable.

9...♕b6 10 ♘f3

10...♗f5

10...♗g4 is an important, and possibly more solid alternative. 10...♗f5 is the more ambitious move, which of course is why it was Tal's choice, as Black intends to occupy the e4 square with his pieces. 11 0-0 ♘bd7 12 h3 ♗xf3 13 ♗xf3 ♖ae8 and Black has a nice Benoni game, although both sides have their pluses. The reason that Tal was so fond of the Benoni is because it suited his style perfectly; the flexibility of the opening, the fluid piece development and tactical

chances that could abound gave full flight to his incredible chess imagination. May I add for the same reasons Bobby Fischer was a fan of this opening as well! In fact Bobby and Tal were firm friends, so perhaps it was Tal's influence that encouraged Bobby to adopt this opening? Black's play in the Benoni tends to be very thematic, and suits a hard worker, as the same plans and ideas pop up time and time again.

11 ♘h4 ♘e4 12 ♘xe4 ♗xe4

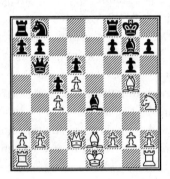

13 0-0-0

Castling into it! A bold and probably rash decision against such a notable tactician as Tal. White steps into the full glare of Black's raking bishops, which in combination with the black queen, already aimed at the enemy queenside, become an unstoppable force. The critical test of Black's idea, and a variation that has been tested many times, was 13 f3! ♕xb2 14 ♖c1! Now Black has two alternatives:

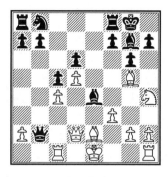

A) 14...h6 15 ♗xh6 ♛xd2+ 16 ♗xd2 ♗f6 17 g3 Now again the path diverges. 17...g5 I believe that Black should try and retain the dark-squared bishop whenever possible in the Benoni; that bishop has much more influence over the game than the light-squared one in this opening – for example, once that bishop disappears, the pawns on d6 and c5 become much more vulnerable (17...♗f5; or 17...♗xh4 18 gxh4 ♗f5 has been tried many times, but it seems White has the better chances after, for example, 19 ♗f4 ♖d8 20 ♖g1±) 18 fxe4 gxh4 19 ♗f4 ♘d7 20 ♗xd6 ♖fe8 21 ♗d3 hxg3 22 hxg3 ♗e5 and Black had sufficient compensation for the pawn in the shape of his grip on the dark squares, and in particular e5, to hold on in the game Polugayevsky – Gufeld, USSR Championship 1966;

B) 14...♛xd2+ 15 ♔xd2 (15 ♗xd2 ♗f6!) 15...♗xd5!? is an interesting idea; Black already gains two pawns for the piece, and hopes to win a third as d5 is then chronically weak. (15...♗f5 has been tried with

success before – after 16 ♘xf5 gxf5 17 ♗d3 Black's game looks ugly, but the knight quickly gets to e5 or b6 from where it will pressurise the weak c-pawn) 16 cxd5 ♖e8!? (16...♘d7 may well be an improvement, Black avoids the problems with ♖b1) 17 ♖b1!? with a fairly unclear position, although this is not supposed to be an opening book, so I have deviated from the path somewhat! But what I have tried to demonstrate is the difficulty that a player is confronted with when faced with an opening of which he has little experience. Presumably Chukaev was unaware of these variations, didn't feel comfortable with dropping the pawn on b2, and chose his own path. This was to prove fatal.

13...♘a6!

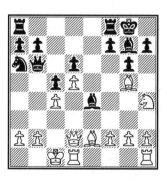

Remarkably, White is already defenceless! He cannot prevent the threatened incursion of the knight to b4, after which his queenside is torn asunder by the combined power of Black's army. We can do a simple mathematical calculation here:

Black is attacking with four pieces, the queen on b6, the knight on a6, the bishop on g7 and the bishop on e4. White is only defending with only one, the queen. A poor contest!

14 f3

14 a3? will not do, because of 14...♛b3! 15 f3 (15 ♗d3 ♗xd3 16 ♛xd3 ♛xb2 mate) 15...♛a2 16 fxe4 ♛a1+ 17 ♔c2 ♛xb2+ 18 ♔d3 ♛xa3+ 19 ♔c2 ♘b4+ 20 ♔b1 ♛a1 mate and White is slain in his bed, a variation that I doubt took Tal more than a couple of seconds to calculate. 14 ♗f3 ♘b4! (14...♖fe8 and 14...♗xf3 are also not bad, but once you see the strength of ♘b4 it is not necessary to look for alternatives.) 15 ♗xe4 ♘xa2+ 16 ♔c2 (16 ♔b1 ♘c3+ 17 ♔c2 ♘xe4-+) 16...♛xb2+ 17 ♔d3 ♛b3+ 18 ♔e2 ♘c3+ -+.

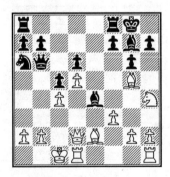

14...♘b4!

This kind of combination is child's play to Tal.

15 fxe4 ♘xa2+ 16 ♔b1

16 ♔c2 ♛xb2+ 17 ♔d3 ♛b3+ 18 ♛c3 ♛xc3 mate.

16...♘c3+ 17 ♔c1

17 ♔c2 would have been considered by White. 17...♘xe4 18 ♛c1 ♘xg5 19 ♛xg5 ♛xb2+ 20 ♔d3 ♛d4+ (20...♛c3+ is also a lot of fun) 21 ♔c2 ♛c3+ 22 ♔b1 ♛b2 mate is a nice demonstration of the power of Black's bishop on g7! Basically – don't castle queenside in the Benoni!

17...♘xe4 18 ♛c2 ♘xg5

Now we can see that White is hopelessly lost. Not only is he two pawns down (which would be enough in itself) but he has yet to solve the problem of his king's safety, which is still threatened by the latent power of the bishop on g7.

19 ♘f3 ♘xf3 20 ♗xf3 a5! 21 ♖d3

Alternatives are hard to come by.

21...a4 22 ♖e1 ♛b4 23 ♖e7 ♖fe8

23...a3 is very powerful as well. Essentially, everything wins.

24 ♖xe8+ ♖xe8 25 ♔b1 b5!

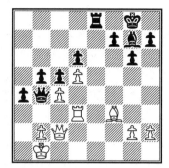

Opening up the game still further, a natural impulse for an attacking player.

26 ♖a3

26 cxb5 c4 27 ♖a3 (27 ♖d1 ♖e3) 27...♖e1+ 28 ♗d1 ♖xd1+ 29 ♕xd1 ♕xb2 mate.

26...♖e1+ 27 ♔a2 ♕xa3+ 0-1

A nice little game, though on the surface nothing special. But the reason I wanted to show this particular encounter is that it demonstrates how important it is to be switched on right from the start of the game. White lost because of one mistake; he castled queenside, after which it was impossible to find a defence. Probably this was due to lazy calculation. Rather like the previous game, White rejected the complications of 11 f3 in favour of a move he regarded as 'safe'. This is an easy mistake to make in the opening, the phase of chess I regard as probably the most important, as it defines the contours of the game. It's very easy to think "I only need to start calculating and thinking in the middlegame, it's the opening, I can't take too long, I know all this stuff." Mistake! One wrong turn can lead to defeat in the opening, especially in this day and age of super strong computers and specialised preparation.

3

B.Spassky – M.Tal

USSR Championship, Riga 1958

Nimzo-Indian Defence

Boris Spassky was one of the great champions and, like Tal, an attacking player *par excellence*. In fact I remember I was first entranced by chess when I saw the James Bond film with Sean Connery *From Russia with Love* on TV as a boy (I was born more than 10 years after the film came out, in 1976.). There the Spectre agent Kronsteen overwhelms his Canadian opponent, Adams, with a finish that was based on one of Spassky's games – a famous King's Gambit that he used to defeat David Bronstein. "Wow, what an amazing combination!" I thought, and immediately fell in love with the game (oh, and James Bond movies of course). The fact that Kronsteen was later killed by a female agent working for Blofeld (who bore more than a passing resemblance to some of the less attractive East European women FMs) was by the by. Chess is very rarely portrayed well in films – a clear exception being the excellent *The Luzhin Defence* with John Tuturro and Emily Watson, based on the book by the famous Russian writer Vladimir Nabokov, who also wrote *Lolita*. The film follows the tragic life of the fictional eccentric Russian grandmaster Alexander Luzhin, played by Tuturro, who falls in love with with Natalia, played by Watson, and struggles to reconcile the possibility of a normal existence outside of chess with his obsession for the game.

Boris Spassky is the only world champion that I've faced in an over-the-board encounter (I've also played a few blitz games against David Bronstein, who narrowly missed out on the world championship title against Botvinnik.). I played Boris in a French league match a few years ago. The game was fairly uneventful until Boris opined "would you like a draw?"– words delivered in a heavy booming Russian accent, so loud that the whole room was able to hear (and it was a large room). I declined but was so torn by the idea of trying to defeat my hero that I made him a reciprocal offer a few moves later!

1 d4 ♘f6 2 c4 e6 3 ♘c3 ♗b4 4 a3

The Samisch variation. In those days it was relatively popular, but has subsequently fallen out of favour somewhat, as several methods of playing have been worked out that give Black at least equality.

4...♗xc3+ 5 bxc3 c5 6 e3 ♘c6 7 ♗d3 e5 8 ♘e2 e4

8...d6 is an important alternative, but as usual Tal plays the more aggressive and ambitious move, already trying to target the weak pawn on c4.

9 ♗b1 b6! 10 ♘g3 ♗a6

11 f3

11 ♘xe4 ♘xe4 12 ♗xe4 ♗xc4 13 ♗d3 ♗xd3 14 ♕xd3 d5 and Black is fine. This line would not have suited Spassky, who was always looking for ways to give his fantasy full flight.

11...♗xc4 12 ♘f5

12 fxe4 d6 13 ♕f3 0-0 14 e5 dxe5 15 ♕xc6 exd4 was the typically crazy continuation of one of the games of grandmaster of disaster 'gentleman' Jim Plaskett, who is now enjoying his retirement in Spain after netting a quarter of a million on

the quiz show *Who wants to be a millionaire?* – nice work if you can get it! Not sure chess pays quite as well! Black has good compensation for the piece, as White's king is stuck in the centre.

12...0-0

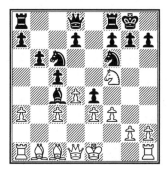

13 ♘d6!

This is Spassky's idea. Exchange the bishop on c4 and make it possible to castle. Though he doesn't castle for another ten moves anyway! Doubtless Spassky saw many of these variations, after all it would be surprising if he didn't at least consider 13 fxe4, but probably rejected the move on general grounds, as the move he played in the game at least ensures his king will not remain stuck in the centre. Sometimes it's not possible to calculate everything and you have to trust your intuition!

13 fxe4 – why did Spassky reject this obvious move? After all, his centre looks quite imposing. Let's take the line on a few moves to find out why.

13...d5 – Black counterattacks in the centre immediately, the drawback being that it gives White a powerful outpost on d6 for the knight after he plays e5 (13...d6! is the sensible choice. Black keeps the white king restrained in the centre. 14 ♕f3 ♖e8) 14 e5 ♘e4 15 ♕g4 g6 16 ♗xe4 dxe4 17 ♘d6.

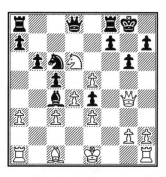

When he rejected fxe4, Spassky would have had to consider the two realistic candidate moves that Tal seems to have at his disposal here, 17...♗d3 and 17...f5.

A) 17...♗d3 18 ♘xe4? (18 h4! looks quite strong. White tries to launch a crude attack, but with his knight rooted to d6 it's quite a powerful one. The e4 pawn is irrelevant, taking it only helps Black to exchange the knight and free his position. Then 18...f6 19 h5 fxe5 20 ♕e6+ ♔g7) 18...f5! 19 exf6 ♗xe4 20 ♕xe4 ♕xf6 and with White's king stuck in the centre, Black's initiative is formidable.

B) 17...f5!?

B1) 18 ♕g3 f4 19 ♕g4 (19 exf4

cxd4 20 ♘xc4 ♕d5 21 ♘d6±)
19...♗d3 20 h4 with an attack;

B2) 18 ♕h3 – the problem with
...f5 is it's very inflexible; Black
leaves White's imposing pawn
chain, c3, d4, e3, e5 unmolested and
the knight on d6 casts a malevolent
eye over Black's position.

13...♗d3

13...♗a6? 14 ♘xe4±

14 ♗xd3

14 ♘xe4 ♘xe4 15 ♗xd3 (15 fxe4
♕h4+ 16 g3 ♕xe4-+) 15...♕h4+
will not do for White.

14...exd3 15 ♕xd3 cxd4 16 cxd4

16...♘e8!

Tal immediately tries to eject the
knight from d6. 16...♕e7?! 17 ♘f5
♕e6 18 e4? (After 18 ♘g3! d5
19 0-0 ♖fe8 20 ♗d2, in general
White has won the opening battle, as
he has got rid of his weak pawn on
c4, the cause of so many headaches
for him in so many lines, and has a
strong centre, so possibly we have to
go back and find improvements for
Black earlier on.) 18...d5 19 e5 ♘xe5-+.

17 ♘f5 d5 18 a4!

A very fine idea from Spassky, he
immediately hits on the best
diagonal for the bishop.

18...♘d6?!

18...g6! 19 ♘g3 (19 ♘h6+ ♔g7
20 ♗a3 ♘d6 is fine for Black;
19 ♗a3 gxf5 20 ♗xf8 ♔xf8
21 ♕xf5 ♘f6) 19...f5 20 0-0 ♘f6
21 ♗d2 ♕d7 looks a better try,
playing in true Nimzo-fashion,
trying to restrain White's centre!

**19 ♘xd6 ♕xd6 20 ♗a3 ♘b4
21 ♕b3 a5 22 0-0 ♖fc8**

White's advantage lies primarily
in his greater preponderance in the
centre. He will try to exchange all
the pawns on the queenside where
he will be left with an extra pawn on
the other side, while Black is still
left with a weak pawn on d5. The
opening has gone wrong for Tal, and
at this point he was surely hunkering
down for a long defence.

**23 ♖ac1 ♕e6 24 ♗xb4 axb4
25 ♔f2!**

Spassky involves the king! In fact
there was no other good way of

covering the e-pawn. 25 e4? dxe4
26 ♕xe6 fxe6 27 fxe4 ♖xc1
28 ♖xc1 ♖xa4 29 ♖c6 b3 30 ♖xb6
♖xd4 31 ♖xb3 ♖xe4∓.

25...♕d6 26 h3 ♔f8

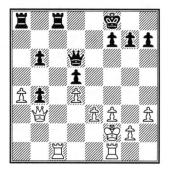

27 ♖c2!

White prepares to double rooks,
after which all of Black's pawns will
drop off like ripe apples. White's
advantage has already taken on
ominous proportions.

**27...♖xc2+ 28 ♕xc2 g6 29 ♖c1
♕d7**

29...♕f6 30 g3 and it's not clear
how Black has improved matters.

30 ♕c6! ♕xc6 31 ♖xc6 ♖a6 32 a5

Spassky calculates a long
variation, at the end of which it is
clear that he is the one pushing for
the win. 32 ♔g3 ♔e7 33 ♔f4 ♔d7
34 ♖f6?? b3! 35 ♖xf7+ ♔e6 36 ♖c7
b2; 32 ♔e2 ♔e7 33 ♔d3 ♖xa4
34 ♖xb6 ♖a2 35 g4 ♖h2.

**32...b3 33 axb6 b2 34 b7 b1=♕
35 ♖c8+ ♔g7 36 b8=♕ ♖a2+
37 ♔g3 ♕e1+ 38 ♔h2 ♕xe3
39 ♖g8+ ♔f6**

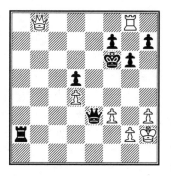

Black's king has been uprooted
and despite the level material it is
clear that Black is very close to
defeat. But can he be tipped over?

40 ♕d6+

What alternatives did Spassky
have here? Presumably this was the
sealed move, as in those days they
had the dreaded adjournments.
40 ♕d8+ ♕e7 41 ♕xd5 ♕c7+
42 ♕e5+ ♕xe5+ 43 dxe5+ ♔xe5
won't do; 40 f4 will not do either –
as Black can immediately make a
draw with 40...♖xg2+ (40...♕xd4
41 ♕d8+ ♔f5 42 ♕d7+) 41 ♔xg2
♕e2+ 42 ♔g1 ♕e1+ 43 ♔g2 ♕e2+
44 ♔g3 ♕e3+ 45 ♔g2.

40...♕e6 41 ♕f4+ ♕f5

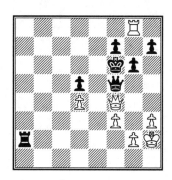

42 ♕d6+

What about the immediate 42 ♕g3 ? Spassky (and Tal of course) would have to analyse this as well. However it would seem that the queen is better posted on f5 than on e6, for example, 42...♖a6 (42...♖d2!?) 43 ♖d8 and Black can even go into a theoretically drawn endgame after 43...♔g7 44 ♕e5+ ♕xe5+ 45 dxe5 f6 46 ♖d7+ ♔h6 47 ♖xd5 fxe5 48 ♖xe5 g5. I think this is one of the hardest things about chess: you can play extremely well, win a pawn in the endgame and it's still a draw! No wonder Tarrasch said all rook endgames were drawn. Perhaps there should be a points system whereby the 'moral' winner gets an extra quarter of a point if the game ends up in a draw? Okay, I jest somewhat.

42...♕e6

43 ♕g3!

Tightening the noose. White now threatens h4, when h6 will not do because after ♕f4+ White can simply capture the h-pawn.

43...♕e3 44 h4 ♖e2

44...♖a4 45 ♕d6+ ♕e6 46 ♕d8+ ♕e7 47 ♕xd5 ♕c7+ 48 ♔h3+-.

45 ♕d6+ ♕e6

46 ♕f4+

The tempting winning try 46 ♕d8+ ♕e7 47 ♕xd5 is refuted by 47...♖xg2+! 48 ♔xg2 ♕e2+ 49 ♔g3 ♕e1+ 50 ♔f4 ♕d2+ and the much maligned black king helps to ensure that his white counterpart can't escape the perpetual. ♖xg2 is a recurring idea.

46...♕f5 47 ♕h6!

Spassky changes course, and a new phase begins.

47...♔e7!

47...♖e7 – of course it takes a brave man to leave the king on f6 – 48 ♖d8 (48 g4? ♕xf3 49 ♕g5+ ♔e6) 48...♖e2 49 ♕f8!

48 ♕f8+ ♔f6 49 ♕g7+ ♔e7 50 ♖a8! ♕d7

50...♕f4+ 51 ♔h3 ♕f5+ 52 ♔g3 doesn't change matters.

51 ♕f8+ ♔f6

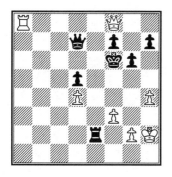

What candidate moves suggest themselves? 52 ♖a6+, 52 ♕h8+ 52 ♕d8+ and 52 ♖d8.

52 ♖a6+?

Spassky shows the first signs of fatigue. I'm curious to know why he didn't play the extremely strong 52 ♖d8! after which a fine game would have been concluded in his favour. Black cannot contain the simultaneous threats to the d-pawn and his king. Presumably all the to and froing of the rooks and queens was having a confusing effect. Oversights and blunders often happen deep into games, where the emotional and physical investment starts to catch up with the players. But that's why it's so important to keep your discipline at all times and keep looking for candidate moves. Keep to the basics. Of course in this game they would have had breaks, because of the adjournments, but no doubt Spassky was extremely tired, as up until this point he was well on course to win the title – but in those days tournaments took on a torturous quality compared to the holiday events of today, often lasting several weeks, and in some masochistic examples, months.

A) 52...♕f5 53 ♕h8+ ♔e7 54 ♖e8+ ♔d7 55 ♖xe2+-;

B) 52...♕e7 53 ♕h8+ ♔f5 54 ♖xd5+ ♔f4 55 ♕b8+ ♔e3 56 ♖e5+;

C) 52...♕b5 Black tries to keep on the e8 square 53 ♖d6+ ♖e6 (53...♔f5 54 ♕xf7 mate) 54 ♕d8+ ♔g7 55 ♖xe6 fxe6 56 ♕e7+ +-;

D) 52...♕c7+ 53 ♔h3; 52 ♕h8+ ♔e7 53 ♕xh7 ♖d6+ 54 ♔h3 ♕e6+ 55 g4 ♖h2+ 56 ♔xh2 ♕e2+ 57 ♔g3 ♕e1+ 58 ♔f4 ♕d2+ 59 ♔e5 ♕e3+ 60 ♔xd5 ♕xf3+; 52 ♕d8+ Black can simply exchange queens, as the ending is a theoretical draw.

52...♖e6

Now he has to win the game all over again and, desperate to do so, he overstretches and even loses.

53 ♕h8+ ♔e7 54 ♖a8

54...♖e1!

Of course, Tal is alive to the danger. 54...♖e2 would have allowed Spassky to transpose back into the winning position after 55 ♕f8+ ♔f6 56 ♖d8.

55 ♔g3

Now 55 ♕f8+ ♔f6 56 ♖d8 will not do, as after 56...♕c7+ 57 ♔h3?? (57 ♕d6+ leads to a drawn endgame, as we saw earlier) 57...♖h1+ 58 ♔g4 h5 is mate.

55...h5 56 ♔f2

Spassky tries to push that irritating rook away.

56...♖e6 57 ♖c8 ♖d6 58 ♕f8+ ♔f6 59 ♖e8 ♖e6 60 ♕h8+

60 ♖d8 ♕b5.

60...♔f5 61 ♕h6 ♔f6 62 ♕h8+ ♔f5 63 ♖d8 ♕c6

63...♕b5!? 64 ♕h6 ♕e2+ 65 ♔g3 ♕e1+ 66 ♔h3 ♕h1+.

64 ♖c8

64 ♕g7 ♖e7.

64...♕a6 65 ♔g3?

Spassky is really pushing the boat out. 65 ♕h6 is correct.

65...♕d6+ 66 ♔h3

66 ♔f2 ♕f4.

66...♖e1

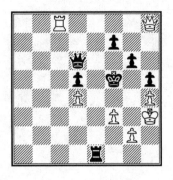

67 g3

67 g4+ hxg4+ 68 fxg4+ ♔f4! 69 ♕h6+ ♔e4 70 ♖e8+ (70 ♔g2 ♕e6 71 ♕g5 ♕xc8 72 ♕e5+ ♔d3 73 ♕xe1 ♕xg4+ -+) 70...♔f3! Maybe this was what Spassky missed when he played 65 ♔g3? Calculating such a variation is easy for a player of Spassky's class when fresh, but at the end of a long battle...

67...♖g1 68 f4

Now White's pawns are fixed on unfortunate squares, but the game is still not over...

68...♖e1

69 ♖c2?

An exhausted Spassky finally succumbs, no doubt frustrated by his inability to put the game away against Tal's obdurate defence. 69 ♕f8 is met by 69...♕e6! 70 ♖c6 ♖h1+ 71 ♔g2 ♕e4+; 69 ♖e8! is the only move to stay in the fight, but it was hard to switch to defence after pushing for a win for so long: 69...♖e4 70 ♖e5+ ♖xe5 71 dxe5 ♕e6 72 ♕b8 ♔e4+ 73 ♔g2 d4 74 ♕b1+.

69...♕e6!

A startling transformation has taken place! Now Spassky is unable to save himself.

70 ♖f2

70 ♕c8 ♕xc8 71 ♖xc8 ♖e4 72 ♖c7 f6.

70...♖h1+ 71 ♔g2 ♕e4+ 72 ♖f3 ♔g4 73 ♕c8+ f5

0-1

A remarkable game, a true battle! This defeat must have shattered Spassky. I often feel that chess is like a form of mental boxing, not only because the contenders tend to feel battered and bruised after the contest (in the case of chess it's more mental and emotional than

physical) but also because you can play a great game for six or seven hours, and after those many hours of mental and emotional investment, lose your concentration for a vital moment and get knocked out at the end! This is what happened to Spassky in this game. He lost concentration at some point and it led to his tragic defeat. Chess can be a cruel game!

It is easy to criticise Spassky for the way he overstretched. In that game it backfired horribly, but the truth remains that kind of fighting attitude gained him more victories than losses and paid off in the long run. Really it is only the players who are willing to take these kind of risks that can attain the kind of heights that Spassky was able to reach. The kind of player who doesn't fight, who agrees to a draw every time it looks like the game is heading for equality, won't progress very far in the long run. Not only that, but it creates a kind of fear in your opponent's mind if he knows he has to scrap to the bitter end in order to gain a result. Fischer took this kind of fighting spirit to its extremes, he detested easy draws and fought on until only the kings were left, or he had extracted every last drop out of the position. With this kind of competitive attitude of playing on until the death, not only will you learn more about this great game, but you will learn more about yourself, and your own limitations and abilities. Having said all that Spassky agreed a 6 move draw in his next game! (sorry, I joke.)

4

M.Bobotsov – M.Tal

Student Chess Olympiad, Varna 1958

King's Indian Defence

1 d4 ♘f6 2 c4 g6 3 ♘c3 ♗g7 4 e4 d6

Tal wasn't a great King's Indian theoretician like Fischer, but he felt very comfortable in the complex tactical middlegames that would evolve from this opening.

5 f3 0-0 6 ♘ge2 c5 7 ♗e3 ♘bd7 8 ♕d2 a6 9 0-0-0 ♕a5

9...♕c7 is a perfectly reasonable alternative, if Black doesn't wish to enter the complexity of the game continuation. Then 10 ♔b1 e6!?.

10 ♔b1

10...b5!

Black must strike while the iron is hot, as White intends the manoeuvre

♘c1-b3, after which he will have a strong grip on the centre and the queen excursion will look somewhat silly. But Tal must have calculated this well, as it involves a queen sacrifice! Nowadays this kind of sacrifice is meat and drink to King's Indian players but at the time this game was played it was quite groundbreaking. Just for the sake of argument, and even though this position is now well rooted in theory (Black nearly always plays ...b5 in this position) let's just have a look at what happens if Black plays an alternative. Dear reader, I want you again to imagine some candidate moves!

10...cxd4 11 ♘xd4 ♘c5 – Black intends ...♗c8-d7, followed by b5.

A) 12 ♘b3!? ♘xb3 13 axb3 ♖e8 (13...♕b4 14 ♔a2 b5 15 ♘d5 ♘xd5 16 cxd5 ♕xd2 17 ♖xd2 ♗d7 18 ♗g5±) 14 ♘a4 ♕xd2 15 ♖xd2.

B) 12 ♘d5!

B1) 12...♘xd5 13 ♕xa5 (13 cxd5±) 13...♘xe3 14 ♖d2±;

B2) 12...♕d8 13 ♗h6 looks like a pleasant advantage for White. So the slightly 'slow' idea of cxd4 and ♘c5 won't work.

10...♖b8 11 ♘c1!

A) 11...b5 12 ♘b3 ♕c7 (12...♕b4 13 ♘d5 ♘xd5 14 cxd5 ♕xd2 15 ♖xd2 c4 16 ♘a5±) 13 dxc5;

B) 11...cxd4 12 ♗xd4 ♘c5 13 ♘d5 is similar.

10...♖e8 11 ♘d5 ♘xd5 12 cxd5±

So do none of the other moves apart from 10...b5 work? Well, not exactly, but it is surprisingly hard to find counterplay with the alternatives. Grandmasters like Tal understood the value of the saying 'time is money' – basically every move counts. When I see games played at a lower level, they are often littered with what I would call 'little' moves, i.e. slow, considerate moves. Tal played big, booming moves that screamed at his opponents! And when you are Black you should fight for the initiative! And this is exactly what Tal does in this game.

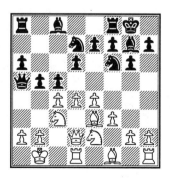

11 ♘d5!?

11 dxc5 tends to be what White does these days. 11...dxc5 (11...b4 12 ♘d5 ♘xd5 13 ♕xd5 ♘xc5 14 ♕xa8 ♗b7 15 ♕a7 ♖a8 16 ♗xc5) 12 ♘d5 ♘xd5 13 ♕xa5 (13 cxd5 ♕xd2 14 ♖xd2 f5! 15 ♘f4 ♘e5 with an attack) 13...♘xe3 14 ♖c1 ♘xc4 15 ♖xc4 bxc4 16 ♘c3 ♖b8 17 ♗xc4 ♘e5 18 ♗e2 is a slightly improved version of the queen sacrifice from White's point of view, but still Black is not without his chances.

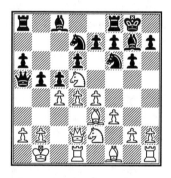

11...♘xd5!

If Black retreats with 11...♕d8 then the whole idea of playing ...♕a5 looks somewhat ridiculous. And it's not as if ♘d5 harms White. This bold sacrifice is now commonplace in this position and Tal understood that the time he would gain, by kicking White's pieces around, and the hold Black would gain over the dark squares, allied to White's slightly shaky king position, would more than compensate for the material deficit. On the other hand, a queen is still a queen! But the fact that this sacrifice is still considered relatively sound by theory shows the strength of his practical decision!

12 ♕xa5

It's not as if White had no choice but to accept the queen sacrifice. He could equally have politely declined with 12 cxd5 ♕xd2 13 ♖xd2 which has also been tried in a number of games. There is nothing new under the sun! Then 13...f5 and the game is unclear (13...c4 14 ♘c3 ♘b6 15 ♗g5 ♖e8 is also reasonable for Black, who will eventually play e6 – and he has an imposing clump of pawns on the queenside to boot.).

12...♘xe3

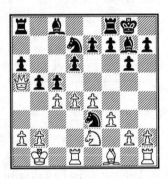

Confronted with such a position against such a dangerous tactician as Tal, I'd wager that 99.9 percent of players would be very nervous with the white pieces here. So what choice has White got?

13 ♖c1?!

13 ♖d3! looks like the only other possible candidate move. White tries to hold on to as much material as possible, as after 13 ♖c1 he is forced to give back an exchange, at least. 13 ♖d3 was tried by the very strong Chinese grandmaster Bu Xiangzhi, who broke a record at the time by becoming the world's youngest ever grandmaster at the age of 13.

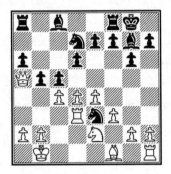

That game went 13...♘xc4 14 ♕e1 ♘db6?! 15 ♕c1 b4? (15...cxd4 16 ♘xd4 ♗d7 17 b3 ♘e5 18 ♖d1 ♖fc8 19 ♕d2 d5 20 f4!) 16 ♖d1 ♗d7 17 ♘f4! and Bu went on to win.

However 14...♖b8 15 h4 (15 ♕c1 cxd4 16 ♘xd4 ♘c5 17 ♖d1 ♗d7 18 b3 ♘e5 19 ♕d2 actually looks better for White, as he has managed to eject the strong knight from c4) 15...cxd4 16 ♘xd4 ♘c5 17 ♖d1 ♗d7 was tried in one game, and Black went on to win. He may only have two pieces and a pawn for the queen, but in this sort of position where White lacks targets, the queen is often less than a match for the minor pieces.

13...♘xc4 14 ♖xc4

14 ♕e1?! cxd4 gives Black too much.

14...bxc4

A critical position. Bobotsov has no less than 8 credible candidate moves here but none of them seem to solve his problems! Let's put ourselves in his shoes. 14 dxc5, 14 ♕c7, 14 ♕a4, 14 ♕c3, 14 ♕d2, 14 ♘c3, 14 ♘f4 and the move he played in the game, 14 ♘c1.

15 ♘c1?

15 dxc5 ♘xc5 16 ♘c3 (16 ♘f4? ♖b8∓) 16...♗e6 leaves Black with good compensation;

15 ♕c7 cxd4 16 ♕xc4 ♘e5 17 ♕xd4 ♘xf3 18 ♕d5 ♗e6∓; 15 ♕a4 cxd4 16 ♕xc4 ♘e5 transposes to the above variation, as does 15 ♕c3 cxd4 16 ♕xc4;

15 ♕d2 ♖b8! keeps the pressure on;

15 ♘c3 cxd4 16 ♘d5 e6 17 ♘e7+ ♔h8 18 ♗xc4 ♘e5 looks good for Black;

15 ♘f4! places the knight far more actively than in the game, where it espies the d5 square, and indeed this has been played in a few games. We have still not left the path of theory! (although it should be reiterated that

Tal was the first to play this queen sacrifice.) Still it would seem that Black has all the trumps after, for example, 15...♗xd4 (15...cxd4 16 ♗xc4 ♘e5 17 ♗b3) 16 ♗xc4 ♖b8 17 b3 ♘e5.

15...♖b8! 16 ♗xc4 ♘b6 17 ♗b3 ♗xd4 18 ♕d2

Surprisingly there is nothing better, as the natural 18 ♘e2 runs into the nice shot 18...♗xb2!

18...♗g7 19 ♘e2 c4 20 ♗c2 c3!

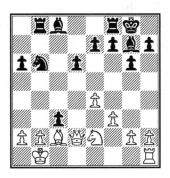

Now Black is winning. Tal mops up efficiently.

21 ♕d3

21 ♘xc3 ♘c4.

21...cxb2 22 ♘d4 ♗d7 23 ♖d1 ♖fc8 24 ♗b3 ♘a4! 25 ♗xa4 ♗xa4 26 ♘b3

26 ♖e1 ♖b4-+.

26...♖c3 27 ♕xa6 ♗xb3 28 axb3 ♖bc8 29 ♕a3 ♖c1+ 30 ♖xc1 ♖xc1+ 0-1

White makes only one real mistake (14 ♘c1?) and is run over!

Tal's sense of the initiative was too strong. What lessons can be drawn from this game? That in dynamic, sharp positions, the smallest, most insignificant looking error can lead to a rapid defeat. Basically it's another reason why calculation is so important. While many of us rely heavily on intuition, and I would count myself among that number, without the ability to make exhaustive analysis of complicated variations, it is often impossible to traverse the tactical minefield with which we are continually confronted with in chess. One classic mistake in calculation that pops up time and time again, is that you look at a sharp idea, where your position seems to hang by a thread, you spend ages looking at it, and you finally convince yourself that it's okay and you play it. But you miss another move straight away that your opponent plays, which is far stronger! That is why most mistakes in calculation come under pressure. It's easy to lose your discipline if your position is deteriorating. So maintain your discipline and force yourself to keep looking at candidate moves!

Chapter 2

Self Handicapping

Self handicapping is a term borrowed from psychology (not from horse racing, where the horses are given the licence to handicap themselves, just in case you are wondering) – whereby a person will put a number of blocks, both mental and real, in their own way to stop themselves from achieving their goals and true potential. Of course this also applies to chess, but some are more guilty than others. For example, whenever a player loses he will blame the fact that he got out of bed too late to prepare properly, or that he stayed out too late the night before, or that he was ill, or even that he was late for the game (although this has been put to the test now that FIDE has recently introduced yet another ridiculously Draconian rule which states that a player will be defaulted if he does not arrive punctually for the start of the game.) or that his mobile phone went off, etc etc. The whole point of this is to avoid a situation where he is fully exposed, i.e. he no longer has any excuses, and any defeat cannot be attributed to outside influences, he/she fears that in that scenario they will be exposed as simply not good

enough. Of course it's very scary to escape from this comfort blanket, because the alternative is often too appalling to contemplate – that we simply aren't good enough. Whenever you have excuses to fall back on, such a scenario can always be avoided to a certain degree, though it is my belief that the stronger the player, the less they are guilty of self-handicapping, as they have more or less removed the mental blocks that lead to fear of defeat. But even strong players are quite guilty of self-handicapping at times, and I believe it was Tal himself who said that he never defeated a healthy opponent, so he must have encountered plenty of this himself. We can all be drawn to failure, perhaps to some of us it is more interesting (and more comforting) than the opposite. The tabloids are obsessed with the apparent downfalls of Britney Spears and Michael Jackson – and numerous celebrities who have destroyed their careers with drugs, affairs and so on. Who wants to read about a happily married couple? It's boring. Let's read about Michael Jackson, who goes bankrupt, millions in debt, forcing him to sell all his memorabilia from his glory days for pennies – only then to die in tragic circumstances. Such a scenario is mirrored in chess by the downfall of the legendary Bobby Fischer, who, hounded by the American authorities, ended up making anti-Semitic outbursts that seemed fuelled more by mental illness than any grip on reality. Nowadays, of course, we are all suffering from the credit crunch – so chess should give us the perfect form of escapism from our everyday woes.

5

M.Tal – P.Benko

Candidates Tournament,
Curacao 1962

French Defence

1 e4 e6 2 d4 d5 3 ♘c3 ♘f6 4 ♗g5 dxe4 5 ♘xe4 ♘bd7

Benko choses a relatively solid line of the French. This Hungarian grandmaster had a pretty awful

record against Tal, so much so that he was convinced that the Latvian was hypnotising his opponents with his intense stare, and even turned up for one of his encounters with Tal donning a pair of dark sunglasses, in an effort to avoid Tal's penetrating glare. Mind you, it didn't help him much as he lost that game as well. Another form of self-handicapping? As I said, chess players are often afraid of admitting that they simply lost to a stronger player.

6 ♘xf6+ ♘xf6 7 ♘f3 c5 8 ♗c4 cxd4 9 0-0 ♗e7 10 ♕e2 h6

10...a6!? with the idea that after 11 ♖ad1 b5 12 ♗b3 h6 13 ♖xd4 ♕b6 the queen is not blocking the b-pawn.

11 ♗f4

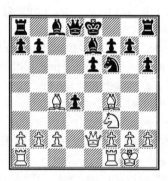

11...0-0

11...a6!? 12 ♖ad1 b5 13 ♗b3 0-0 14 ♘xd4 ♕b6 15 ♘f5!. In general in these lines, the bishop on f4 does a good job of preventing the queen from finding the more comfortable square of c7, where it laterally defends the bishop on e7. If Black can complete his development in such lines then he tends to stand well; Karpov in particular has made a career out of proving Black's chances in such positions. However there's always a grave danger he will get 'killed in his bed'.

12 ♖ad1 ♗d7 13 ♖xd4 ♕b6

14 ♖d3

14 ♕d2, eyeing up the vulnerable h6 point, was Tal's improvement against his perennial opponent, Lajos Portisch, in their world championship quarter final in 1965. 14...♗c6 15 ♗xh6!? A typically adventurous Tal sacrifice! The consequences are unclear but, more importantly, he takes Portisch out of his comfort zone, as the Hungarian was a notably strong positional player, but felt much less comfortable in sharp positions, characterised by the need to calculate difficult variations and where everything hangs by a thread.

A) 15...gxh6 16 ♕xh6 ♗xf3 17 ♕g5+ ♔h8 18 ♖h4+ ♗h5 (18...♘h5 19 ♕xe7 ♖g8 20 ♕f6+! +-) 19 ♗d3! and Black is seemingly powerless against the threats of ♖xh5 and ♕h6, for example 19...♖fd8 20 ♖xh5+ ♘xh5 21 ♕h6+ ♔g8 22 ♗h7+ ♔h8 23 ♗g6+ ♔g8 24 ♕h7+ ♔f8 25 ♕xf7 or 25 ♕h8 mate;

B) 15...♗xf3 16 ♗xg7! (16 ♕g5 ♘e8 17 ♕xe7 ♕xd4) 16...♖fd8 17 ♕h6 ♘h7 18 ♗d3 f5 19 gxf3 (19 ♕g6 ♗h5!) 19...♖xd4 20 ♗xd4 ♕xd4 21 ♕xe6+ ♔f8 22 ♗c4 (22 ♕xf5+ ♘f6) 22...♕g7+ (22...♔e8 23 ♕f7+ ♔d8 24 ♗e2! is a nice switchback, as Black cannot then meet the twin threats of ♖d1 and ♕xh7 adequately) 23 ♔h1 ♘g5 24 ♕xf5+ ♘f7 25 ♖g1 ♕f6 (25...♗g5 26 ♖xg5) 26 ♕g4 ♘h6 (26...♕h8 27 ♕g6 ♘h6 28 ♕xh6+; 26...♔e8 27 ♗b5+) 27 ♕g8+ and mate next move;

C) 15...♘e4 16 ♕f4 gxh6 17 ♖xe4 ♗xe4 18 ♕xe4 and White had reasonable compensation for the exchange, although at this point

Portisch didn't stand that badly, but the exhaustive calculation of these variations had taken its toll and Tal later broke down his defence. It was on just such slayings of Black's castled king that Tal built his reputation!

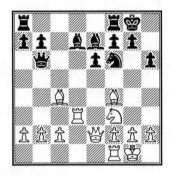

14...♗b5

14...♗c6!? 15 ♘e5 (15 ♖fd1 ♖fd8 16 ♘e5 ♗e4).

A) 15...♖ad8

A1) 16 ♘xf7!? ♖xf7 17 ♕xe6 ♗d5 (17...♘d5 18 ♗e3 ♕a5 19 ♖fd1 maintains the pressure; 17...♖d5 18 ♖xd5) 18 ♖xd5! ♕xe6 (18...♘xd5 19 ♗xd5+-) 19 ♖xd8+ +-;

A2) 16 ♖fd1;

A3) 16 ♖xd8 ♕xd8 (16...♖xd8? 17 ♘xf7 ♔xf7 18 ♕xe6+ ♔e8 19 ♕f7+ ♔d7 20 ♗e6 mate) 17 ♖d1;

A4) 16 ♖g3 ♘e4 17 ♖b3 ♕c5 18 ♘xc6 ♕xc6 19 ♗b5 ♕d5;

B) 15...♖fd8 Which rook!? In some variations it may be better to have the option of walking the king out via f8;

C) 15...♖fd8? 16 ♘xf7! ♖xd3

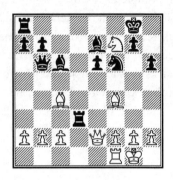

C1) 17 ♕xe6 ♗d5 (17...♖d4 18 ♘xh6+ ♔h8 19 ♘f7+ ♔g8 20 ♘g5+ ♔h8 21 ♕h3+) 18 ♘xh6+ ♔f8!;

C2) 17 cxd3 ♔xf7 18 ♕xe6+ ♔e8 (18...♔g6 19 ♕xe7) 19 ♖e1 ♕d8 (19...♕c5 20 ♗d6) 20 ♕f7+ ♔d7 21 ♗e6 mate;

D) 15...♗e4 16 ♖g3 ♔h8 and it is not so easy to break down the black king's defence; in some variations Black can call on the bishop on e4 for assistance. 17 ♘d7 (17 ♕d2 ♘h5! 18 ♗xh6 ♘xg3 19 hxg3 gxh6 20 ♕xh6+ ♔g8-+) 17...♘xd7 18 ♕xe4 ♗f6 19 ♖b3 ♕a5 and Black is defending.

15 ♗xb5 ♕xb5

It would seem that the exchange of light squared bishops has helped nullify White's attacking chances somewhat, which is probably a reason why Tal chose to improve with 14 ♕d2 against Portisch; however it would not be possible to become world champion if Tal wasn't adept at 'getting blood out of a stone'.

16 ♘e5 ♕xb2

Was Benko forced to take this pawn? What other options did he have?

16...♘d5 (not 16...♖fd8?? 17 ♖xd8+) 17 ♗xh6! gxh6 18 c4 ♘f4? (18...♕b6 19 cxd5+-) 19 ♕g4+;

16...♖ad8

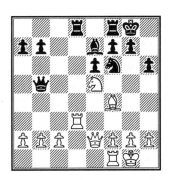

A) 17 ♗xh6 ♖xd3 (17...gxh6?? 18 ♖g3+) 18 cxd3 gxh6-+;

B) 17 c4 ♕a6 was one solid option for Black, nevertheless White also has his trumps; the pawn on c4 stops the knight from coming to the centre, for example.

18 b3 ♖xd3 19 ♘xd3 ♖d8 20 ♖d1;

So we can conclude that the solid 16...♖ad8 would have presented Black with equality; maybe Benko was already searching for more?

17 ♖g3

17 ♖b3 ♕d4!∓ (17...♕xa2!? 18 ♖xb7 ♘d5).

17...♖fc8?

Again we must ask ourselves, was Benko forced to allow the capture on h6? Could he have prevented this somehow? 17...♔h8! looks like the only move to prevent the capture, doesn't it? What would you do as White in this position? If there is a drawback to this move, it's that there is now only one piece defending f7.

A) 18 ♗xh6 seemingly won't do: 18...gxh6 19 ♕e3 (19 ♕d2? ♕xe5 20 ♕xh6+ ♘h7 defending g7) 19...♘g8 (19...♔h7 20 ♕d3+ ♔h8 21 ♕e3) 20 ♕f4 ♗g5! (20...♗f6 21 ♖xg8+ ♔xg8 22 ♕xf6 isn't so clear) 21 ♘xf7+ ♔g7 22 ♖xg5+ hxg5 23 ♕xg5+ ♔xf7;

B) The 'crude' 18 ♖h3!

B1) 18...♘g8 19 ♕h5 (19 ♘g4 ♗f6) 19...g6

B1a) 20 ♘xg6+ fxg6 21 ♕xg6 (21 ♗e5+ ♔h7-+) 21...♖xf4 22 ♖xh6+ ♘xh6 23 ♕xh6+ ♔g8 24 ♕xf4 ♕f6∓;

B1b) 20 ♕e2! Another strong switchback. Having forced numerous weaknesses on Black's kingside, with this retreat White creates the powerful threat of ♘xg6 and ♗e5. 20...♗f6 (20...♔g7 21 ♘d7; 20...♕b6 21 ♘d7; 20...♕xa2 21 ♕e3! h5 22 g4 ♘f6 23 ♗g5 ♔g7 24 gxh5 with an attack) 21 ♘d7±;

B2) 18...♘h7 19 ♕h5! ♔g8 20 ♗xh6 would have been too obvious for Tal;

B3) 18...♘d5 19 ♗xh6 gxh6 20 ♕h5 is a winning sacrifice;

B4) 18...♔g8!

B4a) 19 ♗xh6 gxh6 20 ♕e3 (20 ♖xh6 ♔g7 21 ♕e3 ♘d5) indeed looks very obvious and dangerous; but there is the strong defence 20...h5! (20...♖fd8 21 ♕xh6+-; 20...♘h7? 21 ♕xh6 ♕xc2 22 ♘d3! won't do) 21 ♖g3+ (21 ♕h6 ♕xe5

22 ♖g3+ ♘g4) 21...♔h7 (21...♘g4 22 ♘xg4 hxg4 23 ♖xg4+ ♔h7 24 ♕h3+ ♗h4 25 ♕xh4 mate) 22 ♕d3+ ♔h8 (22...♔h6 23 ♘xf7+ ♖xf7 24 ♕g6 mate) 23 ♕e3 ♘h7! 24 ♕h6 ♕xe5.

So it seems that 17...♔h8 was a sensible choice, and it may well have been that Tal would have had to take the draw after all. But I'm sure Benko didn't think the line he chose in the game was bad either!;

B4b) With 19 ♖g3 White can force a repetition, but Tal would doubtless have chopped both his arms off before acquiescing to a draw here; possibly Benko understood that from a practical point of view it was dangerous to allow Tal 'at least a draw'.

18 ♗xh6

Now Tal has what he always aimed for – an attack. Black's king will be vulnerable for the rest of the game.

18...♗f8

18...♘e8? 19 ♕h5! The shots are coming from everywhere; 18...g6

19 ♘xg6 fxg6 20 ♕xe6+ ♔h7
21 ♕f7+.

19 ♕e3

19...♕xc2

19...♖xc2 20 ♗xg7! ♗xg7
21 ♖xg7+ (21 ♕h6? ♘e8)
21...♔xg7 22 ♕g5+ ♔h7 (22...♔f8
23 ♕xf6 ♖c7 24 ♘g6+ picks up the
errant black queen) 23 ♕xf6 ♖f8
24 ♕h4+ ♔g7 25 ♕g5+ ♔h8
26 ♘d7! ♕g7 27 ♕h4+ wins too
much material. 19...♘d5!? is one
possible 'computer-like' defence,
counter-intuitively moving the
knight away from the kingside.
When defending seemingly
indefensible positions, computers
often resort to suggesting moves that
seem to defy logic, but apparently
hold the defence together by a sharp
tactical thread. May I point out
though that in common with the
majority of games in this book, I
have not gone over this game with a
computer, but having played and
analysed with a computer before, I
am more than aware of their
incredible defensive qualities!
20 ♕g5 (20 ♕e4!?) 20...f6 21 ♕g6?

(21 ♕g4! ♕xe5 22 ♗xg7 ♔f7
23 ♗xf8 ♖xf8 24 ♕g7+ ♔e8
25 ♕xb7 ♖d8 26 ♖g7 does look
very dangerous though) 21...♕xe5
22 ♗xg7 ♘f4 is a defence that is
easy to overlook. That is why it is
important to check every line,
especially when you think you are
on the verge on winning – there is
often a sting in the tail. 19...♘h5?!
20 ♖g5 ♖c3 (20...f6 21 ♖xh5±;
20...♕c3 21 ♕e4±) 21 ♕e2 ♘f4
22 ♕g4+-.

20 ♖e1!

A move that I believe would be out
of the radar of most players. Tal
realises that he can go no further
with his attack so takes time out to
overprotect the e4 square! Most
profound. But again, if we use the
theory of looking at as many
candidate moves as possible, then
♖e1 comes to our attention, as Black
'intends' to play the defence ♕e4.
This move, in the best traditions of
Nimzowitsch, also overprotects the
knight on e5.

20...♖c7?!

20...♕e4 21 ♕xe4! (21 ♗xg7? is met by 21...♕xe3! 22 ♗xf6+ ♕xg3-+) 21...♘xe4 22 ♖xe4 and the c1 square is covered. 20...♕f5! 21 h3! keeping the pressure on; it is useful to give the king some breathing space before carrying on with the attack (21 ♖f3 ♕h5) 21...♘d5 (21...♖c2 22 ♖g5 ♕h7 23 ♘xf7!) 22 ♕b3.

21 h3 ♖ac8?!

21...♕f5! 22 ♖g5 (22 ♖f3 ♕h5) 22...♕e4 23 ♕xe4 ♘xe4 24 ♖xe4 f6 25 ♖gg4 fxe5 26 ♖xe5±.

22 ♗xg7!

Now his position has been strengthened to the maximum, Tal cashes in.

22...♗xg7 23 ♖xg7+ ♔xg7 24 ♕g5+ ♔f8 25 ♕xf6

White doesn't even have a single pawn for the exchange, but the activity of his remaining pieces means that Black's defence is very difficult.

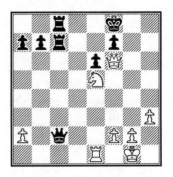

25...♕h7

If 25...♕c3 (25...♕f5!?) 26 ♕h8+ (26 ♘g6+ ♔e8) 26...♔e7 27 ♕h4+

A) 27...f6 28 ♘g6+ ♔d6 (28...♔f7 29 ♕h7+ ♔e8 30 ♕g8+ ♔d7 31 ♕xe6+ ♔d8 32 ♕e8 mate) 29 ♖d1+ ♔c6 30 ♕a4+ ♔b6 (30...b5 31 ♕a6+ ♔c5 32 ♕d6+ ♔c4 33 ♕xe6+) 31 ♖b1+ ♔c5 32 ♕b5+ ♔d4 33 ♖d1+ ♔e4 34 ♕e2+ ♔f5 35 ♕g4 mate;

B) 27...♔e8 28 ♖e3 Black's problem is that he lacks counterplay, while White's combined force of rook, queen and knight casts a spell around the black king. Perhaps only Karpov could defend such a position, but at this moment in time he wasn't around! (28 ♕h8+).

26 ♖e3! ♕f5 27 ♕h8+ ♔e7 28 ♕h4+

28...♕f6?!

28...f6 29 ♕b4+ ♔e8 30 g4!
(30 ♘f3?! ♔f7) 30...♖c1+
(30...♕xe5 31 ♖xe5 fxe5 32 ♕b5+
♔e7 33 ♕xe5±) 31 ♔g2 ♕b1
32 ♕d6 ♖g1+ (32...fxe5 33 ♕xe6+
♔f8 34 ♖f3+) 33 ♔f3 fxe5
34 ♕xe6+.

29 ♕b4+ ♔e8?!

29...♖c5 30 ♕xb7+ ♖8c7 31 ♕b4±.

30 ♕b5+ ♔f8

30...♔e7 31 ♖f3.

31 ♖f3

31...♕d8?

The final mistake. Resistance was
still possible with 31...♕g7 after
which White has a few attacking
tries: 32 ♘d7 32 ♕b4, and 32 ♖g3.

A) 32 ♘d7+ ♔e7 33 ♘f6 does
seem highly promising; White uses
the knight as a shield to keep in the
black king and queen. The problem
though is that Black can give up his
queen with 33...♕xf6 34 ♕b4+ ♖c5
35 ♖xf6 ♔xf6 36 ♕xb7 ♖8c7 after
which it is doubtful White can win;

B) 32 ♕b4+ ♔e8 33 ♕f4 (33 ♖g3
♕xe5 34 ♖g8+ ♔d7; 33 ♕d6 ♕f8)
still with a dangerous looking attack
as Black has to keep a keen eye on
f7;

C) 32 ♖g3! 32...♕f6 33 ♕b4+
♕e7 34 ♕f4.

32 ♕b4+ ♔e8 33 ♖g3 1-0

There is no defence to ♖g8.
Another good example of the
extreme mental pressure to which
Tal subjected his opponents – Benko
didn't seem to make any obvious big
errors, but bit by bit he was led to his
defeat.

6

M.Tal – E.Geller

USSR Championship, Riga 1958

Ruy Lopez

If Tal was a dangerous counter-
attacker with the black pieces, he
was even more deadly when given
the advantage of the first move. He
could control the game and more
easily lead the game towards
the kind of insanely complicated
positions that he revelled in.

**1 e4 e5 2 ♘f3 ♘c6 3 ♗b5 a6
4 ♗a4 ♘f6 5 0-0 ♗e7 6 ♖e1 b5
7 ♗b3 0-0 8 c3 d6 9 h3 ♘a5**

The Chigorin variation, which has
never really lost its popularity as one
of Black's main replies to the Ruy
Lopez.

10 ♗c2

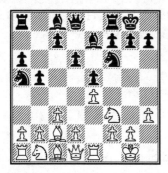

10...c5

Just lately the surprising pawn sacrifice 10...d5!? has featured in a number of games. Black's idea, unlike in the Marshall, is that while the black knight is presently rather out of play on a5, it also has the advantage that when White captures on d5 he is not hitting the knight with tempo. 11 exd5 e4! 12 ♘g5 (12 ♗xe4 ♘xe4 13 ♖xe4 ♗b7 14 d4 ♗xd5 gives Black some compensation for the pawn in the shape of the two bishops, though I rather suspect that White should be on top in this kind of situation. It would be interesting to know what Tal would have made of this 10...d5!? idea. The problem these days is that every novelty and pretty much every move known in the opening is analysed to death by super-computers, so it is becoming more and more difficult to be truly original and inventive in this phase of the game.) 12...♘xd5 13 ♘xe4 f5! 14 ♘g3 f4 15 ♘e4 f3 is rather unclear.

11 d4 ♗b7 12 b4!?

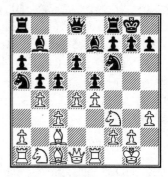

Tal goes his own way in the opening! More 'normal' would be 12 ♘bd2 cxd4 13 cxd4 exd4 14 ♘xd4 ♖e8 15 ♘f1 ♗f8 16 ♘g3 which is the main line of the Romanishin variation. But Tal was keen to take his opponents into uncharted territory as soon as possible, and force them to think for themselves!

12...cxb4 13 cxb4

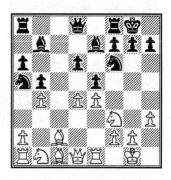

13...♘c4

13...♘c6 would also seem quite logical. 14 a3 exd4 (14...♘xd4 15 ♘xd4 exd4 16 ♗b2 a5 17 ♗xd4 axb4 18 axb4 ♖xa1 19 ♗xa1 d5

20 e5 ♘e4 21 ♕d4 with a slight advantage)

A) 15 ♘xd4 ♘xd4 16 ♕xd4 ♘d7 (16...♘xe4 17 ♗xe4 ♗f6 18 ♗xh7+ ♔xh7 19 ♕d3+ g6 20 ♘c3 ♖c8 21 ♗b2 is about equal) 17 ♖a2 ♘e5 looks fine for Black;

B) 15 ♗b2 ♘e5 16 ♘xd4 (16 ♗xd4 ♘fd7 17 ♘c3 ♗f6) 16...♘c4 17 ♗c3 g6 18 ♘d2 (18 a4 ♕b6) 18...♖c8 I think Tal may have played ♘c6 as it immediately 'puts the question' to White, i.e. it exerts pressure on White's centre, therefore it probably gives him more chances to go wrong. However it is difficult to believe that there is anything wrong with ♘c4 either.

14 ♘bd2

A) 19...♗xb4 20 ♘xf7! ♖xf7 (20...♕xd1 21 ♖exd1 ♖xf7 22 ♖d7+-) 21 ♗xf7+ ♔xf7 22 ♕b3+ ♕d5 23 ♕xb4 ♖c2 24 ♖ad1 ♕f5 25 ♕b3+;

B) 19...♕xd1 20 ♖exd1 ♖cd8 (20...♗xb4 21 ♖d7 ♘c5 22 ♗xf7+ ♔h8 23 ♖d4! ♗a5 24 ♘g6+ hxg6 25 ♖h4 mate

...is one nice variation) 21 ♖xd8 ♗xd8 22 ♖d1 and White has everything in order. d5 is the normal 'equalising'" move for Black in the Ruy Lopez, as if Black can get it in effectively it tends to relieve all the tension in the centre. However, as we can see, it was never that easy to 'equalise' against Tal!

15 exd5!

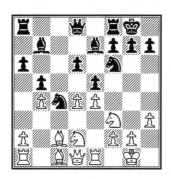

14...d5!?

Geller rejects the 'solid' 14...♖c8 because of 15 ♘xc4 ♖xc4 (15...bxc4 16 d5±) 16 ♗b3 ♖c8 (16...♖xb4? 17 ♗a3 ♖xb3 18 ♕xb3 exd4 19 ♘xd4 ♗xe4 20 f3±) 17 ♗b2 ♘xe4 18 dxe5 dxe5 19 ♘xe5 as it looks as if White is having all the fun;

15 dxe5?! ♘xe4 16 ♘xe4 (16 a3? ♘c3! wins) 16...dxe4 17 ♕xd8 ♖axd8 18 ♗xe4 ♗xe4 19 ♖xe4 ♖d1+ 20 ♔h2 ♗xb4∓

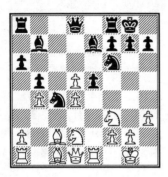

15...exd4

Black had two other realistic candidate moves that needed to be calculated here:

15...♗xb4? 16 dxe5

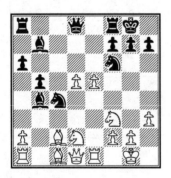

A) 16...♘xd2 17 ♗xd2

A1) 17...♗xd2 18 ♕xd2 ♘xd5 19 ♘g5! with the initiative, e.g. 19...h6 (19...g6 20 e6±) 20 ♕d3 g6 21 ♘e6 (21 ♘xf7!?);

A2) 17...♘xd5 18 ♗xh7+! ♔xh7 19 ♘g5+ ♔g8 (19...♔g6 20 ♕c2+ f5 21 exf6+ ♔xf6 22 ♖e6 mate) 20 ♕h5 ♘f6 (20...♖e8 21 ♕xf7+

♔h8 22 ♕h5+ ♔g8 23 ♕h7+ ♔f8 24 ♕h8+ ♔e7 25 ♕xg7 mate) 21 exf6 ♕d3 22 ♗xb4+-;

B) 16...♘xd5 17 ♘xc4

B1) 17...bxc4 18 ♗xh7+! ♔xh7 19 ♘g5+ ♔g8 (19...♔g6 20 ♕c2+ f5 21 exf6+ ♔xf6 22 ♖e6 mate) 20 ♕h5 ♘f6 21 exf6 ♕d3 22 fxg7 ♔xg7 23 ♘e6+! fxe6 (23...♔g8 24 ♖e3 wins) 24 ♗h6+ ♔g8 (24...♔f6 25 ♕g5+ ♔f7 26 ♕g7+ is similar) 25 ♕g4+ ♔f7 26 ♕g7+ ♔e8 27 ♖xe6+ ♔d8 28 ♕xb7+- Such sacrifices were meat and drink to Tal.

B2) 17...♗xe1 18 ♘d6 pours a cold shower as Black will inevitably lose a piece.

15...♘xd5!? is a more challenging try. Then 16 ♘xc4 bxc4

A) 17 dxe5 ♘xb4 with an initiative;

B) 17 ♘xe5! ♗xb4 18 ♗d2 ♗xd2 19 ♕xd2 c3 20 ♕d3 g6 21 ♗b3±;

C) 17 ♖xe5 ♘xb4 (17...♗xb4) 18 ♗e4 ♗xe4 19 ♖xe4 ♗f6 with the idea of ...♕d5;

D) 17 a3?! ♘c3 18 ♕d2

D1) 18...♗xf3? 19 ♕xc3 ♗b7 (19...♕xd4 20 ♕xd4 exd4 21 ♖xe7) 20 dxe5±;

D2) 18...exd4 19 ♕xd4 ♕xd4 20 ♘xd4 ♗f6∓ I doubt that Geller analysed these lines very much; he probably just saw that exd4 looked more than acceptable on general grounds and trusted to his intuition.

16 ♘xc4

16 ♘xd4 ♕xd5 17 ♘2f3 ♗xb4∓

16...bxc4 17 ♕xd4 ♗xb4

17...♘xd5 would presumably have been carefully considered by Geller.

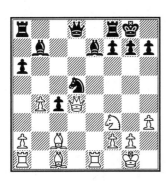

Now White has no less than four reasonable candidate moves.

A) 18 ♕e4?! g6 only seems to strengthen Black's position;

B) 18 ♗d2 ♗f6 (18...♘xb4! 19 ♕xd8 ♖fxd8 20 ♖xe7 ♘xc2 21 ♖c1 ♗xf3 22 ♖xc2 ♗d5∓) 19 ♘e5 ♕c7 offers Black good play for the pawn;

C) 18 ♗b2

C1) 18...♗f6! 19 ♕e4 g6 20 ♗xf6 ♕xf6 21 ♖ab1 (21 a3? ♘xb4 22 ♕xb7 ♘xc2)

C1a) 21...♖ab8 22 ♕xc4? ♖fc8

C1a1) 23 ♕b3 ♖c3 24 ♕b2 ♘f4 with a tremendous attack (24...♖xf3 25 gxf3 ♕g5+ 26 ♔h2 ♕f4+ 27 ♔g1 ♕g5+);

C1a2) 23 ♕d3 ♘f4;

C1b) 21...♕c3!? 22 ♖ed1 ♖fe8 and Black has good control over the centre of the board;

C2) 18...c3 19 ♗a3 ♗f6 looks more than okay for Black;

D) 18 ♕xc4 ♗f6 19 ♖b1 ♘c3 20 ♖b2 ♖c8 (20...♗d5! 21 ♕f4 ♘xa2 22 ♖b1 ♘c3∓) 21 ♕d3 ♕xd3 22 ♗xd3 ♖cd8;

E) 18 a3 ♗f6 19 ♕e4 (19 ♘e5 ♖e8 20 f4 ♕c7 looks very active for Black) 19...g6 20 ♗h6 ♗xa1 (20...♖e8 21 ♕xe8+ ♕xe8 22 ♖xe8+ ♖xe8 23 ♖d1 ♗b2 24 ♗c1±) 21 ♗xf8 (21 ♖xa1 ♕f6∓) 21...♗c3∓

All in all, it is not easy to suggest a good continuation for White after 17...♘xd5! which is probably why this 12 b4 idea hasn't generally been repeated since. In my own experience grandmasters often play moves in the opening and early middlegame quite quickly, relying heavily on their highly tuned intuition, to save time for the inevitable crisis later on. But this is often a mistake! It all depends on the position. Fair enough if it's quite a dull, quiet game, but here there is a lot going on and every move is important.

18 ♖b1?!

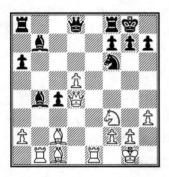

Tal, on the other hand, is alive to all the possibilities! It is not so hard to identify ♖b1 as a candidate move, the difficulty is seeing how things will develop. Many players would look at ♖b1 and think "hmmm, interesting move, but do I have enough for the exchange?" and wouldn't have the courage to play it. But one thing Tal didn't lack was courage, at times his play bordered on reckless, but it was very effective! 18 ♖d1 ♗xd5 19 ♕h4 was the more sedate continuation, and perhaps more sensible.

18...♗xe1

18...♘xd5! again had to be calculated.

White had a dangerous looking 'Greek gift' sacrifice but it would appear that things are not so clear in that case:

A) 19 ♖d1;

B) 19 ♗d2! ♗xd2 20 ♕xd2 (20 ♘xd2 ♗c6 is probably about equal) 20...♗c6 21 ♘e5 and White is active in the centre;

C) 19 ♕e4 g6;

D) 19 ♗xh7+? 19...♔xh7 20 ♘g5+ ♔g6 (20...♔g8 21 ♕h4 ♘f6 22 ♖xb4±) 21 ♕h4 ♖h8! (21...♗xe1 22 ♕h7+ ♔f6 23 ♖xb7 ♕c8 doesn't seem to offer enough for White either) 22 ♕e4+ f5 23 ♕e6+ ♕f6 24 ♖xb4 ♘xb4 25 ♕xc4 ♖he8.

19 ♖xb7 ♖e8

19...♕xd5!? 20 ♕xd5 ♘xd5 21 ♘xe1 ♖ab8! 22 ♖xb8 ♖xb8 23 a3 and material is effectively level, but White will walk his king over to try to neutralise the c-pawn, after which he can get to work with

his minor pieces. 19...♘xd5
20 ♘xe1±; 19...♗a5 20 ♗g5!!

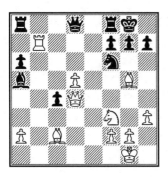

A) 20...h6 21 ♗h4

A1) 21...g5 22 ♘xg5 ♕xd5
23 ♕xf6 hxg5 24 ♕h6+-;

A2) 21...♖e8 22 d6 ♖b8 23 ♖xb8
♕xb8 24 ♗xf6 gxf6 25 ♕xf6 ♖e6
26 ♗h7+-+;

A3) 21...♖e8 22 d6 ♖e6 23 ♗xf6
(23 d7!? ♗b6 24 ♕xc4 and already
White has a massive d-pawn for the
exchange) 23...♕xf6 24 ♕d5 ♗d8
25 d7 ♖d6 26 ♕xc4 and the d-pawn
is very dangerous;

A4) 21...♕xd5 22 ♗xf6 ♕xb7
23 ♕g4+-;

B) 20...♕xd5 21 ♕h4 (21 ♗xf6
♕xb7 22 ♕h4 h6 23 ♕g4 What's
impressive in all these lines is how
all White's pieces are contributing to
the attack, while Black's extra
exchange is surprisingly ineffective.
Explaining 19 ♖xb7 is simple – Tal
liked to attack!);

19...♖b8 20 ♖xb8 ♕xb8 21 ♘xe1.

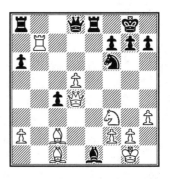

20 d6!

Tal opens a line to his favourite
square, f7. 20 ♗g5 ♖e2!? 21 ♕xc4
♗xf2+ 22 ♔f1 ♖xc2 23 ♕xc2 ♗g3
isn't a stupid idea. Black tries to give
back some material in an attempt to
quench White's ferocious initiative.

20...♕c8

Again Geller had alternatives;
20...♖b8 runs into the prosaic
21 ♖xb8! (but not 21 ♘g5? ♕xd6
22 ♘xe6 ♕xe6∓) 21...♕xb8 22 d7
♖d8 23 ♘xe1 ♖xd7 24 ♕xc4 and
White should win. Then again,
20...♖e6 21 ♗f4 and White's rook
on the seventh rank, the weak
f7 pawn, and the monster pawn
on d6 offer more than enough
compensation for the exchange.

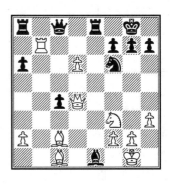

21 ♗g5?

Played with elan, but bad! The simple 21 ♖c7 would have kept Tal's disadvantage to a minimum, but when could Tal resist a combination!? He was seduced by the beautiful lines when Black takes the rook, but he isn't even forced to do so! Nevertheless the simple capture of the rook would have led to a decisive advantage for Black.

21...♖e2?!

21...♕xb7! calling Tal's bluff. Then after 22 ♗xf6 ♖e2 (22...gxf6 23 ♕g4+ ♔h8 24 ♕f5+–) ...

...what would you do now?

A) 23 ♕g4 g6 24 d7 (24 ♕f4 ♗xf2+ 25 ♔h2 ♗e3) 24...♖xc2;

B) 23 ♗xh7+!

B1) Upon 23...♔xh7 I'm sure Tal had calculated 24 ♕h4+ ♔g8 25 ♕g5 ♗xf2+ 26 ♔h2 ♔f8 (26...g6 27 ♕h6) 27 ♕xg7+ ♔e8 28 ♕g8+ ♔d7 29 ♕xf7+ ♔c6 30 ♕xc4+ ♔xd6 31 ♕xe2.

B2) But 23...♔h8! seems to pour cold water on the whole concept.

B2a) 24 ♕g4 gxf6 25 ♗f5 (25 ♕h5 ♔g7) 25...♖g8–+;

B2b) 24 ♕xc4∓;

B2c) 24 ♕f4 ♗xf2+! (24...♔xh7 transposes into the main variation, 24...♗d2 25 ♕h4; 24... gxf6 25 ♗f5 ♔g7 [25...♗xf2+ 26 ♔h2] 26 ♕g4+ ♔f8 27 ♕h5 and mates.) 25 ♔h2 ♔xh7! and White no longer has ♕h4 check, so is losing.

22 ♖c7 ♕e6 23 ♘xe1 ♖xe1+ 24 ♔h2 ♖d8

24...♕e5+ 25 ♕xe5 ♖xe5 26 ♗xf6 gxf6 27 d7 ♖d5 28 ♗e4 loses.

25 ♗xf6

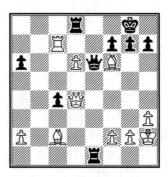

25...gxf6??

Having looked to be over the worst, Geller finally cracks under the pressure and Tal reaps the reward for his bold play! After the obvious 25...♕xf6! White's initiative is starting to run out: 26 ♕xf6 (26 ♕xc4 ♕xf2) 26...gxf6 27 d7 ♔f8∓

26 ♖e7

Oops!

26...♕xd6+ 27 ♕xd6 ♖xd6
28 ♖xe1 ♖d2 29 ♖c1 ♖xf2 30 ♗e4
♖xa2 31 ♖xc4 a5 32 ♖c8+ ♔g7
33 ♖c7

Tal won many times this way. His high-risk style in this game was no doubt objectively incorrect, but in a sense that didn't matter. What mattered was that in a competitive game he subjected his opponents to constant pressure – and the lengthy calculation that they were forced to make in search of a refutation of his attack more often than not led to blunders. As Karpov said, Tal taught us to defend. By submitting his games to stringent analysis, methods were found to combat this kind of attack, and defensive technique improved.

1-0

A journey through the mountains of chess madness

We have already touched upon the mental deterioration suffered by Fischer – which no doubt will continue to be subject of debate for many years. Some said that he was psychophrenic, others that his obsession with chess and his subsequent withdrawal into a hermit-like existence triggered a breakdown. Whatever the reason, madness and chess have always had a close relationship. The enormous challenges posed by the game attract obsessive personalities. You have to be consumed by the game to reach the level of a Fischer or a Morphy, who also had a nervous breakdown and died in straitened circumstances. Because chess is such an unfathomable game, those who seek its greatest secrets will always flirt on the edge of insanity, albeit a form locked within the game itself. Tal was one such player – perfectly sane but drawn towards insanity on the chessboard. He seemed to overwhelm his opponents in a tidal wave of complexity from which they were frequently unable to emerge.

7

M.Tal – L.Polugaevsky

USSR Championship,
Tbilisi 1959

Sicilian Defence

1 e4 c5 2 ♘f3 d6 3 d4 cxd4
4 ♘xd4 ♘f6 5 ♘c3 a6 6 ♗g5

The razor sharp ♗g5 variation, which still strikes fear into every Najdorf player – myself included!

6...♘bd7

6...e6 7 f4 is now generally accepted as the main line, after which Black has the option of 7...♕b6!?, the Poisoned Pawn variation first popularised by Fischer and also used with success by Garry Kasparov. Other replies are 7...♗e7 8 ♕f3 ♕c7; 7...♘bd7 8 ♕f3 ♕c7; 7...♘c6!?; 7...h6; 7...♕c7!?; while 7...b5!? is a variation named after the erudite and hard working Russian Lev Polugaevsky, who single-handedly developed and practised it at grandmaster level – presumably after becoming discouraged by other main lines. Black's energetic reply is based on the tactic 8 e5 dxe5 9 fxe5 ♕c7! 10 exf6 ♕e5+ regaining the piece. Theory now regards the Polugaevsky variation as being slightly dubious, but that's another story. In our age of super computers, which exert a heavy influence on contemporary opening theory, what are the chances of today's players having an opening variation named after them!? On the other hand, 'the Rybka variation' doesn't have quite the same ring to it!

7 ♗c4 ♕a5 8 ♕d2 e6 9 0-0

9 0-0-0 was also tried several times around this time with general success. A year earlier, in the USSR Championship at Riga 1958, Polu tried 9...b5 against Spassky who continued 10 ♗b3 ♗b7 11 ♖he1 ♗e7 12 f4 ♘c5 13 e5!? and won. Another reason why Polugaevsky

was soon burning the midnight oil over his innovatory 7 … b5.

9...♗e7

9...h6 was Korchnoi's improvement against Tal in round 18 of the same tournament. (Incidentally, some of these old world class tournaments were real slogs – even lasting several months. If the pampered modern pro were subjected to such a war of attrition he would no doubt sue the organisers for emotional overload!) After 10 ♗h4 ♗e7 11 ♖ad1 ♘e5 12 ♗b3 came 12...g5!, a typical idea in the Najdorf whereby Black secures the e5 square for the knight. Black doesn't fear the weaknesses on the kingside as for the time being his king is very safe in the centre and can always be sent to the queenside later. After 13 ♗g3 ♘h5! 14 ♗a4+!? b5 15 ♗xe5 dxe5 16 ♘c6 ♕c7 17 ♘xe7 ♔xe7 18 ♗b3 ♘f6, despite the detention of his king in the centre, Black's doubled pawns have control of the centre squares and in fact Korchnoi went on to grind down his opponent in the endgame.

Korchnoi was something of a *bête noir* for Tal, whose overall score against the warhorse from Leningrad was truly awful! Even Korchnoi could not explain his overwhelming superiority, although he was an arch materialist who would grab a pawn or accept a sacrifice at any opportunity unless he saw a clear refutation. Fischer too had this tendency but, unlike Korchnoi, he had a *bad* score against Tal when he was young. Perhaps this can all by explained by personal psychology but then again if you look at games between Korchnoi and Tal, the latter rarely got the chance to sacrifice! Most likely Korchnoi had such respect for Tal's flair for sacrificial combinations that he nipped all danger in the bud. I heard a funny story about Korchnoi from one of his team-mates. During the game he would think of the worst possible way he could insult his opponent after the game and then enjoy watching him squirm after having both his chess and personal ego crushed. However the Bosnian grandmaster Ivan Sokolov subsequently prepared an antidote – he met insult with an even greater insult! Perhaps this trading of insults will become an art form – and without any interference from Rybka and Fritz!

10 ♖ad1 ♘c5?

As will soon become clear, the knight is not as well placed here as it is on e5, since it is more vulnerable to attack. Therefore 10...h6 11 ♗h4 ♘e5 12 ♗b3 g5, transposing into the Korchnoi game, was more to the point.

11 ♖fe1

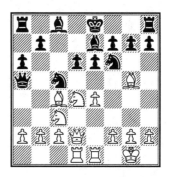

11...♗d7

11...b5?! 12 ♗d5! (12 ♘c6 ♕c7 13 ♘xe7 ♕xe7 is only slightly better for White) 12...exd5 (12...♘xd5 13 exd5±; but 12...♗b7 13 ♗xb7 ♘xb7 14 ♘c6 ♕c7 15 ♘xe7 ♕xe7 reduces his disadvantage) 13 exd5 ♗d7 (13...♗b7 14 ♘f5) 14 ♗xf6 gxf6 15 ♕e3 is winning; 11...h6 12 ♗h4 g5 13 ♗g3 Now this doesn't have as much purpose as when the knight can come to e5, nevertheless it may have been safer. 13...♘h5 14 a3 ♘xg3 15 hxg3 ♕c7 16 b4 ♘d7 17 ♗xe6 fxe6 18 ♘xe6 ♕c6 19 ♘d5 ♔f7 20 ♘ec7 is the kind of sacrifice that Tal wouldn't have thought twice about – so Polugaevsky was probably keen to complete his development as soon as possible.

12 a3!

This is the problem. Black must lose time and – more importantly – lose control over the e6 square.

12...♕c7 13 b4 ♘a4 14 ♘xa4 ♗xa4

15 ♗xe6!

Typical Tal – he should have patented this sacrifice!

15...fxe6 16 ♘xe6

Of course Tal would have analysed Black's alternatives when he sacrificed on e6.

16...♕xc2

16...♕c6 17 ♘xg7+ ♔f7 18 ♘f5 doesn't look at all appetising – White has three pawns and a raging attack for the piece.

A) 18...♖he8 19 ♗xf6 ♗xf6 and if the very promising attacking try 20 ♕h6 isn't to his liking, White can also recover some booty with 20 ♘xd6+ ♔g8 21 ♘xe8 ♖xe8;

B) 18...♘xe4 19 ♕d4 ♗xg5 (19...♗f6 20 ♗xf6 ♘xf6 21 ♖e7+ ♔g6 22 ♘h4+) 20 ♕g7+ ♔e8 (20...♔e6 21 ♘d4+) 21 ♘xd6+; 16...♕d7 17 ♘xg7+ ♔f7 18 ♘f5± It seems that Polugaevsky, with his great experience of the Sicilian, knew that any attempt to defend such a position against the attacking genius of Tal would be hopeless, and therefore concluded that 16...♕xc2 was necessary.

17 ♕d4!

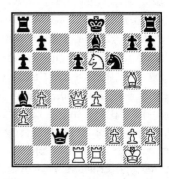

The key move. White can simply play this 'quiet move' emphasising the somewhat hapless nature of Black's pieces (queen on c2, bishop on a4) and the exposed position of his king.

17...♔f7

17...♔d7 18 ♖c1 ♕a2 19 ♘c5++–; while 17...♖g8 18 ♖c1 (18 ♘xg7+ ♖xg7 19 ♗xf6 ♗xf6 20 ♕xf6 ♖g8

21 ♕e6+ isn't bad either) 18...♕a2 19 e5 dxe5 (19...♕xe6 20 exf6) 20 ♖xc5 ♔f7 (What else is there?) 21 ♘xg7! ♗d8 (21...♖xg7 22 ♖xe7+ ♔xe7 23 ♕xf6+ +-) 22 ♗xf6 ♗xf6 23 ♖c7+ ♔g6 24 ♕g4+ is one way to rip away Black's crumbling edifice.

18 ♖c1!

18 e5 dxe5 19 ♕xe5 ♕xf2+ 20 ♔xf2 ♘g4+ 21 ♔g1 ♘xe5 and the white rook is exposed to attack on d1.

18...♕a2 19 e5

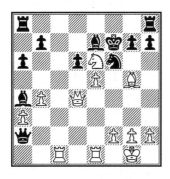

19...dxe5

Also 19...♕xe6 needed to be calculated. 20 exf6 ♗xf6 21 ♗xf6 (21 ♖c7+ ♔g8) 21...♕xf6 22 ♕d5+ (22 ♖c7+ ♔f8 23 ♕c4 ♗e8) 22...♔f8 White's position looks overwhelming, but the final blow still has to be found. 23 ♖e6 (23 ♕xb7 ♖e8 24 ♖e3 ♖xe3 25 fxe3 ♕e6 26 ♖f1+ ♔e8) 23...♕f7 (23...♕f4 24 ♖c4! doesn't improve matters; 23...♕d8 24 ♖c4!) 24 ♕xd6+ (24 ♖c3 ♗c6 25 ♕xd6+ ♔g8) 24...♔g8

A) 25 ♖c7 ♕f5 26 h3± (26 ♖xg7+ ♔xg7 27 ♖e7+ ♔g8 28 ♕g3+ ♕g6);

B) 25 ♖e7 25...♕f6 26 ♕d5+ ♔f8 27 ♖xb7±

Doubtless, with his rook out of the game on h8 and White's rooks going on the rampage, Polugaevsky must have felt his position was untenable in the long run – even if he didn't see a forced win for his opponent.

20 ♕xe5

20...♕xf2+?!

Black has this trick, but even an endgame can't fully quench White's initiative. For example, 20...♖ac8 21 ♘xg7! ♔xg7 22 ♕xe7+ ♕f7 23 ♗xf6+ wins. But in light of the game continuation 20...♖he8!? may have been a better try. After enduring the kind of attack seen here, it's tempting to try and simplify to an apparently tenable endgame as soon as possible. But this is often an impossible task.

A) 21 ♗xf6 ♗xf6 22 ♖c7+ ♔g8;

B) 21 ♘xg7!? ♔xg7 22 ♖c7

B1) 22...♔g6 23 ♗xf6 ♗xf6
24 ♕g3+ ♔g5 (24...♔f5 25 ♖c5+!)
25 ♕d3+ ♔f6 (25...♔h5 26 ♖xh7+
♗h6 27 ♕f5+) 26 ♕f3+;

B2) 22...♕f7 23 ♖xe7 ♖xe7
24 ♕xe7 ♕xe7 25 ♖xe7+ ♔g6
26 ♗xf6 ♔xf6 27 ♖xb7 looks like a
draw. But…

C) 21 ♘c7!? ♕xf2+ (21...♗f8
22 ♘xe8 ♖xe8 23 ♕c7+±) 22 ♔xf2
♘g4+ 23 ♔g1 ♘xe5 24 ♖xe5±;

**21 ♔xf2 ♘g4+ 22 ♔g1 ♘xe5
23 ♖xe5**

Black is seemingly over the worst,
but in fact the difference in the
activity of the two armies proves far
too great.

23...♗xg5

23...♗d6 24 ♖f1+! ♔g8 (24...♔g6
25 ♖d5 and the bishop is forced to
retreat to the pathetic square f8)
25 ♖d5 ♗f8 26 ♖df5 ♗d6 27 ♘xg7!
♔xg7 28 ♗f6+ ♔g8 (28...♔h6
29 ♗xh8 ♖xh8 30 ♖f6+ and wins)
29 ♖g5+ +-; 23...♗f6 24 ♖c7+ ♔g6
(24...♔g8 25 ♗xf6 gxf6 26 ♖g7
mate) 25 ♘f4 mate; 23...♖he8

24 ♖f1+ ♔g8 25 ♘xg7! (This knight
sacrifice on g7 is a recurring theme)
25...♔xg7 26 ♗xe7±

24 ♘xg5+ ♔g6 25 ♘e6!

The knight returns, that g7 square
is just too tempting...

25...♖he8

25...♔f6 26 ♖e3 ♗b5 27 a4! ♗xa4
28 ♖f1+ ♔g6 29 ♖g3+ ♔h6
30 ♖f4+-; 25...♖ac8 26 ♖f1 (26 ♘c5
♖he8 27 ♖xe8 ♗xe8) 26...h6
27 ♖e3! ♔h7 28 ♖f7±

26 ♖e3! ♖ac8 27 ♖f1 ♗b5

27...♖e7 28 ♘f8+ decides.

28 ♖g3+ ♔h6 29 ♘xg7

29...♖f8?!

29...♗xf1 30 ♘xe8 (30 ♘f5+ ♔h5
31 h4 ♖g8) 30...♖xe8 (30...♗xg2
31 ♘d6+-) 31 ♔xf1 and with the
black king cut off, it looks doubtful
that he will be able to hold the
difficult endgame. However this
may have been a better chance, as
White will still have to prove his
technique whereas in the game he
simply continues with the attack...

30 ♖e1!

Decisive.

30...♖f6 31 h3 ♖c2 32 ♖e4 ♖c4 33 ♖e5 ♖c1+ 34 ♔h2

Tal fed his family on Sicilian sacrifices and any aspiring 1 e4 player could do a lot worse than study his methods. An attractive feature of this game is the way he continued his attack even after the queens were exchanged.

1-0

8

M.Tal – V.Smyslov

Candidates Tournament,
Bled/Zagreb/Belgrade 1959

Sicilian Defence

1 e4 c5

Earlier in the tournament Tal won a highly impressive sacrificial game against Smyslov's Caro-Kann Defence, which in fact went on to attain legendary status. I give the game without notes, as it has been scoured over so many times (even by Kasparov in his classic series, *My Great Predecessors*) that while it would be churlish to say that there is nothing new to add, as chess is such an inexhaustible game, I have deliberately elected to feature games in this book that are less well known – in other words games that haven't

been analysed to death. Here is the complete score: 1 e4 c6 2 d3 d5 3 ♘d2 e5 4 ♘gf3 ♘d7 5 d4 dxe4 6 ♘xe4 exd4 7 ♕xd4 ♘gf6 8 ♗g5 ♗e7 9 0-0-0 0-0 10 ♘d6 ♕a5 11 ♗c4 b5 12 ♗d2 ♕a6 13 ♘f5 ♗d8 14 ♕h4!? bxc4 15 ♕g5 ♘h5 16 ♘h6+ ♔h8 17 ♕xh5 ♕xa2 18 ♗c3 ♘f6? 19 ♕xf7! ♕a1+ 20 ♔d2 ♖xf7 21 ♘xf7+ ♔g8 22 ♖xa1 ♔xf7 23 ♘e5+ ♔e6 24 ♘xc6 ♘e4+ 25 ♔e3 ♗b6+ 26 ♗d4 Tal-Smyslov, Round 8, Candidates 1959 (In this tournament the players had to play each other four times.) Certainly one of Tal's most famous victories – if not his most famous. Typical of his style, he intuitively gave up a piece to create just one threat – but that was enough to win the game!

2 ♘f3 d6 3 d4 cxd4 4 ♘xd4 ♘f6 5 ♘c3 e6

The Scheveningen variation, utilised most effectively by Kasparov in his titanic clashes with Karpov.

6 ♗e2

Perhaps surprisingly, Tal avoids the wild complications of 6 g4!? but it should be noted that Tal wasn't a great theoretician in the mould of say, a Fischer. But then again neither was Smyslov.

6...a6 7 0-0 ♘bd7

7...♗e7 8 f4 0-0 9 a4 ♕c7 is a more common move order, followed by placing the knight on c6.

8 f4 b5 9 ♗f3 ♗b7 10 a3

The logical 10 e5!? has been tried many times, however it would seem that Black's chances are good after 10...♗xf3 11 ♘xf3 dxe5 12 fxe5 ♘g4 13 ♕e2 b4! 14 ♘e4 ♘dxe5∞.

10...♕c7 11 ♕e1 ♗e7 12 ♔h1

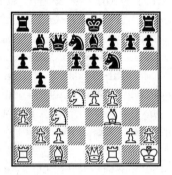

12...♖b8!

Smyslov is paying attention! This 'mysterious rook move' is directed against White's pawn thrust g4, which may not be so effective if Black hasn't castled. It also has another purpose, it discourages the pawn push e5. 12...0-0 is the more normal continuation, then 13 g4! d5?! 14 e5 ♘e4 15 ♘xe4 dxe4 16 ♗xe4 ♘c5 17 ♗xb7 ♕xb7+ 18 ♔g1±. A player lacking concentration may have carelessly played 12...♖c8?! after which comes 13 e5! dxe5 14 fxe5 ♗xf3 15 ♘xf3±.

13 b3

Tal calmly develops.

13 g4 springs to mind. Why did Tal reject this? I get the impression in this game that Tal was avoiding

any possible preparation in order to defer the fight until later in the middlegame. 13...h6! (13...♘b6 14 g5; 13...d5? 14 exd5±)

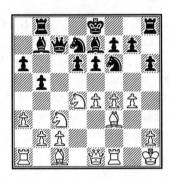

A) 14 f5 e5 15 ♘de2 ♘b6;

B) 14 ♗d2 g5! 15 fxg5 (15 f5 e5 16 ♘de2 h5 17 gxh5 g4 18 ♗g2 ♘xh5∓) 15...hxg5 16 ♗xg5 d5 and Black has good counterplay. So g4 is not so effective if the black rook is still on h8!;

C) 14 g5?! hxg5 15 fxg5 d5! g4 is a bit careless, but if the white player doesn't look at Black's possible candidate moves, it may be easy to overlook the modest ...h6! idea. Now if 13 e5? dxe5 14 fxe5 ♘xe5 15 ♗xb7 ♖xb7 we see the difference, the rook defends b7 and after 16 ♗f4 ♗d6 favours Black.

13...0-0

Why not try 13...h6!? anyway? Well, after 14 ♗b2 (14 f5 e5 15 ♘de2 ♘c5 16 ♘g3 h5 17 h4 ♘g4 18 ♗g5 ♗xg5 19 hxg5 h4! 20 ♗xg4 hxg3+ 21 ♗h3 ♕c6 22 ♘d5 ♘xe4 with an attack) 14...g5 comes 15 e5! which is more effective now that Black has weakened his kingside.

For example: 15...dxe5 16 fxe5

A) 16...♕xe5 17 ♕xe5 (17 ♕f2 ♗d6 18 ♕g1 ♗xf3 19 ♘xf3 ♕c5 20 ♘e4 ♘xe4 21 ♗xh8∞) 17...♘xe5 18 ♗xb7 ♖xb7 19 ♖ae1 ♘ed7;

B) 16...♘xe5 17 ♘dxb5!

14 ♗b2 ♖fe8

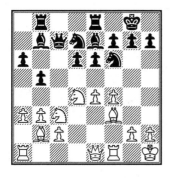

15 ♕g3

So far Tal's play has been very unpretentious, resisting any temptation to make the pawn thrust g4 (which also, it may be added, would weaken his own king position.) 15 g4!?, after which 15...d5 (15...♘c5 16 g5 ♘fd7±; 15...e5?! 16 ♘f5 exf4? 17 g5 ♘xe4 18 ♘xe4 ♗xg5 19 ♘xg7 ♕xc2 20 ♘xe8 ♖xe8 21 ♕c3 ♕xc3

22 ♘xc3+-) 16 e5 ♘e4 17 ♘xe4 dxe4 18 ♗xe4 ♘c5 19 ♗xb7 ♕xb7+ 20 ♔g1 ♖bc8 (or perhaps 20...♖bd8!? 21 ♕e2 ♖d5 22 ♖ad1 ♖ed8 23 ♘f3) is one possible continuation. White is a pawn to the good, but his king is somewhat draughty and against a counter-attacker of Smyslov's calibre this might be more important than any possibility of a superior endgame.

15...♗f8 16 ♖ae1 e5 17 ♘f5?!

Very bold, Tal was never one to contemplate retreat! 17 ♘de2 was 'safer' 17...♘c5 18 fxe5 dxe5 (18...♖xe5 19 ♘d5) 19 ♘g1 ♘e6 20 ♘d5 ♘xd5 21 exd5 ♘f4 22 ♗xe5!

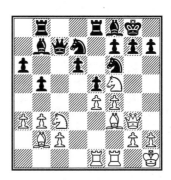

17...♔h8

17...g6! creates a threat of taking on f4, and also prepares to post the bishop on the suberb square g7 in case of a retreat by the white knight, but of course Tal wouldn't retreat!

A) 18 fxe5;

B) 18 ♕g5 exf4 19 ♘h6+ ♗xh6 (19...♔g7?!) 20 ♕xh6 ♘e5 21 ♕xf4

♕e7 and Black's strong knight on e5 cuts out any possible danger on the a1-h8 diagonal;

C) 18 fxe5 ♘xe5 19 ♕h4 ♕d8;

D) 18 ♘e3 exf4 19 ♕xf4 ♗g7 is fine for Black.

In general I can find no advantage for White after 17...g6, as Black's forces are excellently co-ordinated. No doubt the move Smyslov chose in the game was okay as well, but Tal frequently came out of the opening no better!

18 ♕h4!? exf4 19 ♕xf4 ♘e5

19...g6!? 20 ♘h6 (20 ♘d5 ♗xd5) 20...♗xh6 21 ♕xh6 ♘e5 again seems to offer no great problems for Black.

20 ♖e3 g6

21 ♘h6?

Objectively this move is rather pushing White's chances, and probably from a 'higher truth' point of view deserves a question mark. 21 ♘g3 was safer but after 21...♗g7 it would be obvious that Black is covering all entry points and stands very comfortably indeed; in fact it is often a noted feature of the Sicilian that if Black survives White's early initiative then he generally stands better. Tal was adept at putting as many obstacles in his opponent's path as possible; in fact to him it didn't really matter if he was objectively better, equal or worse; what mattered was simply that he was able to out-think his opponent!

21...♗g7

21...♗xh6 22 ♕xh6 ♕e7 (not 22...♘fg4?? 23 ♗xg4 ♘xg4 24 ♘d5+), with the idea of ♘fd7 gaining total control over the e5 square, isn't bad either. Then 23 ♗e2 ♘fd7 24 ♖h3 f6∞.

22 ♘d5

White must act quickly if he wishes to take advantage of the threatening placement of the knight on h6. But if the game is anything to go by, Tal's attack was misconceived. Also 22 ♘g4 ♘fxg4 (22...♘exg4 23 ♗xg4 ♘xe4 24 ♘xe4 ♗xb2 25 ♘xd6) 23 ♗xg4 ♘xg4 24 ♕xg4 ♔g8∓

22...♘xd5!

22...♗xd5 23 exd5

A) 23...♗xh6! is a simpler solution than the game continuation, so from a practical point of view may have been preferred. 24 ♕xh6 (24 ♕xf6+ ♗g7 25 ♕f4 ♕xc2 26 ♗xe5 ♖xe5 27 ♖xe5 ♗xe5 28 ♕xf7 ♕xb3∓) 24...♕xc2

A1) 25 ♖e2 ♕d3;

A2) 25 ♗xe5 ♖xe5 26 ♖xe5 dxe5 27 ♕g5 (27 ♗d1 ♕d3) 27...♕f5∓;

A3) 25 ♗a1 ♔g8 (25...♘fd7 26 ♗e4 ♕d2 27 ♗c3 ♕a2 28 ♖h3-+) 26 ♗d1! ♕c1! 27 ♗e2 ♘fg4! 28 ♖xc1 ♘xh6∓;

B) 23...♕xc2 24 ♗xe5 dxe5 25 ♘xf7+ ♔g8 26 ♘xe5 clearly favours White.

23 exd5 f6

This is very tempting as it leads to the win of a piece, but Black had a few reasonable alternatives, e.g. 23...♖f8 and it is not clear what White is doing, or 23...f5!? and in general I think Black has the advantage here.

24 ♗e4

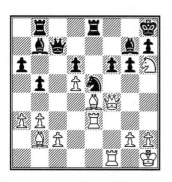

24...g5

I wonder what Tal had planned against the thrust 24...f5? – of course 25 ♘xf5! (not 25 ♖h3 ♗xh6 26 ♕xh6 fxe4) since ♘g3 with ♗f3 would hardly be in his chess vocabulary. Nevertheless the consequences of this sacrifice are rather unclear and, if anything, favour Black, rather like the game.

A) 25...gxf5 26 ♕xf5 ♗h6

A1) 27 ♕f6+ ♕g7 28 ♕xd6 ♗xe3 29 ♖f5 is one crazy idea, White is a rook and piece down but his attack isn't easily repelled; 29...♖bd8? (29...♔g8 30 ♖xe5; 29...♖ed8 30 ♕e6 ♗c8 31 ♕xe5 ♕xe5 32 ♗xe5+ ♔g8 33 ♖f3!) 30 ♖xe5!;

A2) 27 ♕h5! ♕g7 (27...♖f8 28 ♖ef3 ♕g7 29 ♖f7!) 28 ♖g3 ♖f8! 29 ♖xf8+ ♖xf8 30 ♗d3 ♕f7!;

B) 25...♖f8 26 ♖h3 gxf5 27 ♗xf5 ♖f6 (27...h6 28 ♖xh6+ ♗xh6 29 ♕xh6+ ♔g8 30 ♗e6+ +-) 28 ♖xh7+ ♔g8 29 ♕h4 ♕f7 (29...♗xd5!? 30 ♕xf6? ♗xg2+) 30 ♗e6? ♕xe6.

25 ♕f5 ♗xh6 26 ♕xf6+ ♗g7

Smyslov would not like to have unleashed the power of the bishop on b2 after 26...♕g7 27 ♕xd6; it is simple enough to see that White has two pawns and a mighty initiative for the piece: 27...♖bd8 28 ♕c5±.

27 ♕f5

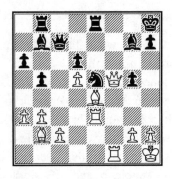

27...♘g6

I wonder if in the case of 27...♗h6 Tal would have repeated? Most likely he would have done, as anything else really runs into trouble – 28 ♕h3 ♖f8!

28 ♖h3 ♗xb2

28...♖f8?? 29 ♖xh7+ ♔xh7 (29...♔g8 30 ♕e6+ ♔xh7 31 ♕xg6+ ♔g8 32 ♕h7 mate) 30 ♕xg6+ ♔g8 31 ♕h7 mate.

29 ♕xg6 ♖e7

Forced, to defend both h7 and f7.

30 ♖h6

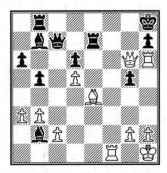

What does Tal intend with this move? How should Smyslov defend now? It would seem that in any case

Black is over the worst, but it would by no means be easy to realise the extra piece.

30...♖g8

30...♗e5 31 ♕xg5 ♖g8 32 ♕h5 ♗c8 33 ♗g6 ♖eg7 34 ♖f7 ♖xf7 35 ♗xf7 ♖g7; 30...♖g7! looked like a possible improvement. 31 ♕h5! (31 ♕xd6 ♕xd6 32 ♖xd6 ♗xa3 33 ♖e6 ♖d8∓; 31 ♕f5 ♖e8 32 ♕f3 ♕e7!) 31...♕e7 (31...♗e5!?) 32 ♖e6 ♖f8!

31 ♕f5 ♗c8

31...♖eg7!

32 ♕f3

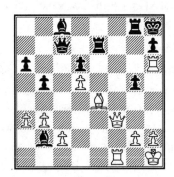

32...g4

There is also 32...♗e5; or even better 32...♖eg7! 33 ♕d3 ♕e7 34 c4 (34 c3 ♗xc3 35 ♕xc3 ♕xe4 36 ♖xh7+ ♔xh7 37 ♕h3+ ♕h4) 34...♖f8!

33 ♕d3 ♗e5

33...♕c3? 34 ♗xh7; 33...♖gg7 34 ♖f8+ (34 ♗xh7? ♖xh7 35 ♖f8+ ♔g7 36 ♕xh7+ ♔xf8) 34...♖g8.

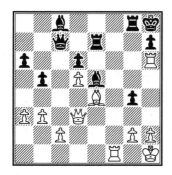

34 c4!

Tal finds any chance, however small! The problem that Black faces is that his pieces are tied down to the h7 square, which makes any freeing attempt surprisingly difficult.

34...bxc4 35 bxc4 ♖eg7

Other possibilities were 35...♕d7; or 35...♕a7 met by 36 c5 dxc5 37 d6 ♖d7 38 ♗d5.

36 c5!

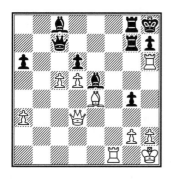

36...dxc5?

This complicates matters. 36...♕e7!, attempting to trade Black's passive rook with ♖f8, whilst also taking advantage of the fact that White has a back rank problem, was an idea that Smyslov

seemed to overlook for a long period of the game. Then 37 cxd6 (37 c6 ♖f8 38 ♖xf8+ ♕xf8 39 ♗xh7 ♖f7!) 37...♗xd6∓.

37 d6!

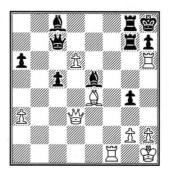

37...♕a7?

This is too passive. Better is 37...c4! – these kind of in-between moves are often difficult to spot – 38 ♕d5 (38 ♕d1 ♕c5) 38...♗xd6 39 ♖xd6 (39 ♕xd6 ♕xd6 40 ♖xd6 ♖c7∓) 39...♗b7!

38 ♗d5 ♖d8

38...♖e8 39 ♕e4! with the crushing threat of ♕xe5 and rook to f8 check.

39 ♕e4! ♗d4 40 ♕f4 ♖gd7 41 ♖f6!

41 ...♔g7 42 ♕g5+ is mating.

1-0

On the surface a flawed game, and certainly Smyslov was close to winning for long periods. But in a way it's a good illustration of Tal's 'all in' style. Less brave souls probably wouldn't have got into the trouble that Tal did in this game, but the fact that yet again he was able to get Smyslov into the kind of position in which the ex-world champion felt uncomfortable, to draw him into his own world of chess insanity and one in which he really had to calculate and couldn't simply use his great positional skill, was the key. It's interesting that when annotating the game between these two players from earlier in the tournament, given earlier, Kasparov alluded to the fact that Tal showed great psychological insight in eschewing a clearly better endgame, as he probably (rightly) sensed that Smyslov would be more at home there than in the kind of tactical morass in which Tal revelled. It helps to be aware of your opponent's strengths and weaknesses. Incidentally Tal, having qualified from this tournament, went on to defeat Botvinnik in 1960 in a sensational match and become the youngest world champion up to that time. Sadly, the following year, he lost his title to the same opponent in a match where both players scored badly with Black (in particular Tal). Perhaps at that time defensive technique, particularly with the Black pieces, hadn't been fully worked out. It is significant that Anand scored two victories with Black against Kramnik in their 2009 world championship match. But, in his defence, Tal was already exhibiting signs of the health problems that were to blight him later in his life. Moreover, in those days, he was obliged to give Botvinnik a quick rematch, which was to his disadvantage. Later, whenever some promising young chess player was mentioned, Tal would reply "at that age I was already world champion!" Indeed, Tal will always be fondly remembered in chess players' hearts as the first great attacking player of the modern era.

Chapter 3

Simply Shirov

Alexey Shirov burst on the chess scene in the early nineties. Along with players such as Kramnik, Topalov and Anand, he was part of a new wave of attacking chess talent who eventually challenged the hegemony of Karpov and Kasparov – who had so dominated the chess world in the seventies and eighties. However, more than any of those players, Shirov's swashbuckling attacks and fearless play evoked memories of his great predecessor and fellow Latvian, Mikhail Tal – although it should be emphasised that Shirov brought his own highly individual style to the chess table. He also introduced a number of interesting ideas in the openings, for example the 7 g4 pawn sac in the Semi-Slav – which he and his compatriot Alex Shabalov soon made very popular.

9

A. Shirov – V.Akopian

Interzonal, Biel 1993

Semi-Slav Defence

1 d4 d5 2 c4 c6 3 ♘c3 ♘f6 4 ♘f3 e6 5 e3 ♘bd7 6 ♕c2 ♗d6 7 g4!?

A move that became popular around this time as Shirov and Shabalov were winning some breathtaking games with it. White takes advantage of the fact that the g7 square is now undefended.

7...dxc4

7...♘xg4 8 ♖g1

A) 8...♘h6 9 e4!? (9 ♖xg7? ♕f6 10 ♖xh7 ♖xh7 11 ♕xh7 ♘f8-+);

B) 8...♘xh2 9 ♘xh2 ♗xh2 10 ♖xg7 ♕f6 11 ♖g2 with compensation; 7...♗b4!? 8 g5 ♘e4 9 h4∞.

8 ♗xc4

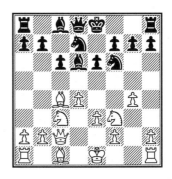

8...b5?!

Alexey Shirov makes this move look like a forced loss! I tried 8...e5!? a few times in a tournament in Gibraltar a few years back, and managed to draw with a couple of world class players. I was impressed when Alexey, who was playing in the same tournament, came up to me afterwards and asked me about the games. What impressed me most was that such a strong player would be interested in the opinion of a patzer! Alexey seems very down earth compared to many top grandmasters. I once met Kasparov (or rather met in the loosest sense of the word) at a function after a handicap match that he played against the English businessman Terry Chapman. Slightly the worse for wear after downing a couple of bottles of Becks, I lurched over to Garry and patted him on the back, congratulating him on his great victory over Chapman – which was met by what was surely the greatest blanking of my life. Garry simply stared straight ahead, as if I wasn't there (didn't he know who I was?). Since there were plenty of people around to observe this incident, it was one of those moments when you wish the ground would swallow you up. Anyway back to the game...

9 g5 ♘d5!

A) 10 ♘xd5 cxd5 11 ♗xd5?? (11 ♗e2 e4) 11...♕a5+;

B) 10 ♗xd5 cxd5 11 ♘xd5 0-0;

C) 10 ♘e4 ♗b4+ 11 ♗d2 ♕e7∞.

9 ♗d3 ♗b7 10 g5 ♘d5 11 ♘e4 ♗e7 12 ♗d2

White also has the option of playing 12 a3, which Shabalov has employed with success. Generally speaking, in such positions if Black can get in the move... c5 without anything horrible happening to him he'll be doing very well as the bishop on b7 will come to life. However it's not always easy to do this and castling kingside is usually risky because White has a cramping pawn on g5, which will lead to all sorts of combinations with ♘f6, etc.

12...♕b6?!

It turns out the queen is not very well placed on this square. What would Shirov have done after 12...♖c8 ?

A) 13 ♖c1 c5 14 dxc5 b4 (14...♗xc5   15   ♗xb5   ♗xe3? 16 ♘d6+);

B) 13 ♘c5 ♘xc5 (13...♗xc5 14 dxc5 ♕c7 15 ♗xh7 ♘e5 16 ♗e4 ♘xf3+ 17 ♗xf3 ♖xh2 18 0-0-0 g6 19 e4±) 14 dxc5 ♗xg5 15 ♗xh7 ♗f6 (15...g6? 16 ♗xg6; 15...f5 16 ♗g6+ ♔f8 17 e4! ♗xd2+ ·18 ♕xd2 ♘e7 19 exf5 ♕xd2+

20 ♔xd2 exf5 21 ♖ag1 ♖h6 22 ♘e5±) 16 ♗d3 a5 17 a3 ♖h3 18 ♔e2 looks quite promising for White; Black has the better pawn structure but his knight is about to be kicked by e4 while his bishop on b7 is a bit of a dead rubber. Nevertheless I think this would have been best as it would have minimised the damage.

Other moves are:

12...♘b4 13 ♗xb4 ♗xb4+ 14 ♔e2 ♕e7 15 a3 ♗d6 16 b4 e5 17 ♘c5! ♗xc5 18 dxc5 g6 19 h4±;

12...0-0 13 ♘c5 ♗xc5 14 dxc5 g6 15 h4 f5 16 h5 with an attack.

13 ♖c1!

Controlling the c5 square and getting ready to plonk a knight on that square, thereby burying the bishop on b7.

13...♘b4 14 ♗xb4 ♗xb4+ 15 ♔e2

The king is perfectly safe on this square.

15...c5?

Akopian, a very active player, desperately seeks counterplay rather than allow White to establish a bind on the queenside and suffocate the b7 bishop. But when you embark on tactics against Shirov you really need to be sure of what you are doing! What other options did he have? Was his position so bad that he already had to start tactical operations?

Here are some other possibilities:

15...0-0? 16 a3 ♗e7 17 b4 a5 (17...♖fd8 18 ♘c5 ♘f8 19 h4 and White's game plays itself) 18 ♘c5!;

15...e5 16 dxe5 ♗e7 (16...c5 17 a3±; 16...♕c7 17 e6 fxe6 18 ♕b3±) 17 ♕b3 a6 18 e6±;

15...g6?! 16 ♘c5 ♗xc5 17 dxc5 ♕c7 18 ♕c3 e5 19 ♘d2±

15...♗e7! looks relatively safest,

...e.g. 16 ♘c5 ♗xc5 (16...♘xc5 17 dxc5 ♕c7 18 ♗xh7! g6 19 ♗xg6 fxg6 20 ♕xg6+ ♔f8 21 ♘d4 ♗c8 22 ♘xe6+ ♗xe6 23 ♕xe6 and White has four pawns for the piece – which is clearly too much.) 17 dxc5

♕a5 18 a3 (18 ♗xh7 ♕xa2) 18...b4! 19 axb4 ♕xb4 20 ♗xh7? ♖xh7 21 ♕xh7 ♗a6+ 22 ♔d1 0-0-0 with an attack. I think this position is a good example: Akopian, fearing that he would be worse after passive moves, goes for the active move but one that only accelerates his defeat! I'm sure that he was less than convinced about 15...c5 in the game, but may have talked himself into it.

16 a3!

The refutation, after which White is a relatively safe pawn to the good. On 16 ♘xc5?! ♖c8!; 16 dxc5!? ♘xc5! 17 ♘xc5 ♖c8 18 ♕b3 ♗xc5 19 ♕xb5+ ♔e7 it will not be an easy task to convert the extra pawn as the two bishops make a formidable combination.

16...c4 17 axb4 ♗d5

17...cxd3+ 18 ♕xd3 a5 19 bxa5 ♖xa5 20 ♘c5±

18 ♘fd2 0-0 19 ♖hg1

19...e5

19...cxd3+ 20 ♕xd3 ♖ad8 doesn't help – White has the powerful

21 ♘f6+± Also good for White are 20...a5 21 ♘f6+ ♗xf6 22 gxf6 g6 23 e4 ♗c4 24 ♘xc4 bxc4 25 ♕e3 ♔h8 26 ♕h6 ♖g8 27 ♖g3+-; or 20...f5 21 gxf6 ♘xf6 22 ♘xf6+ ♖xf6 23 f4±

20 dxe5

20...♖ad8

After 20...♘xe5 21 ♘f6+ gxf6 22 ♗xh7+ ♔h8 White has the 'power move' 23 ♕f5! ♕e6 (23...♘d3 24 ♕h3+-) 24 gxf6 ♕xf5 25 ♗xf5+-

21 ♘f6+! ♘xf6 22 ♗f5 ♘h5 23 ♗xh7+ ♔h8 24 ♗f5 ♗e6

Or 24...♖fe8 25 ♗g4 g6 26 ♗xh5 gxh5 27 f4 with a crushing position.

25 ♘f3 g6

Otherwise there is no way to bring the knight into the game, and in any case White was presumably threatening g6 himself.

26 ♗xe6 ♕xe6 27 ♖cd1 ♕e7 28 ♕c3 ♖d3 29 ♖xd3 cxd3+ 30 ♕xd3 ♕xb4 31 ♕d4

31...♛b3

31...♛e7 32 ♖a1 ♖a8 33 e6+ and the black king is exposed yet further; or 31...♛xd4 32 ♘xd4 a6 33 ♖a1 ♖e8 34 f4+-

32 ♘d2! ♛e6

32...♛c2 33 ♖a1 ♘g7 34 e6 fxe6 35 ♖xa7 ♖g8 36 ♔f1 and as the attempt to escape from the pin with 36...♔h7 is simply met by 37 ♘e4 Black is in great difficulties.

33 ♛d6 ♛c8

33...♛xd6 34 exd6 ♖d8 35 ♘e4 and Black will inevitably drop one of the queenside pawns, leaving him two pawns worse off. Meanwhile 33...♛e8 is met by 34 ♖a1.

34 ♖c1! ♛g4+ 35 f3 ♛g2+ 36 ♔d3

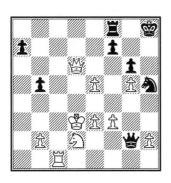

36...♔g7

36...♔g8 37 f4 ♘g7 38 ♘e4 ♘f5 39 ♘f6+ ♔g7 40 ♛xf8+! ♔xf8 41 ♖c8+ is one nice variation, showing the bind that the white pawns have over the kingside.

37 f4

Despite the fact that White's king is looking slightly precarious on d3, Black has no good way of getting to it.

37...♛h3

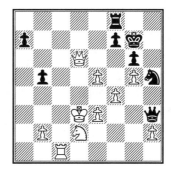

38 e6! fxe6

38...♛xe6 39 ♛xe6 fxe6 is a hopeless endgame for Black – not only is he a pawn down but all his pawns are scattered and weak. White can continue with either 40 ♖c7+ or 40 ♘e4.

39 ♖c7+ ♔g8 40 ♔c2 ♛f5+

40...♘g7 41 ♛e7 ♘h5 42 ♘e4 ♛g2+ 43 ♔b3+-

41 e4

Akopian had no wish to see the nice finish; 41...♛g4 42 f5! cutting off the queen's defence of e6, after which his position crumbles. A nice game from Shirov, the variation with g4 complements his direct style perfectly – and he never gave Akopian a moment's respite.

1-0

The first time I saw Shirov play was at the Istanbul Olympiad in 2000 where he was representing Spain. I was astonished to see him staring into space for almost the entire duration of the game – essentially playing blindfold – but it didn't seem to do him any harm, as he racked up a rather large score, brutalising some of his opponents along the way. This included a distressed Van Wely, who I witnessed shaking his head in disbelief after having his Najdorf Sicilian dismantled in double quick time.

Shirov is not alone in the world elite for his ability to play at the same level (and better on occasion) without sight of the board. Players such as Ivanchuk, Kramnik and Morozevich are noted for their blindfold skill. Of course Shirov and the above-mentioned players are regular fixtures at the annual Amber blindfold/rapidplay event, held in Monaco and now Nice. Far from the old wives tale of blindfold chess being detrimental to your mental health, I think it can improve your game, certainly your calculating ability, as not only do you have to permanently hold the current

position in your head but you also have to constantly visualise variations. Let's face it: in chess we are essentially playing blindfold anyway – we are constantly carrying positions around in our heads – well at least I am. :-)

Another way you can try to improve your calculation is to have a go at solving chess studies – some of which are so difficult that only complex mental gymnastics will lead you to the answer. Probably the best 'chess problem' solver in the world is John Nunn, and he's always been recognised as an excellent calculator. Moreover in a recent interview Kramnik said that one of the ways he kept fit was to go to the swimming pool and try to solve difficult chess studies in his head. Takes all sorts! In the following game Shirov faces the indestructible Korchnoi, a man to whom the word 'retirement' is anathema.

10

V.Korchnoi – A.Shirov

Biel 1992

Catalan Opening

1 c4 e6 2 g3 d5 3 ♗g2 c6 4 ♕c2 dxc4 5 ♕xc4 b5 6 ♕c2 ♗b7 7 d3 ♘f6 8 ♘c3

Korchnoi was always a fan of the Catalan and scored many fine victories with this opening. Possible is 8 ♘d2!? heading for the b3 square in some lines.

8...a6 9 a4 ♗e7 10 ♘f3 ♘bd7 11 0-0 0-0 12 ♖d1 ♖c8 13 e4

If 13 ♗f4 ♕b6 (intending ...c5) 14 ♕b3 ♘c5 15 ♕b4 ♖fe8 16 ♗e3 ♘g4 17 ♗d4 e5! 18 ♘xe5 ♘xe5 19 ♗xe5 ♘xd3.

13...♕b6 14 axb5 axb5

14...cxb5?! reduces some of his influence in the centre: 15 ♗e3 ♕c7 16 ♕e2±

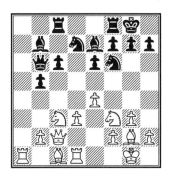

15 d4?!

True to his style, Korchnoi plays the most forcing move – however, although in the game he wins a piece, Black seems to get plenty of compensation. Therefore 15 d4 may be somewhat premature and 15 ♗e3!, putting the question to the queen, would be more circumspect. 15...♕c7 (15...♗c5 16 d4±)

A) 16 d4!? ♕b8 (16...♘g4 17 ♗f4 ♗d6 18 ♗xd6 ♕xd6 19 h3±; 16...e5 17 dxe5 ♘xe5 18 ♘xe5 ♕xe5 19 f4 ♕h5 20 h3±)

A1) 17 h3 c5! (17...b4 18 ♘a4 c5 19 ♗f4 cxd4!) 18 d5 exd5 19 ♘xd5 ♗xd5 20 cxd5 ♗d6 and Black has a good grip on the dark squares;

A2) 17 e5! ♘d5 (17...♘g4 18 ♗g5! f6 19 exf6±) 18 ♘xd5 cxd5 19 ♕d3 b4 20 ♘g5!?± (if 20 ♗g5 ♖fe8 21 ♗xe7 ♖xe7 22 ♘g5 ♘f8).

B) 16 ♖dc1 ♕b8 17 h3±

15...c5! 16 d5 exd5

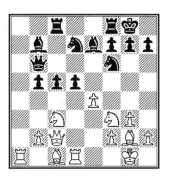

17 e5?

Remarkably, this very natural move seems to be a mistake! Other possibilities are 17 ♘xd5 and also 17 exd5, e.g. 17...b4 (possible 17...♗d6!? when Black is doing a good job of blockading the d-pawn; also 17...c4 with such ideas as ...♘g4, targeting the f-pawn – White may regret playing his rook to d1! – and...♗c5, or ♘c5-d3/b3, or b4.) 18 ♗e3 ♗c5 19 ♗xc5 ♘xc5 and Black is fine) 18 ♘a4 ♕c7 19 ♘h4 g6 20 b3 ♗d6.

17...d4!

17...♘g4?! was an interesting alternative.

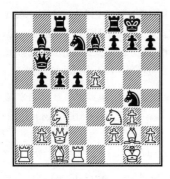

A) 18 ♗f4 d4! 19 ♘e4 ♛g6;

B) 18 ♛e2 d4 19 ♘xb5 d3! 20 ♛xd3 ♗xf3 21 ♗xf3 (21 ♛xd7 ♖fd8-+) 21...♘gxe5-+;

C) 18 ♖xd5!? ♗xd5 (18...b4 19 ♖xd7+-) 19 ♘xd5 ♛e6 20 ♘f4 ♛c4 21 ♛xc4 bxc4 22 ♗h3! ♘gxe5 23 ♘xe5 ♘xe5 24 ♗xc8 ♖xc8 25 ♘d5±; but Black has 18...♛e6! 19 ♖d1 b4 20 ♘e2 ♘gxe5∓

D) 18 ♘xd5 ♗xd5 19 ♖xd5 would look like a beautiful Catalan for White, if it were not for 19...♛e6!;

E) 18 ♗h3!

...seems to cast a cloud over Black's idea, though. 18...♘dxe5 19 ♘xe5 ♘xe5 20 ♗xc8 ♖xc8

E1) 21 ♛f5 d4! (21...♛e6 22 ♛xe6 fxe6 23 ♖a7!; 21...♗f6 22 ♘xd5) 22 ♛xe5 ♗d6 (22...♗f6 23 ♘d5!; 22...♛c6 23 ♘e4! ♛xe4 24 ♛xe4 ♗xe4 25 ♖e1 f5 26 f3+-) 23 ♘d5 ♛c6;

E2) 21 ♘xd5 21...♛e6 22 ♛e4 ♗f8 23 ♗f4!± (23 ♖a7!?). In these lines White has too much control over the centre for Black to claim enough compensation for the exchange.

18 exf6 ♘xf6

I'm sure that any computer would really like White here, but in a practical sense Black's position is easier to play. In fact it's very easy – simply push the pawns! On the other hand it's is not clear where White should put his pieces.

19 ♘b1

Korchnoi tries to retain the e2 square for his queen.

19 ♘e2 is insufficient:

A) 19...♖fd8 20 ♗g5 (20 ♘f4 c4) 20...h6 21 ♗xf6 ♗xf6 22 ♘f4 c4!

23 ♘e1 d3 24 ♕d2 b4 and the pawns are starting to roll.

B) 19...♗e4! 20 ♕d2 ♕b7 21 ♘h4 ♖fd8 22 ♘f5 ♗f8 and it's not clear what White is doing.

19...♖fd8

There is also 19...♗e4 20 ♕e2 ♖fe8 21 ♘bd2 ♗d5.

20 ♕e2

In general there are a large number of possible moves for both sides but it is unlikely to change the assessment of the position – that Black has very good, perhaps in a higher sense even winning compensation.

20...♗f8

21 ♗d2

What alternatives did Korchnoi have? It would seem he has four or five reasonable candidate moves: 21 ♗d2, 21 ♗g5, 21 ♘bd2 21 ♘h4 and 21 ♘e1. Here are some possible continuations:

21 ♗g5 h6 22 ♗xf6 ♕xf6 leaves Black very well co-ordinated,

e.g. 23 ♘bd2 d3! 24 ♕f1 (24 ♕e3 c4) 24...c4 and b2 is increasingly weak, while Black also threatens the overwhelming ...b4 and ...c3;

21 ♘bd2 c4! and White isn't doing anything while Black has an obvious plan of pushing the pawns.

21 ♘h4 ♗xg2 22 ♘xg2 c4 23 ♗g5 h6 24 ♗xf6 ♕xf6 25 ♘d2 d3 26 ♕g4 ♕xb2! 27 ♖ab1 ♕c2 28 ♖xb5 c3 29 ♘e3 cxd2 30 ♘xc2 dxc2 is one illustration of the strength of Black's pawns.

21...b4!

21...c4? 22 ♗a5!

22 b3

Korchnoi desperately tries to blockade the c4 square. The drawback is that this pawn simply drops off! 22 ♗g5 is met by 22...c4.

22...♗d5!

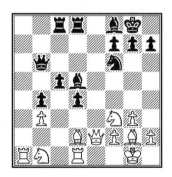

23 ♖e1?!

23 ♕d3! may have been a better try. After White drops the b-pawn Black must in the long run be winning; White has no way of

creating enough tactical counterplay to prevent Black from pushing the pawns. For example: 23...c4 (23...♖a8!? 24 ♖xa8 ♖xa8) 24 bxc4 ♗xc4 25 ♕f5 ♗e2 26 ♖e1 d3 and the knight on b1 is a sorry picture, but at least White has managed to fracture the black queenside pawns. (26...♖c5 27 ♕f4 ♗d6 28 ♕xd4 ♗xg3 is real mess) 27 ♗e3 ♗c5 28 ♗xc5 ♖xc5 with compensation.

23...♗xb3 24 ♖a6 ♕b7

24...♕b8 25 ♗f4!

25 ♘xd4

25 ♖xf6 gxf6 26 ♘xd4 ♗d5 27 ♗xd5 ♕xd5∓

25...♗d5

It was important that when Shirov played his queen to b7 – allowing the knight discovery – he didn't fear ghosts. Accurate calculation reveals that Black's pawns offer more than enough compensation for the piece.

26 ♗xd5 ♖xd5 27 ♘c2

27 ♘f3 ♖e8 28 ♕c4 ♖xe1+ 29 ♘xe1 ♖d4 30 ♕f1 c4!; or

27 ♘b3 ♖e8 28 ♕f1 ♖xe1 29 ♗xe1 ♖d1! 30 ♖a1 ♕d5-+

27...♖cd8!

On 27...♖e8 comes 28 ♘e3.

28 ♖xf6

28 ♘e3!? is still possible.

A) 28...♖xd2 29 ♘xd2 ♖xd2 30 ♕xd2 ♕xa6 31 ♘d5 (31 ♖c1 ♘e4) 31...♘xd5 32 ♕xd5 c4 33 ♖e8 is tricky, e.g. 33...g6 34 ♕c5!;

B) 28...♖e5;

C) 28...♖d3 29 ♖xf6 gxf6 30 ♘g4 ♗g7 31 ♗h6 ♕f3!? 32 ♕e8+ (32 ♕xf3 ♖xf3-+) 32...♗f8.

28...gxf6 29 ♗f4 ♕d7 30 ♘e3 ♖d4 31 ♘c4

31 ♘g4 ♕e6! 32 ♕xe6 fxe6 33 ♘xf6+ ♔f7 34 ♘g4 ♖d1.

31...♕e6! 32 ♘bd2

32 ♘e3 c4 doesn't help.

32...♕xe2 33 ♖xe2 ♖a8 34 ♖e1 ♖a2 35 ♖e8 ♔g7 36 ♗e3 ♖d5 37 g4 ♖c2 38 h4 h5 39 g5 fxg5 40 hxg5 b3 41 ♖b8 b2!

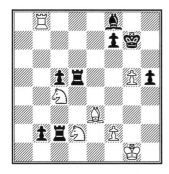

42 ⊗g2

Unfortunately for Korchnoi, 42 ☖xb2 is met by 42...☖dxd2! 43 ♗xd2 ☖xc4 44 f4 ♗d6 45 f5 ♗f4 and the white kingside pawns are more vulnerable than strong.

42...♗e7 43 f4 f6! 44 ☖b7

After 44 gxf6+ ♗xf6 there is the crushing threat of ...♗c3.

44...⊗g6! 45 ⊗f3

45 ☖xe7 ☖dxd2+ 46 ♘xd2 ☖xd2+ −+

45...fxg5 46 ☖b6+ ⊗g7 47 ⊗e4 gxf4

48 ♗xf4

An admission of defeat. But would White have had any chances of holding after 48 ⊗xd5 fxe3 49 ♘f3

♗f6 (Also there is 49...☖f2 50 ⊗e4 e2 51 ☖xb2 ☖xf3 52 ☖xe2 when White can put up some resistance but is probably losing in the long run) 50 ♘xe3 ☖c1

A) 51 ♘f5+ ⊗g8 52 ☖b8+ ⊗f7 (52...⊗h7 53 ☖b7+ ⊗g6 54 ♘5h4+ ♗xh4 55 ♘xh4+ ⊗g5 56 ♘f3+ ⊗f4 57 ♘d2 ☖c2 58 ♘b1 h4 is also good) 53 ☖b7+ ⊗g6 54 ♘5h4+ ♗xh4 55 ♘xh4+ ⊗g5 transposes.

B) 51 ♘d2 ♗c3 52 ♘ec4 h4! and White is not in a position to hold back all the passers.

48...☖d4+ 49 ⊗f5 ♗f6! 50 ☖b7+

50 ♗h6+ ⊗xh6 51 ☖xf6+ ⊗g7 52 ☖b6 ☖dxd2.

50...⊗g8 51 ⊗xf6 ☖xf4+ 52 ⊗g6 ⊗f8 53 ⊗xh5

53...☖f2

Breaking the blockade on d2.

Shirov showed great insight in realising that his chances were superior with two pawns and greater development for the piece – good calculation is in fact good judgement. Moreover, in favouring one tempting line over another, experience also plays a large part – and Shirov truly showed great chess wisdom at an early age.

0-1

The PCA, the Professional Chess Association set up by Garry Kasparov and Nigel Short just before their world championship match in 1993, was the breakaway rival to FIDE, the body governing world chess. Sadly the PCA is now defunct, but they did organise a world championship cycle which culminated in Kasparov beating Anand in New York in 1995. I believe the PCA went under as it lost its sponsorship from the computer firm Intel.

The chess world is constantly finding it difficult to attract sponsors, possibly because chess is a harder sell than, for example, poker which is easier to understand and also has the gambling element – which means that even a very poor player can beat the best player in the world if the cards fall right, something that is very unlikely in chess where the luck factor is far less. However, a player like Shirov will always attract the sponsors because, as well as being very strong, he plays consistently entertaining chess.

In the present day and age there are a huge number of very strong chess players, so you need something special to stand out from the crowd – and Shirov certainly has that. In fact he was instrumental in setting up the ACP, the Association of Chess Professionals, which was founded to protect chess players from the stranger demands of FIDE. In fact not too long ago FIDE came in for a lot of criticism (what's new?) with the high-profile withdrawal of Magnus Carlsen and Michael Adams from their Grand Prix circuit. This came in response to FIDE's decision, halfway through the season, to downgrade the importance of the Grand Prix in relation to the world championship cycle.

FIDE was also criticised for its treatment of Vasily Ivanchuk during the Chess Olympiad in Dresden 2008, where the Ukrainian was threatened with disqualification from the tournament (along with the rest of the Ukrainian team) for failing to take a drugs test after a traumatic defeat in the last round against Gata Kamsky. The resulting defeat against the USA dashed Ukraine's medal hopes. Apparently Ivanchuk was seen kicking a wall afterwards, (I've done something similar – I've punched a wall – but that was *during* a game after I had blundered. Fortunately for the wall I won the game anyway) which may appear unseemly, but it seems indicative that FIDE is more concerned with pleasing the IOC, in an effort to get chess recognised as an Olympic sport, than in showing sympathy towards a player who is clearly in a vulnerable state. To me the Olympics have always seemed the most overrated sporting event of all. It only comes around every four years and most of the events are over in 10 seconds, not to mention the drugs scandals. I'm not sure what drugs can be used to enhance chess performance anyway – unless a Rybka chip can be ground down into a soluble form. Another ridiculous rule that FIDE has experimented with at the Olympiad is to default a player who is a second late for the start of the game. FIDE has yet to make this rule widespread practice but is debating it. Of course such Draconian measures, which also include the somewhat harsh mobile phone rule – one ring and you lose – are more likely to alienate ordinary chess players than anything else.

Another change considered by FIDE is the introduction of an elite grandmaster title – as a reaction to the deluge of grandmasters which has resulted in a devaluation of the title. I have no idea how many grandmasters there are, though I would guess over a thousand. Apparently, though, the percentage of grandmasters to the number of people actually playing the game has greatly decreased – in terms of grandmasters compared to 2200 players, the figure stands at 0.055 – and in relation to all other players, grandmasters only represent 0.012 of the total chess population! But despite that, I would personally be in favour of scrapping the grandmaster title altogether – along with the IM title – there are so many of each now that I no longer feel the titles have any relevance. Today it's all about ratings. In my view it's grossly unfair that, for example, an international master with a higher rating than his grandmaster counterpart will receive appreciably worse conditions. For example, in golf or tennis there are no titles – your world ranking is everything. Why shouldn't it be the same in chess? Mind you, FIDE has tightened up the rules on gaining grandmaster norms – now 33 percent of your opponents have to be grandmasters.

Conditions

This brings me to the subject of conditions (I love a good rant : -)) Chess conditions are getting worse and worse. In England, there is a weekend chess circuit where the average first prize will be something around the 300 pounds mark. Once I have paid my entry fee, got the train and picked up the hotel bill, I will be lucky if I make 150 pounds profit, and that's if I win. What you tend to find is that everyone else has the same idea, so it's basically a lot of talented sharks fighting over an increasingly small pot. Tournament prize money in England hasn't risen in line with inflation – in the seventies the top prize would be about 300 pounds as well, but that would be worth several thousands today. As far as I can see the only good thing about playing weekenders is that the venues tend to be easy to find – you just follow the slightly awkward social outcast shuffling along carrying a shopping bag. Given that it's almost impossible in this country to make a living from playing chess, you tend to have a few stark alternatives – join the real world and get a proper job (no chance), do lots of soul destroying junior coaching, or simply move abroad, to somewhere like Spain where there are far more tournaments and chess isn't looked down upon like it is in this country.

11

A.Shirov – A.Chernin

PCA World Championship, Groningen 1993

French Defence

1 e4 e6 2 d4 d5 3 ②c3 dxe4 4 ②xe4 ♗d7

The 'Fort Knox' variation – so called because it's as hard to break down as the gold vaults in Texas. It tends to be favoured by players who are happy to defend.

5 ②f3 ♗c6 6 ♗d3 ②d7 7 0-0 ②gf6 8 ②g3

8 ②ed2!?

8...♗e7 9 b3 0-0 10 ♗b2 ♗xf3 11 ♕xf3 c6 12 c4

12...♖c8

12...♕a5!? is also considered by theory. White nearly always reacts to it with 13 a3! followed by ♖ad1, since taking on a3 is not an option for Black as the rook simply returns to a1.

13 ♖fe1 ♗f8

Shirov has also had to meet 13...②f8. Against Hubner in Munich the same year, play went 14 h4! ♕c7 15 ♖ac1 ②g6?! 16 h5 ②h4 17 ♕e3 ♗d6 18 ②e4! ♗f4 19 ②xf6+ gxf6 20 ♕e4 f5 21 ♕e2 ♗xc1 22 ♖xc1 and despite being an exchange to the good Hubner's knight was in trouble and in the game was unable to solve his problems.

14 ♖ad1 ♕a5 15 ♗b1 g6 16 h4!

Always a useful move, as it will be impossible to storm Black's kingside 'fortress' – unless White can force some weaknesses over there.

16...♗g7 17 ♗c3 ♕c7 18 h5

18...b5

What other plans did Black have? The young Ukrainian player Andrei Volokitin, in his annotations to a game he won against Nakamura in Lausanne, said that White is better off putting his pawn on c3 in the Fort Knox, as with the pawn on c4 the d-pawn becomes a target for Black's pieces. Interesting insight but probably overly cautious! Nevertheless Black could keep one eye on the d-pawn with 18...♖ad8!? 19 hxg6 (19 h6 ♗h8) 19...hxg6 20 ♘e4 ♘xe4 (20...c5 21 d5! ♘xe4 22 ♗xe4) 21 ♗xe4

A) 21...c5 22 d5! (22 ♗xb7 cxd4 23 ♗xd4 ♗xd4 24 ♖xd4 ♘e5

25 ♕e4 ♖xd4 26 ♕xd4 ♘xc4!) 22...exd5 (22...♗xc3 23 ♕xc3 e5 24 d6±) 23 ♗xd5 ♘e5 24 ♕g3±;

B) 21...e5!? 22 d5 f5 23 d6! (23 ♔b1 e4 24 ♕e3 ♗xc3 25 ♕xc3 ♕e5) 23...♕b6! (23...fxe4 24 dxc7+-; 23...♕b8 24 ♔b1 e4 25 ♕g3 ♗xc3 26 ♕xc3 c5 27 f3±) 24 ♔b1 e4 25 ♕g3 ♗xc3 26 ♕xc3 ♖e6 27 ♖d2∞.

18...e5!?

A) 19 hxg6 hxg6 20 dxe5 ♘xe5 21 ♕f4 ♘fg4! (21...♘fd7 22 ♘e4±);

B) 19 d5 cxd5 20 cxd5⩲

So it would seem that White is at least slightly better in all variations. Not really surprising though, given that he enjoys the advantage of the two bishops, he should be better! Indeed, in the hands of a dangerous attacking player like Shirov, the two bishops can become a very potent force. With 18...b5, a standard idea in this variation, Black hopes that White will exchange on b5, gifting the superb square on d5 to the black knights.

19 h6!

19...♗xh6?

Quite simply Chernin didn't want the pawn hanging over his head on h6 for the rest of the game, and who can blame him? Any check then by White might well be mate but I still would have preferred the humble retreat 19...♗h8 20 ♘e4 bxc4 21 bxc4 ♖ad8± (21...♘xe4!? 22 ♗xe4 ♖ac8±). I guess Black's problem is that he doesn't have room for manoeuvre since any pawn break with ...c5 or ...e5 is likely to open up the game for White's two bishops.

20 d5!

Now Alexey is happy – tactics are imminent!

20...cxd5

20...♗g7 21 dxc6+–; 20...exd5 21 ♗xf6.

21 ♗xf6 bxc4 22 ♗b2

Unlike in the previous game where Black had two pawns for the piece (in this case Black has three pawns), White's extra piece is likely to prove

very useful, as his forces are aimed menacingly at Black's kingside.

22...cxb3

Black would very much like 22...♗g7!? to work, because in theory the removal of one of the bishops should greatly increase his defensive chances – but Alexey would obtain an attack even then! 23 ♗xg7 ♔xg7 24 ♕c3+ (24 bxc4 ♕xc4 25 ♖c1 ♕b4! and White has a lot of work to do, if he is better at all.) 24...♔g8 (24...♘f6 25 ♗d3!) 25 bxc4 (25 ♗d3!?) 25...♘b6 (25...♖ac8 26 ♗d3! ♘c5 27 ♗f1±)

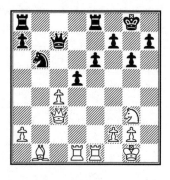

A) 26 ♘h5!? gxh5

A1) 27 ♕d3 f5 28 cxd5 ♖ad8 (28...♘xd5 29 ♖xe6 ♖xe6 30 ♕xd5 ♖ae8 31 ♗xf5 ♕f7 32 ♗xe6 ♖xe6±);

A2) 27 ♖e5 f5;

B) 26 c5! ♘a4 27 ♕d4! ♘xc5 28 ♖c1± ♖ac8 29 ♖c3 ♕a5 30 ♖ec1+–

23 ♘h5!

Alexey needs no invitation!

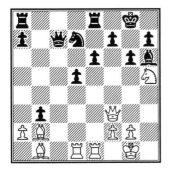

23...f5

How should White increase the pressure after 23...♗g5? By 24 ♕g4! ♕d8 25 ♕d4 e5 (it would take a brave man to play 25...♔f8 26 ♕g7+ ♔e7 27 ♖xd5+–) 26 ♕xd5+– Other replies are 23...♕d8 24 ♕c3+; 23...gxh5 24 ♕xh5 when 24 ... ♕f4 is met by the elegant switchback 25 ♗c1!; and finally 23...bxa2 24 ♘f6+ ♘xf6 25 ♕xf6 e5 26 ♖xe5!

24 ♖xd5!

Bravo! Black's position collapses like a house of cards.

24...gxh5

24...exd5 25 ♕xd5+ ♔f8 26 ♗a3+ +–

25 ♖xf5! ♘f8 26 ♖xh5

Now apart from still having a raging attack, White is almost back to level material.

26...bxa2 27 ♗xa2

27...♗g7

27...♕f4 was another try. Then 28 ♕h3! ♗g7 (28...♕d2 29 ♗c3 ♕xa2 30 ♖xh6 and Black is not long for this world.) 29 ♗xg7 ♔xg7 30 ♗b1 h6 31 ♖e3! ♖ab8 32 ♗c2! ♘h7 33 ♖g3+ ♘g5 34 ♖hxg5+! hxg5 35 ♕h7+ ♔f6 36 ♖f3+– Here Black is only defending with the queen and knight – hardly sufficient against the heavy pressure of White's attacking force.

28 ♕g4

28...♔h8

White is having a lot of fun in this position.

28...♖ad8

A) 29 ♖g5 ♘g6 30 ♖xe6? (30 ♗xe6+ ♔h8 31 ♖xg6 ♗xb2) 30...♖xe6 31 ♕xe6+ ♔h8 32 ♖xg6 ♖d1+;

B) 29 ♖c1!? ♕f7 30 ♗xg7 ♕xg7 31 ♖g5 ♘g6 32 ♗xe6+ ♔h8 33 ♗f5 ♖d6!;

C) 29 ♗xg7 ♕xg7 30 ♖g5 ♘g6 31 ♗b1 (31 ♖xe6 ♖xe6 32 ♗xe6+ ♔h8 33 ♗f5 ♕e5 34 g3 ♕e1+ 35 ♔g2 ♖d1!) 31...♕c3 32 ♖f1 (32 ♗xg6? ♕xe1+ 33 ♔h2 hxg6 34 ♖xg6+ ♔f7 35 ♖g7+ ♔f8 36 ♖g8+ ♔e7 seems to throw a spanner in the works.) 32...♕d4 (32...♖d4 33 ♕h5) 33 ♕h5+- When you have a winning position it's easy to believe that everything wins, but it's important to remember that there are always hidden resources.

29 ♗xg7+ ♕xg7 30 ♖g5 ♘g6

30...♕f7 31 ♕d4+ e5 32 ♗xf7 exd4 33 ♖g8 mate.

31 ♗b1 ♕c3 32 ♖d1 ♕f6

32...♖ad8 33 ♗xg6 ♖xd1+ 34 ♕xd1 hxg6 35 ♖xg6+-

33 ♖d7!

Now White introduces the deadly threat of ♖xh7. But can't he play 33 ♗xg6 – and Black resigns doesn't he? No. 33...♖g8! is an easy move to miss, which is why it's important to check everything! Then on 34 ♖d7 follows 34...♖xg6 35 ♖h5 h6.

33...♖e7

On 33...♕a1 34 ♕e4! is simplest, e.g. 34...♖g8 35 ♖h5 ♖g7 36 ♕xa8+.

34 ♖xe7 ♕xe7 35 ♗xg6

Now this really is decisive.

35...♖g8 36 ♕d4+

36...♖g7

36...♕g7 is met by 37 ♗f7!!; and 36...e5 with 37 ♖xe5.

37 ♖h5 e5 1-0

38 ♖xe5 is decisive. Shirov made this attack look easy – but that's because he calculated Black's defensive possibilities very well and

chose the most accurate move every time. Another powerful display!

12

E.Bareev – A.Shirov

Linares 1993

Semi-Slav Defence

1 d4 d5 2 c4 c6 3 ♘f3 ♘f6 4 ♘c3 e6 5 ♕b3 dxc4 6 ♕xc4 b5 7 ♕d3 ♗e7 8 a3 0-0 9 e4

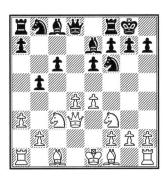

9...c5?!

A fascinating sacrifice, if perhaps slightly flawed. Development above all! Another option would be 9...a6 but that can be met by the aggressive 10 e5 ♘d5 11 ♘e4 and it would seem that Black has to play the slightly risky looking 11...f5!? 12 exf6 ♘xf6 in order to free his position. Typical of his active style Shirov is happy to temporarily sacrifice a pawn in order to avoid being suffocated.

10 dxc5 ♗xc5

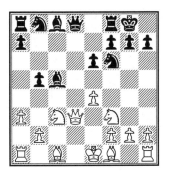

11 ♕xb5?!

In reality, this is a very risky pawn grab.

Also after 11 ♘xb5 ♕b6! (if 11...♘g4 12 ♕xd8 ♖xd8 13 ♘c7 ♗xf2+ 14 ♔e2±) with ideas of ...♗b7 ...♘g4 ...♖d8 and ...♘bd7 – as well as simply taking on f2 – Black has excellent development. Then 12 ♗e3 ♗b7 13 e5 ♘g4 looks more than okay for Black. The idea of sacrificing a pawn for rapid development is most commonly seen in the Grunfeld and Benko against 1 d4 but obviously can be used in other openings as well.

Other moves are:

11 ♗e2 ♘g4 12 0-0 ♕b6 with some initiative;

11 ♗e3? ♕xd3 12 ♗xd3 ♗xe3 13 fxe3 a6 14 e5 ♘g4 15 ♔e2 ♘d7∓;

11 h3 ♕b6 12 ♕c2 ♘c6 13 ♗xb5 ♘d4 14 ♘xd4 ♗xd4 15 ♗d3 ♗b7.

But there is also the 'simple' 11 ♕xd8! ♖xd8, when

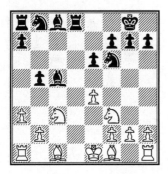

A) 12 ♘xb5 appears to run into 12...♘xe4 13 ♘c7 ♗xf2+ (13...♘xf2 14 ♖g1 ♘e4 15 ♘xa8) 14 ♔e2 ♖d7 (14...♗a6+!? 15 ♘xa6 ♘xa6 16 ♘g5! ♘xg5 17 ♗xg5± [17 ♔xf2 ♘e4+ 18 ♔f3 ♘ac5 19 b4 ♘b3]; 15 ♗f4 (15 ♘xa8?? ♗a6 mate) 15...e5!

A1) 16 ♘xa8 exf4 17 ♘e5 (17 ♖d1 ♗a6+) 17...♖e7∓;

A2) 16 ♗xe5 ♘c6∓;

but

B) 12 ♗xb5 looks best; then 12...♗b7 (12...h6!? 13 0-0 ♗b7 14 ♖e1 ♘g4 15 ♖e2±) 13 ♗g5±;

11...♕c7!

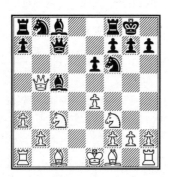

What compensation does Black have here? Well, it's simply in the way of development. Put the white e-pawn on e3 and Black's

compensation would look somewhat ridiculous. but on e4 it is vulnerable, giving a chance for Black to develop with tempo by ...♗b7. It also softens up the route to f2 – the bishop is already pointing to that square – allowing Black to think about moves like ...♘g4. Doubtless again a computer would prefer White here – they normally like having the extra booty – but finding the correct series of moves for White is by no means easy.

12 ♗g5

The idea behind this move is very credible, that White can drop the bishop back to h4 and bolster the f2 square. However the problem is that it leaves White two moves from castling(!) as queenside castling is clearly not an option for White here. 12 ♗e2 (12 ♗d3?? ♗a6-+) looks like the 'safe' move, e.g.

A) 12...♘g4 13 0-0 ♗a6 14 ♕a4 ♗xe2 15 ♘xe2±;

B) 12...♗b7

B1) 13 ♕c4 ♘g4 (13...♘bd7 14 b4 ♗b6 15 ♕xc7 ♗xc7) 14 0-0 ♕b6 15 ♘d1 ♖d8!;

B2) 13 ♕d3 ♖d8 14 ♕c2 (14 ♕b1 ♘g4! 15 0-0 ♗xf2+ 16 ♖xf2 ♕b6 17 ♘d1 ♖xd1+ 18 ♗xd1 ♕xf2+ 19 ♔h1 ♕f1+ 20 ♘g1 ♘f2 mate is a cute finish) 14...♘xe4! 15 ♘xe4 ♗xf2+-+;

B3) 13 0-0! ♘xe4 14 ♘xe4 ♗xe4 15 ♗f4! ♕xf4 (15...♗xf2+? 16 ♖xf2

♕xf4 17 ♘g5 ♕e3 18 ♕e5+-)
16 ♕xc5;

But in fact Black can crank up the
pressure on the f2 point by simple
play;

C) 12...♗a6! 13 ♕a4 ♕b6.

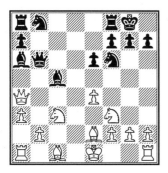

When analysing these lines, it
quickly becomes obvious that the f2
square is an Achilles heel for White
in many variations. Therefore ♗h4
is very logical – and indeed can be
found by the process of elimination
– the bishop can drop back to h4 to
cover that square. But unfortunately
it would seem that White has
problems after this move as well!

12...♘bd7!

Introducing the threat of ...♖b8.

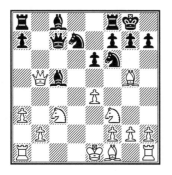

13 ♕a4?!

13 ♕e2 looks very passive. Then
comes 13...a5! and White is having
an awfully hard time getting his
pieces out.

13 ♕c4!? may have already been
the best chance!

A) 13...♖b8 14 b4 ♗a6!? 15 ♕xa6
♗d4! (15...♗xb4 16 axb4 ♕xc3+
17 ♗d2) 16 ♘b5 (16 ♖c1 ♗xc3+
17 ♘d2 ♘xe4) 16...♖xb5 17 ♕xb5
♕c3+;

B) 13...♘g4 14 ♗h4 ♘de5
15 ♘xe5 ♘xe5 16 ♕a2.

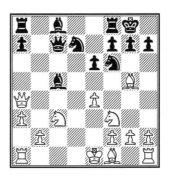

13...♗xf2+!

When considering each move by
your opponent, you should always
think "what drawback does that
move have?" Bareev left a 'tactical
hole', the c5 square, with his last
move.

13...♖b8!? was also possible. Then
14 ♕c2!

A) 14...♗b7 15 ♗d3 ♘g4 16 ♗h4
♘de5 17 ♘xe5 ♘xe5 (17...♕xe5
18 h3) 18 0-0;

B) 14...♘g4 15 ♗h4;

C) 14...♕b6

C1) 15 b4 ♗d4 (15...♗d6!?) 16 ♘xd4 ♕xd4 17 ♖d1;

C2) 15 ♘a4 ♗xf2+ 16 ♕xf2 ♕a5+ 17 ♘c3 ♘xe4 with an attack.

14 ♔xf2 ♘c5!

Now Black's initiative assumes frightening proportions, and each variation becomes incredibly complicated.

15 ♕d4

It was difficult to see which queen move worked best;

15 ♕b4!?

A) 15...♘g4+ 16 ♔g1;

B) 15...♖b8 16 ♘b5! (16 ♗b5 ♘d3+ 17 ♗xd3 ♖xb4 18 axb4 ♕b6+ 19 ♔g3 ♕d6+ 20 e5 ♘h5+ 21 ♔h4 ♕xd3 22 ♔xh5 f6∓) is a real mess;

B1) 16...♘fxe4+ 17 ♔e3 (17 ♔g1) 17...♕b6;

B2) 16...♕b6 17 ♘bd4 ♘cxe4+ 18 ♔e3 (18 ♔g1 ♘xg5 19 ♘xg5 ♕c7);

B3) 16...♘cxe4+

B3a) 17 ♔e3

B3a1) 17...♘g4+ 18 ♔xe4 ♗b7+ 19 ♔d3 ♖fd8+ (19...♘f2+ 20 ♔e2 ♕c2+ 21 ♕d2 ♕xd2+ 22 ♗xd2 ♘xh1) 20 ♔e2;

B3a2) 17...♘d5+! 18 ♔xe4 (18 ♔d4 ♕b6+) 18...♕c2+ 19 ♗d3 f5+ 20 ♔e5 ♕xd3;

B3b) 17 ♔g1! ♕b6+ 18 ♕d4 ♘xg5 19 ♘xg5 ♕xd4+ 20 ♘xd4 ♖xb2 and Black probably has enough compensation, but no more than that;

C) 15...a5! 16 ♕c4 ♗a6 looks like too much to handle for White.

Finally 15 ♕d1 ♘cxe4+ 16 ♘xe4 ♘xe4+ 17 ♔e3 (17 ♔g1 ♘xg5 18 ♘xg5 ♕c5+) 17...♘xg5 18 ♘xg5 ♕c5+ 19 ♔f4 ♕f5+ -+; and...

15 ♕c2 ♞cxe4+! (taking advantage of the pin) 16 ♔g1 ♞xg5 17 ♞xg5 ♕c5+ -+

15...♞g4+

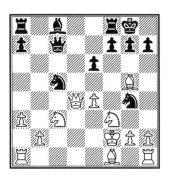

16 ♔g1

16 ♔e2 ♝a6+ 17 ♔e1 ♞b3 18 ♕d1 ♝xf1 19 ♔xf1 (19 ♕xb3 ♝xg2-+) 19...♞xa1 (19...♕c4+ 20 ♕e2 ♕xe2+ 21 ♔xe2 ♞xa1 22 ♖xa1) 20 ♕xa1 ♕b6∓

16...♞b3 17 ♞b5

17 ♕d1? lost on the spot to 17...♕c5+

17...♕b8 18 ♕d6

18 ♕d1 ♕b6+ 19 ♞bd4 ♞xa1 20 ♕xa1 e5-+

18...♞xa1 19 h3 ♞f6 20 ♝d3

20 ♞c7 ♞xe4 21 ♕c6 ♝b7∓

20...♞b3 21 e5 ♞d5 22 ♝c4

It would seem that White has gained some activity as compensation for the lost exchange. However appearances can be deceptive and it is the far superior co-ordination of the black pieces that is the crucial factor.

22...h6! 23 ♝h4

23 ♝xb3 ♕xb5-+

23...♞e3 24 ♝d3

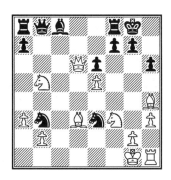

24...♕xd6?!

24...♞f5! seems to me to be a much simpler win. 25 ♝xf5 (25 ♕xb8 ♖xb8 26 ♞xa7 ♝d7 and the knight is getting trapped; or 25 ♕b4 a6 26 ♕xb3 axb5 27 ♕xb5 ♕xb5 28 ♝xb5 ♖b8 29 a4 ♝b7∓) 25...♕xb5 26 ♝e4 ♝b7.

25 exd6

25 ♞xd6!? doesn't look that simple either. Black can try 25...g5 26 ♝f2 ♞d5 27 ♝c4 (27 h4 g4 28 ♞h2 h5) 27...♞a5 28 ♝xd5 exd5 29 ♞d4 ♞c4 and he should be winning. However it seems as if White has rather lost control.

25...♝a6!

Always develop!

26 ♝e7 ♖fb8 27 ♞c7 ♝xd3 28 ♞xa8

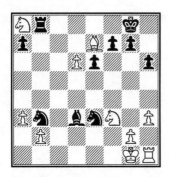

28...♘f5!

Controlling the d-pawn, after which the bishop on e7 starts to look rather pointless. On the other hand 28...♖xa8? 29 d7! would not do.

29 ♘c7

Otherwise Black can simply pick up a pawn with ...♘xe7 and ...♖e8.

29...♗e4!

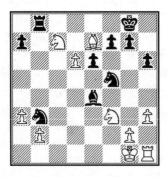

Alexey is back in charge – this move prevents g4 plus there is the additional benefit of being able to withdraw to c6 if the d-pawn should look too dangerous.

30 ♔f2

30 ♔h2 ♘a5 31 b4 ♘c6∓

30...♘c5 31 b4 ♘d3+ 32 ♔e2 ♘f4+ 33 ♔d2 ♘xg2 34 ♘e5 f6! 35 ♖e1

35 d7 ♘xe7.

35...♘xe1 36 ♘d7 ♘f3+ 37 ♔c3 ♖c8 0-1

The imaginative idea ...c5 and later ....♗xf2 set tactical problems that the normally ultra-solid Russian Bareev couldn't handle. Again this might have been good psychology – similar to Tal against Smyslov – since Shirov understood that Bareev's weaknesses tend to be of the calculating variety – why not force him to find a very narrow path? Being aware of the limitations of your opponents as well as their strengths is an essential weapon in the armoury of someone like Shirov.

13

A.Shirov – J.Timman

Biel 1995

Evans Gambit

1 e4 e5 2 ♘f3 ♘c6 3 ♗c4 ♗c5 4 b4

The fabled Evans Gambit, which was reintroduced into tournament play thanks to the efforts of Garry Kasparov and Nigel Short.

4...♗xb4 5 c3 ♗e7

5...♗a5!? is also quite popular.

6 d4

6 ♕b3?! ♘a5 7 ♗xf7+? ♔f8 8 ♕d5 c6.

6...♞a5 7 ♝e2 exd4 8 ♛xd4

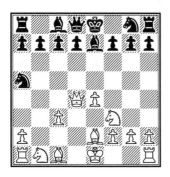

8...d6

8...♞f6 9 e5 ♞c6 10 ♛h4 ♞d5 11 ♛g3 was the continuation of the game Kasparov – Anand, Riga 1995, which I will attempt to analyse later on in the book. Interesting is 8...d5!? 9 ♛xg7 (9 exd5 ♞f6 10 ♛a4+ c6) 9...♝f6 10 ♛g3 dxe4 11 ♞g5 ♝f5∞.

9 ♛xg7 ♝f6 10 ♛g3

10...♛e7?!

This slightly artificial move interferes with the natural square of the king's knight. On the other hand 10...♞e7! was once used by Alexander Onischuk, a former Ukrainian player now resident in the

USA, to achieve a comfortable draw with another Evans Gambit devotee – English grandmaster Nigel Short. After 11 ♝g5 ♞g6 Black gains control over squares on the kingside.

11 0-0 ♝d7?!

This allows the knight to come to d4, although things are still not that clear. 11...♞c6! would have prevented ♞d4 – I must make a confession I never understand these kind of Evans Gambit positions at all – 12 ♜e1 (12 ♝e3? ♛xe4! 13 ♞bd2 ♛g6) 12...♝d7 and in general Black's position looks fine to me. Alternatively 11...♛xe4!? 12 ♜e1 looks incredibly risky, although remarkably 12...♚f8 13 ♝b5 ♛g6 seems to defend, Perhaps one for Fritz?!

12 ♞d4! 0-0-0 13 ♞d2

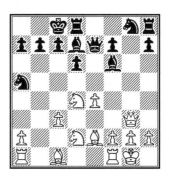

Essentially, as in most positions with castling on opposite wings, both players are committed to attack – White will try and probe along the b-file and Black the same on the g-file. However it would seem in this respect White's trumps are more

significant than Black's, especially if the game continuation is anything to go by. For example, White can simply block the g-file by g2-g3, and while Black can do the same with b7-b6, it would seem that White has other ways in. Also it seems that the white queen can attack in a way that her counterpart cannot.

13...♘c6

Was this really necessary now that White can simply support the knight on d4?

13...h5 14 ♖b1 ♘h6

A) 15 ♗xh5? (of course, opening the h-file only serves to accelerate Black's attack) 15...♖dg8 16 ♕e3 (16 ♕d3 ♗g4 17 ♗xg4+ ♘xg4 18 ♘2f3 ♗e5 with an attack) 16...♗g4!;

B) 15 ♕d3 would be similar to the game, and White has the threat of ♕a6! Then 15...b6 16 ♕a6+ ♔b8 17 ♕xa5+–;

13...♗e5 14 f4 ♗xd4+ (14...♗f6 15 ♖b1) 15 cxd4 ♘f6 16 ♗f3 only helps to reinforce White's central control.

14 ♕e3

14 ♕d3?! ♘e5!

14...h5 15 ♖b1

15 ♘xc6 ♗xc6 16 ♕xa7 is premature; after 16...♗xc3 17 ♖b1 ♘f6 the black king can always run out via d7 if need be.

15...♘h6

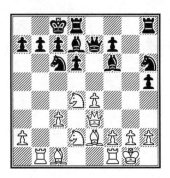

16 ♕d3! b6

Now 16...♘e5 is not possible as it can be met by 17 ♕a6! which is the reason why White didn't simply play ♕d3 earlier. Now the rook is on the b-file 17...bxa6 18 ♗xa6 is mate.

17 a4! ♔b8

If the black bishop were on b7 here, he would be doing well. Unfortunately it isn't.

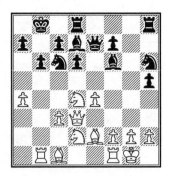

18 a5!

Shirov is only too glad to take the opportunity to open the a-file, which will give him more possibilities for attack.

18...♘xa5 19 ♕a6 ♔a8

Forced, as 19...♘b7 20 ♖a1 ♘a5 21 ♖xa5 bxa5 22 ♗a3 ♔a8 23 ♘b5 ♗xb5 24 ♗xb5 is soon mating.

20 e5!

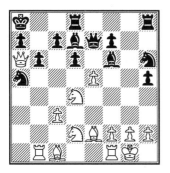

Players like Shirov are constantly alive to every tactical opportunity. White opens the diagonal for the bishop, which Black can only block with a very shaky pawn move.

20...♕xe5 21 ♗f3+ d5 22 ♘c4! ♗c8?

Strangely enough, it's actually the c4 knight that presents the most danger to Black's king. When confronted by the wealth of possibilities that White has after 22...♘xc4 23 ♕xc4 it would be quite easy to go wrong. However in the game White's attacking moves are much more obvious. Sometimes it pays at least to give your opponent the opportunity to go wrong. Though it looks as if the white squares are starting to creak around his king, Black has 23...♗c8! (not 23...c6 24 ♘xc6 dxc4 25 ♘xe5+ ♔b8 26 ♗f4 ♔c8 27 ♘xc4 ♘f5 28 ♖xb6!+-)

...which is a critical test of White's idea. Shirov would then have several continuations, ♘b5, ♘c6, ♕a4, ♕a2 and ♗h6 and Timman may have been worried about so many attacking possibilities

A) 24 ♘c6 dxc4

A1) 25 ♖a1!? a6 (25...a5? 26 ♘xa5+ ♗b7 27 ♘xb7+ ♔b8 28 ♘xd8 ♔c8 29 ♖a8+ ♔d7 30 ♖d1+ ♔e7 31 ♘c6+ +-) 26 ♘xd8+ ♗b7 27 ♗xb7+ (27 ♖xa6+ ♔b8 28 ♗xb7 c6 29 ♘xc6+ ♔xb7 30 ♘xe5 ♔xa6 31 ♘xc4 ♗xc3∓) 27...♔b8 28 ♗c6;

A2) 25 ♘xd8+ ♗b7 26 ♗xb7+ ♔b8 27 ♘c6+ ♔xb7 28 ♘xe5 ♗xe5∓;

B) 24 ♗xh6 ♖xh6 25 ♘c6 dxc4 26 ♘xe5+ ♗b7 27 ♗xb7+ ♔xb7 28 ♘xf7 ♖g6 29 ♘xd8+ ♗xd8∞;

C) 24 ♘b5 ♔b8 25 ♕a4 a6;

D) 24 ♕a2 ♗b7 25 ♘b5 a5 26 ♗e3;

E) 24 ♕a4 ♗b7 25 ♖a1!? (also there is 25 ♘b5 or 25 ♘c6 ♗xc6 26 ♕xc6+ ♔b8) 25 ... a5 (25...a6

26 ♕b5 ♔b8 27 ♖xa6) 26 ♕b5 is interesting; White simply intends to rip open the black queenside with a sac on a5 at some point. Play might continue 26...♕e8 27 ♖xa5+ bxa5 28 ♕xa5+ ♔b8 29 ♗f4 ♕d7 (29...♗e5 30 ♖b1 ♗xf4 31 ♕a6 ♔c8 32 ♕xb7+ ♔d7 33 ♕c6+ ♔e7 34 ♖e1+ ♔f8 35 ♖xe8+ ♖xe8±) 30 ♘b5.

23 ♕xa5 ♕xd4

23...bxa5 24 ♘xe5 ♗xe5 25 ♘c6+-

24 ♕a2!

Someone once said of Tal, that all he needed was an open file to win the game. The same could equally apply to Shirov.

24...♕xc3

24...♕c5 25 ♗e3! is even more crushing than the game, if such a thing is possible. Then 25...♕e7 26 ♗xb6 cxb6 27 ♘xb6+ +-

25 ♗e3!

Shirov brings all the players to the party! 25 ♗b2 wins a piece doesn't it? Not so fast, then comes 25...♕c2! 26 ♖fc1 ♕g6 and Black is still fighting. Now the combined threats of ♖c1, taking on b6 etc, are overwhelming.

25...♗b7

25...♔b8 26 ♘xb6 cxb6 27 ♗xb6 axb6 28 ♖xb6+ ♗b7 looks suicidal against an attacking monster like Shirov, but at the moment Black is two pieces to the good:

A) 29 ♖fb1 ♔c7 30 ♕a7 (30 ♖xb7+ ♔d6) 30...♖b8 31 ♗xd5 ♗d4 32 ♖xb7+ ♖xb7 33 ♖xb7+ ♔d6 34 ♖d7+ ♔e5 and Black may be escaping;

B) 29 ♕a6 ♖d7 30 ♗xd5! and the black king, denuded of all defenders, is not likely to survive much longer.

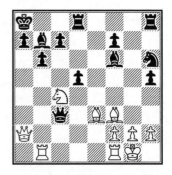

26 ♗xb6! cxb6 27 ♘xb6+ ♔b8 28 ♘xd5

White has stripped the black king bare, and Black cannot resist the threats, for example 28...♕c5 29 ♘xf6. A model game by Shirov of how to attack a king on the queenside. What's most impressive is that it's quite difficult to pinpoint any obvious mistakes by Timman, yet he didn't manage to last beyond 30 moves.

1-0

14

A.Shirov – P.Leko

Investbank, Belgrade 1995

Ruy Lopez

1 e4 e5 2 ♘f3 ♘c6 3 ♗b5 a6 4 ♗a4 ♘f6 5 0-0 ♗e7 6 ♖e1 b5 7 ♗b3 d6 8 c3 0-0 9 h3 ♗b7 10 d4 ♖e8

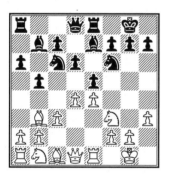

The Zaitsev variaton of the Ruy Lopez, which was employed extensively by Karpov in his matches against Kasparov. Some of the positions that arise in the main line are so complicated that when Kasparov analysed his fantastic struggle against Karpov from the 16th game of their world championship match in 1986, some of the variations ran to several pages long!

11 ♘g5 ♖f8 12 ♘f3

Generally White will use this move order to gain time on the clock (though this seems less relevant now that increment is used) though you will come across the odd player who uses it to try and gain an early draw (You know the type, crushing bore and failed accountant, who you will desperately try to avoid being trapped in a conversation at a party).

12...♖e8 13 a4 h6 14 ♘bd2 ♗f8 15 ♗c2 exd4 16 cxd4 ♘b4 17 ♗b1 c5 18 d5 ♘d7 19 ♖a3

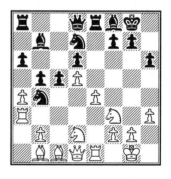

19...f5?!

Far from it for me to question a move that has long been considered playable by theory, but I have always felt that these kinds of positions favour White, as his king is extremely safe and all his pieces are ideally placed to attack the enemy king (and f5 seems to weaken the king's protection as well). 19...c4!? has been tried many times with the basic idea being to get an iron grip on the d3 square with ...♘c5-d3, thereby blunting the power of White's bishop on b1.

**20 exf5 ♗xd5 21 ♖xe8 ♕xe8
22 ♖e3 ♕f7**

22...♕h5 may run into trouble
after 23 ♘e4! ♖e8 (23...♗f7?
24 ♘xd6) 24 g4!?

A) 24...♕f7 25 g5!? (25 ♘fg5?
hxg5 26 ♘xg5 ♖xe3! 27 ♘xf7
♖xh3);

B) 24...♕xh3 25 ♘fg5 ♕h4
26 ♖h3

23 ♘e4

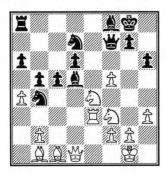

The critical position. Now Black
has to navigate his way through a
dense forest of variations, quite
common for this opening, but it
appears he makes the wrong choice.

23...bxa4?

The young Leko did not have the
experience to possess a Karpovian
sense of danger at this stage in his
career and is readily swept aside by
Shirov in an orgy of controlled
violence! His move is slightly anti-
positional and what's much worse, it
fails to do anything about White's
threat. Leko intends ...♗b3 which
will allow him to play ...d5 with
tempo, but it's just too slow!
However there is 23...♗xe4!

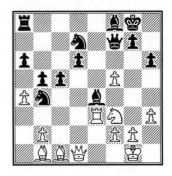

...which we can hit upon by the
simple process of elimination; in
many variations this knight is
threatening to sac itself on g5,
causing Black no end of problems;
so why not chop it off? On the other
hand this move does have the
drawback that it gives up the light
squares to White:

A) 24 ♖xe4

A1) 24...♕xf5 25 ♗d2! ♘c6?
(25...♕f7 26 ♗xb4±) 26 ♖e8;

A2) 24...♖e8! 25 ♗d2 ♖xe4
26 ♗xe4 ♘f6!;

B) 24 ♗xe4 d5 25 ♗b1 ♖e8! (It is
important to exchange as many
pieces as possible, as this will ease
the defence. If 25...d4 26 ♖e6!)
26 ♖xe8 ♕xe8 27 ♗d2 ♘c6 and it
looks as if Black is more than just
clinging on as 28 ♗a2 can be met by
28...c4 though of course there is still
plenty of play left.

23...♖e8 seems to allow two
powerful knight thrusts, i.e.
24 ♘eg5 hxg5 25 ♘xg5 ♗b3
26 ♕d2+− and 24 ♘fg5 ♕xf5 25 g4!
which is also strong;

23...♘f6 24 ♘xf6+ ♕xf6 looks as if it solves Black's problems but unfortunately there is 25 ♗d2!

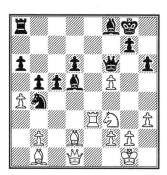

A) 25...♕xb2 26 ♗xb4 ♗xf3 27 ♖xf3 ♕xb4 28 f6! (the prosaic 28 ♕d5+ ♔h7 29 ♕xa8 ♕xb1+ 30 ♔h2 isn't bad either) with a winning attack;

B) 25...♘c6 26 ♗c3 ♕f7 27 f6! and all of White's pieces will contribute to the attack after 27...gxf6 28 ♘h4 ♘e5 29 ♖g3+ ♔h8 (29...♗g7 30 ♘f5) 30 ♗xe5+-

24 ♘fg5!

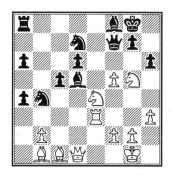

As we have seen before, Shirov isn't one to miss a tactic! Remarkably perhaps, Leko has already gone past the point of no return.

24...hxg5

24...♕e7 25 ♘c3 ♕xg5 26 ♘xd5 looks horrible for Black, who will inevitably suffer a catastrophe on the light squares.

25 ♘xg5 ♕f6

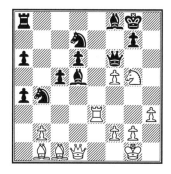

26 ♖e6!

Of course! This move unleashes the b1 bishop, enabling it to fulfil its full potential.

26...♗xe6

26...♕d4 27 ♕h5 (very simple!) 27...♘f6 28 ♖xf6 and mate soon follows.

27 fxe6

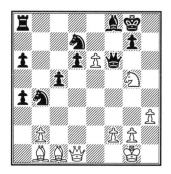

27...g6

27...♘e5 is an attempt to give up the queen to block the attack.

A) 28 f4 ♘ed3! 29 ♕h5 (29 ♗xd3 ♕d4+) 29...♕h6 30 ♕f7+ ♔h8 31 e7 ♗xe7 32 ♕xe7 ♕f6;

B) 28 ♕h5 transposes after 28...♕h6;

C) 28 ♗h7+ ♔h8 29 ♕h5 (you would look at this variation wouldn't you!?) 29...♕h6 30 ♘f7+ ♘xf7 31 ♗xh6 ♘xh6 (31...♔xh7 32 ♗d2+ ♘h6 33 ♗xh6 gxh6 34 ♕f7+ ♔h8 35 e7+-) 32 ♗b1!? is more than likely winning for White despite Black having a rook and two pieces for the queen; White simply threatens g4-g5 and Black doesn't have an answer to this.

28 exd7

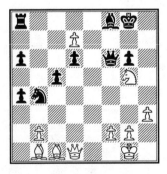

A typical Shirov position – if there is such a thing! Black is an exchange up, but that's the end of the good news. The d-pawn is a monster and the squares around his king have been fatally weakened. And on top of all this White has two raking bishops.

28...♖d8

28...♗h6 29 ♘e4 ♕g7 (29...♕d4 30 ♕xd4 cxd4 31 ♗xh6+-) 30 ♗xh6 ♕xh6 31 ♕xd6+-; or 28...d5 29 ♕g4 (29 ♗d2 ♘c6) with the threat of ♘e6.

29 ♕g4 ♗e7

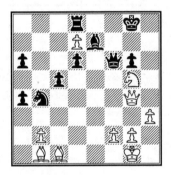

30 h4!

Simply reinforcing the knight and re-emphasising Black's helplessness. 30 ♘e4 is met by 30...♕f5 though the immediate 30 ♘f3 wasn't bad either.

30...d5

Leko tries desperately to block the a2-g8 diagonal at least. 30...♘c6 is met by 31 ♗a2+ (31 h5!?) 31...♔g7 32 ♘e6+ +-

31 ♘f3!?

31 h5!? gxh5 (31...♕d6 32 ♘e6) 32 ♕xh5 ♕g7 33 ♗h7+

31...♔g7

31...♔f7 32 ♗xg6+! ♕xg6 (32...♔f8 33 ♗h6+) 33 ♘e5+; while 31...♕d6 32 ♗xg6 is overwhelming.

32 ♗g5! ♕xb2

32...♕d6 33 ♗xe7 ♕xe7 34 ♕xg6+ ♔f8 35 ♘g5 ♕e1+ 36 ♔h2 ♕e5+ 37 g3 ♔e7 38 ♕h7+! ♔d6 39 ♘f7+

33 ♗h6+ 1-0

Chapter 4

Topalov and the age of computers

Unless you've been hiding in a nuclear bunker for the last 20 years, you can't help but notice the changes that advances in computer technology have wrought upon society. And nowhere is this more prevalent than in chess, where you can now buy just an average chess playing program in your high street shop which will probably be able to outplay most players. Basically, chess computers are now murderously strong and the catalyst for this was undoubtedly Deep Blue's defeat of Kasparov in 1997, a match that sent shock waves around the chess world. If Kasparov is undisputedly the greatest chess player of all time, then Deep Blue is surely his computer counterpart. In fact one of Deep Blue's programmers, grandmaster Joel Benjamin, told me that Deep Blue played a series of training matches against other programs before the Kasparov match. This could hardly have been designed to boost the machine's confidence (computers have no concept of confidence). Deep Blue won every single game against its silicon rivals, which should give you some idea of just how strong it was. Computers like Deep Blue are capable of looking at several billion positions a second. Nowadays the strongest chess playing programs on the market are Rybka, Fritz and Shredder, to name just a few. Practising with these programs can greatly improve your powers of calculation. Not that a human will ever be able to calculate like a computer, but machines sometimes look at moves that people rarely, if ever, do. Working with a program like Rybka will expand your calculating horizons. Moreover such programs are also great sparring partners – after all they will destroy any sense of ego you may have had, as they brutally dismantle your chess game. Computers are also readily available for competitive play on the Internet. Indeed, Internet chess has really taken off in recent years, and the following tongue in cheek article was published in No.4 of *New in Chess*, 2008 under the title of *Diary of an ICC addict*. I'll let you in on a secret. I really hate post-mortems. There's something inherently hypocritical about trying to bash your opponent's brains out throughout a tense 3-4 hour encounter and then sentimentally reminiscing about the contours of the game with him/her afterwards. Imagine how ridiculous it would look if, after a Chelsea – Man United clash in the final of the Champions League, the two teams were to adjourn to a training pitch immediately afterwards to reconstruct possible moves that could have occurred during the game. Or Tiger Woods and Phil Mickelson, after the last hole of the Masters, going back to the final green and Phil trying to hole the 8-footer that he missed first time around – while Tiger gives him friendly advice. It just wouldn't happen. Many times I've had people storm off after a game, but only twice did it happen after they had beaten me. And on each occasion they were strong, world renowned grandmasters who shall remain nameless. Both times I thought it was very rude, but now I see their point. Why spend even more time in the company of an opponent whose chess strength you hold in utter contempt? It might impact in a negative way on their future results to expose themselves to such bad karma. In any case, on the Internet you need not have any concerns about false morality or tipping your hat to any social niceties. You simply do whatever it takes to win. Fortunately, your opponent can't get

even a glimpse of the overwhelming expression of guilt on your face when you flag him (win on time) in a king and rook vs. king and rook ending. Nor do you hear his screams of frustration and anger (though certainly you can imagine them). The ICC (the Internet Chess Club) is the site I play on, and it's by far the most popular of its kind, although its popularity has been challenged in recent years by its main rival Playchess. Playing blitz chess on the Internet is incredibly addictive. I would describe the typical ICC addict's experience as follows; after downloading the software and commencing play, the user experiences a serotonin cascade in the pre-frontal lobe of his brain similar to that which he would experience if he were to use a psychotropic drug. This leads to more and more use, as the addict chases the same high which he finds increasingly difficult to match in his humdrum everyday existence.

The typical day of an ICC addict

Wake up around 2 p.m. Blearily switch on your computer (while blithely ignoring more constructive activites). Check your emails, no new emails. Open ICC. Check who's online. Immediately experience frustration after you type '1' (the command to enter the one minute pairing pool) as you are left waiting for a game. Experience withdrawal symptoms (sweaty palms, high blood pressure) whilst you keep typing '1' over and over again, only to be met with the same irritating message 'you are already in the pool of players waiting to be paired' Eventually you get a game. Throw the mouse at the screen with a scream of pure anger after your opponent flags you in a totally drawn endgame. Throw some insults at him, which makes you feel better, albeit temporarily. Realise it is now four o'clock in the afternoon, it is getting dark outside, and you still haven't got out of bed (you have wireless). Resolve to do something about your situation. Your stomach is grumbling about the lack of food (even ICC addicts need sustenance occasionally), so you wolf down two slices of toast before quickly resuming your activities, exasperated that normal bodily functions like eating should get in the way of your addiction. There is probably an interesting tournament going on – Wijk aan Zee or Linares. You fearlessly mock the play of these overrated and overpaid superstars (while secretly harbouring a jealousy that they are doing something constructive with their lives). Go down to the corner shop to buy a chocolate bar (your first excursion outside your front door for

a couple of days). Along the way you remember there is a Champions League game on the telly that night, and you decide to make a detour to the local boozer to watch it. Unfortunately, however, it's Roma vs. Bayern Munich, and with the score standing at 0-0 you quickly rush back to the house and as you log on to ICC, a pleasant calm feeling returns once again. After three hours, however, you have a raging headache from staring at the screen for so long. You can't take it anymore and log off. You go to You Tube but your search for the video 'Carla Bruni in sexy bikini' achieves no results. Exhausted by your efforts, you fall asleep, resolving for god's sake to do something more constructive tomorrow. Not sure about the last bit! Nevertheless I would say this is pretty accurate :-) Still, there is a solution to all this Internet addiction. Simply pull the plug! Actually one time I adopted a radical approach, I threw my computer out of the window (though such a method should not be recommended). Go outside, get some fresh air. Go to the Himalayas if need be, as they won't have the Internet (in fact they probably do, though you might have to walk for days to find an Internet cafe, and it's doubtful there's much in the way of wireless connection on Everest.) One of the founders of the ICC told me once that it was common for players to ask to be banned from the

ICC altogether, as the addiction was so strong that they were unable to stop themselves. Personally I find the ICC and Internet chess a bit dull – it can hardly replace the real thing – in fact the primary emotion that tends to fly about is one of anger, as insults and swear words are thrown at one another – it's like a chess version of the school playground.

One player who has certainly had his fair share of controversy involving computers is the Bulgarian superstar Veselin Topalov. He was involved in the famous 'toiletgate' scandal during his world championship match with Kramnik, when he accused the Russian, who was making regular trips to the toilet, of using that time to call upon computer assistance. Of course, now that computers are so strong, players using them to cheat in the game has become a real issue, and in fact there have been several cases where players have been caught with their Fritz down, so to speak. In fact a few people have accused Topalov of this sort of thing, with some strange videos coming to light of his controversial manager Silvio Danialov making what appeared to be strange signals towards Topalov during play. While it would be ridiculous to paint Topalov as lighter than light, I think the accusations of cheating are wide of the mark, it would simply be impossible to reach the level that he has, and stay there, while consistently obtaining computer assistance. Players who have done so tend to be found out very quickly – such is the case that you feel they were doing it more for the buzz of the 'sting' than any real monetary desire. Of course it should also be remembered that Topalov was playing elite chess in the days before computers were really strong. Topalov, whose rating is currently about 2810, is one of the very best players in the world today and has achieved some very Kasparovian performances. Can Topalov overtake Kasparov? Perhaps not, as his rating is still well short of the remarkable 2851 rating, a real Bob Beamon-like record that Kasparov created. But he's certainly the best placed of the current players to do so – along with Magnus Carlsen. After all, standards in chess are rising all the time. Each generation taking something from the previous generation and raising the level of play higher and higher.

I think the catalyst for the incredibly high level in top chess these days was the series of matches between Kasparov and Karpov, one of the most epic rivalries in the history of world sport. These two mental gladiators were taking lumps out of each other over a prolonged period of time, and as Kasparov himself said, it was only the new generation, the Anands and the Kramniks, who were able to take the new ideas from those match games forward, while the older generation was essentially left behind.

However, I don't share some people's opinions that players like Capablanca and Steinitz were weak – a strong grandmaster once said that Capablanca was at the level of a current 2200 player. Certainly some of the players around at that time were at a horrible level – they were making terrible blunders that you just wouldn't see now. But players like Capablanca and Morphy were just as gifted as anyone around now – they just didn't have the knowledge or the information that players of today enjoy.

15

V.Topalov – J.Polgar

Novgorod 1996

Sicilian Defence

1 e4 c5 2 ♘f3 e6 3 d4 cxd4 4 ♘xd4 ♘c6 5 ♘c3 ♕c7 6 ♗e3 a6

The Taimanov variation, long known to be a favourite of Judit Polgar.

7 ♗d3

7...b5

7...♘f6 8 0-0 ♘e5 (8...♘xd4 9 ♗xd4 ♗c5 10 ♗xc5 ♕xc5 11 ♘a4!? ♕c7 12 c4±) 9 h3

A) 9...♗c5 10 ♔h1 (10 f4 ♘c6 11 ♘f5 ♕b6 12 ♘xg7+ ♔f8 13 ♗xc5+ ♕xc5+ 14 ♔h1 ♔xg7 15 e5 ♘e8 and I believe that White's position is winning with the pawn on h2 – but with the pawn on h3 it might well be losing because later on the rook cannot gain access to the h3 square. Very deep!) 10...d6;

B) 9...b5 10 f4 ♘c4 11 ♗xc4 ♕xc4 12 ♕d3! ♗b7 13 a4! ♕xd3 14 cxd3 b4 15 ♘ce2 ♗c5 16 ♖fc1 ♖c8?

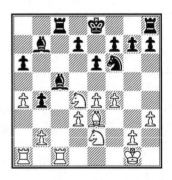

17 ♖xc5! ♖xc5 18 ♘xe6 ♖c2 19 ♘2d4! ♖xb2 20 ♘xg7+ ♔f8 21 ♗c1 ♖xg2+ 22 ♔xg2 ♔xg7 23 ♗b2 and I won a few moves later in a game I played not too long ago against a 2200 player, whose name escapes me, in the Le Touquet tournament in France.

8 ♘xc6 ♕xc6 9 0-0 ♗b7 10 a3 ♘f6 11 ♖e1 ♗e7

11...♗d6!? has been tried by Anand. Then 12 ♘d4 is met by 12...e5 13 ♗e3 ♗c5.

12 ♕f3!

12 f3 looks a bit innocuous, and can be met effectively by 12...♕c7.

12...d6 13 ♕h3

White intends to push the f-pawn and hopes the queen on h3 will deter Black from castling kingside.

13...h5!?

True to her active style, Polgar makes a very aggressive thrust, grabbing space on the kingside. 13...h6!? was also possible, while 13...0-0 14 ♗d4 h6 was Ivanchuk's choice when he reached this position. Personally, I quite like the Taimanov as an opening, since it combines the solidity of something like the Scheveningen with the activity of the Najdorf.

14 ♗g5 ♕c5 15 ♗e3

White doesn't really want to swap queens by 15 ♕e3?! – as usual Black is fine in any Sicilian endgame after 15...♕xe3 16 ♗xe3 ♘g4!?

15...♕c6 16 f3!

White changes tack and elects to play more positionally. If Black is not careful, then White will simply play a4 probing the queenside. Judit needs to generate counterplay quickly.

16...g5!?

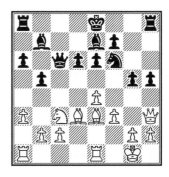

17 a4

Not surprisingly Black has a counter to 17 ♗xg5 in 17...♘g4! (Not 17...0-0-0!? 18 ♕h4 ♕c5+ 19 ♗e3 (19 ♔h1 ♘g4! 20 fxg4 ♗xg5∓) 18 fxg4 (18 ♗xe7? ♕c5+ and mate soon follows; or 18 ♗h4 ♕c5+ 19 ♔h1 ♗xh4) 18...♗xg5 19 gxh5 0-0-0 and despite being two pawns to the good, White's kingside is very exposed, whereas Black has superb control of the dark squares.

17...b4 18 ♘a2

18 ♘e2 g4! (or 18...♖g8!?) with an initiative.

18...g4! 19 fxg4

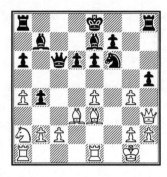

19...d5

Why not 19...♘xg4 ? It hangs the b4 pawn but is that important? After 20 ♘xb4 ♕c7 21 ♗d4 ♘e5 22 a5 it would seem that White has kept control, since 22...0-0-0 is impossible because of 23 ♗b6.

20 c3!

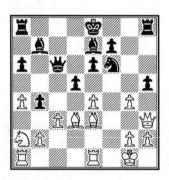

Topalov, himself a very active player who understands the value of time and initiative just as well as Polgar, like her does not take time to pause for breath. Every move counts!

20...bxc3

20...dxe4 21 ♗e2 b3 22 ♘b4! (22 ♘c1 0-0-0 23 g5 ♘d5 24 ♘xb3 ♖dg8 is less clear) 22...♗xb4

(22...♕c7 23 g5 ♘d5 24 ♘xd5 ♗xd5 25 ♖ed1 looks dangerous for Black) 23 cxb4 and as Black cannot castle queenside, he is likely to be under fire in the centre for a while.

But 20...♘xg4! 21 ♗d4 e5 22 exd5 ♕xd5 23 ♗e4 ♕d7 (of course, it looks very dangerous to go into this against Topalov) 24 ♗xb7 (24 ♗xe5 ♗c5+) 24...♕xb7 25 ♗xe5 0-0-0!? (trying at any cost to get in a deadly check on the a7-g1 diagonal) 26 ♗xh8 (26 ♗d4!? may be safest) 26...♕a7+ (26...♖xh8) 27 ♗d4 ♖xd4! 28 cxd4 ♕xd4+ 29 ♖e3 ♗g5 30 ♖ae1 ♗xe3+ 31 ♖xe3 ♕d1+.

21 bxc3 ♘xg4

21...dxe4 22 ♗e2 0-0-0 23 ♘b4! ♕d7 24 ♖ed1±

22 ♗d4!

22...♗c5?

Too slow! 22...e5! may look too weakening, as it gives White the option of taking on d5 and then playing e4, but it does put the question to the bishop on d4. Also Black should try to take advantage of the knight on g4!. There can follow 23 exd5 ♕xd5

A) 24 ♖ab1!? exd4 25 ♗e4 ♕xa2! (25...♕xe4 26 ♖xe4 ♗xe4∓) 26 ♗xb7 ♕f2+ 27 ♔h1 ♕xe1+!-+;

B) 24 ♗e4 24...♕d7 25 ♗xb7 ♕xb7

B1) 26 ♖ab1 ♕d7 (26...♕c7 27 ♘b4! exd4 28 ♘d5) 27 ♗b6 (27 ♗xe5 ♗c5+!) 27...♕xa4 28 ♘b4 looks like a mess;

B2) 26 ♗xe5 0-0-0! (Maybe this was the idea that Judit missed? Black is going for gold – the immediate 26...♕b6+ 27 ♗d4 wasn't effective.) 27 ♗xh8 ♕b6+ 28 ♗d4 ♖xd4.

23 ♗e2!

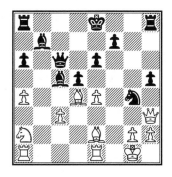

23...♘f6

An admission of defeat, surely? After all, what would you be thinking here as White – the knight on g4 is giving you knightmares! Can Black try anything else?

There is 23...0-0-0 24 e5!? ♕b6 25 ♖ed1 and also 23...♕b6 –

an obvious move that requires calculation but apparently no better than the game;

A) 24 ♖ed1!? renews the threat of taking on g4. Then if 24...e5? (24...♗xd4+ 25 cxd4) 25 ♖ab1 ♕a7

A1) 26 ♗xg4 exd4 27 ♔h1 dxe4 28 cxd4 ♗xd4 29 ♗d7+ (29 ♗xh5 ♗c8) 29...♔f8 (29...♔e7 might be a better try) 30 ♖f1! ♗d5 31 ♘b4;

A2) 26 ♖xb7! ♗xd4+ 27 cxd4 ♕xb7 28 ♗xg4;

B) 24 ♗xg4 ♗xd4+ 25 cxd4 ♕xd4+ 26 ♔h1 hxg4 27 ♕xg4 0-0-0 (27...dxe4 28 ♖ad1 ♕e5 29 h3); 23...e5? 24 ♗xg4 exd4 25 exd5+ +-;

24 e5 ♘e4 25 ♘b4 ♗xd4+

25...♗xb4 26 cxb4 would leave Black with a miserable game; the queen and bishop on c6 are biting on granite.

26 cxd4 ♕b6 27 ♘c2

The position has clarified somewhat and it is clear that Topalov has gained control; Black's bishop is a fairly poor piece (all of the black pawns are on the same coloured squares as the bishop) and his king is safe on either side of the board.

27...♖c8 28 ♖ab1

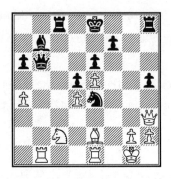

28...♕a7?!

28...♕c7! was more natural. With
♕a7 Black is holding on to the old
idea of pressure down the a7-g1
diagonal – but it's clear that doesn't
work anymore and it was time to
change tack. 29 ♗d3 ♗a8 30 ♗xe4
(now there is no a5 as Black simply
takes it) 30...dxe4 31 ♘e3 ♕c3

A) 32 d5!? ♕xe5 (32...exd5 33 e6
with an attack) 33 dxe6 ♕xe6
34 ♘f5±;

B) 32 ♖ed1.

29 ♗d3 ♖g8

29...♖xc2 30 ♗xc2 ♕xd4+
31 ♕e3.

30 a5 ♗c6 31 ♖b6

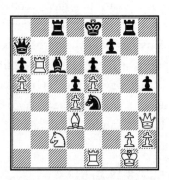

31...♗b5?

Losing directly but Black's
position was very poor anyway as
simply taking on a6 was threatened.

32 ♗xe4 dxe4 33 ♖xe6+! ♔f8

33...fxe6 34 ♕xe6+ ♔f8.

34 ♕a3+ ♔g7 35 ♖e7 ♖c7

35...♕b8 36 ♘e3.

**36 ♖xc7 ♕xc7 37 ♘e3 ♔h8
38 ♖c1 ♕d8 39 d5!**

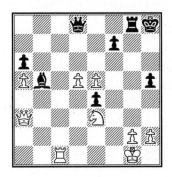

Judit's position is a sorry sight –
her army is fragmented, there are
weak pawns everywhere, not to
mention the exposed nature of her
king.

**39...♕g5 40 ♕c3 ♔h7 41 ♕d4
♗d3 42 d6 h4 43 ♖c7 ♖b8
44 ♖xf7+ ♔g8 45 e6!**

As usual Topalov goes for a tactical solution to a technical problem.

45...♕xe3+

A nice try, but one that just fails. After 45...♖b1+ 46 ♔f2 Black has run out of checks.

46 ♕xe3 ♖b1+ 47 ♕c1

47 ♔f2?? ♖f1 mate would not be too clever.

47...♖xc1+ 48 ♔f2 ♖c6

48...♖f1+ 49 ♔e3 ♖xf7 50 d7! ♖f8 51 e7! is an apt demonstration of the power of the pawn duo.

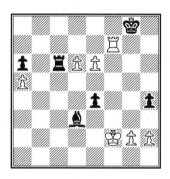

49 ♖d7?!

49 d7 wins in more elementary fashion; 49...e3+ 50 ♔f3! (50 ♔xe3! ♖xe6+ 51 ♔d4 ♖d6+ 52 ♔c5 ♔xf7 53 ♔xd6+-) 50...♖xe6 51 d8=♕+ ♔xf7 52 ♕xd3 e2 53 ♕xe2 ♖xe2 54 ♔xe2 decides.

49...♗b5!

Judit, such an accomplished tactician, struggles valiantly to the end! However it's too little, too late.

50 ♔e3!

50 ♖d8+? ♔g7 51 d7 (51 e7 ♖c2+ 52 ♔e3 ♔f7! 53 ♖f8+ ♔e6) 51...e3+! 52 ♔f3 ♖xe6 53 ♖g8+ ♔xg8 54 d8=♕+ ♖e8 55 ♕xh4 e2 56 ♕e1 ♖f8+!

50...♖c2

50...♖c8 51 ♖b7! ♖d8 52 ♖xb5! axb5 53 e7 ♖e8 54 d7 ♔f7 55 d8=♕; or 50...♔f8 51 ♖f7+ ♔g8 52 d7 ♖d6 53 ♖e7+-

51 ♖c7 ♖e2+ 52 ♔f4 ♖f2+ 53 ♔xe4 ♖e2+ 54 ♔f5

The two pawns are too strong.

54...♖f2+ 55 ♔e5 ♖e2+ 56 ♔f6 ♖f2+ 57 ♔e7 ♖e2 58 d7 ♗xd7 59 ♔xd7 ♖d2+ 60 ♔e8

This is what makes top level chess so difficult – you don't get many chances against the very top players but when you do, you have to take them. Judit had her chances in the opening but failed to take them. Once Topalov gained the advantage he was remorseless.

1-0

Another way in which computers have changed the face of world chess is in preparation – and specifically with Chessbase. This program gives you access to millions of chess games, thereby enabling you to look up your opponent and predict more or less what he will play. There are also drawbacks to this of course. Your opponent can do exactly the same, so it becomes a war of preparation. The player with the superior knowledge will have a huge edge – and access to games even played the previous day can be crucial. One top player compared it to an arms race. However this rather takes away the mystery of the game and you long for the days of just having a beat-up copy of *Informator* and a few old tatty *British Chess Magazines*. A program like Fritz can also be a useful tool for preparation since after Chessbase has told you which opening lines your prospective opponent employs, you simply play some training games against the computer in those variations.

Nevertheless I think it is dangerous to overuse computers as not only can they stifle your imagination, they can also make you lazy as they will do the analysis for you. So, although computers are great analytical tools, in a way they are *too* good and it is all too tempting to sit back and let them do all the work while you are a passive spectator.

16

M.Adams – V.Topalov

Madrid 1996

Trompowsky Opening

1 d4 ♘f6 2 ♗g5

Adams essays the Trompowsky, which he employed a lot in his early career, doubtless inspired by the efforts of his good friend Julian Hodgson, who played nothing else with White. However the Trompowsky is unlikely to give any advantage for White at the highest level, so Adams wisely switched to playing 1 e4 aggressively, and it paid off, enabling him to break through the 2700 barrier and into the world top ten.

2...e6

2...♘e4 3 ♗f4

A) 3...c5 4 f3 ♕a5+ 5 c3 ♘f6 6 ♘d2 is probably the main line;

B) 3...d6 4 f3 ♘f6 5 e4 e5 was shown to me by the late and legendary David Bronstein; his idea was 6 dxe5 ♘h5! 7 ♕d2 (7 ♗e3 dxe5 8 ♕xd8+ ♔xd8 leaves White slightly better in the endgame) 7...♘xf4 8 ♕xf4 ♘d7! 9 exd6 ♗xd6 "and lots of dark squares" or words to that effect by the great man!

C) 3...d5 4 e3 c5!? 5 ♗d3 ♕b6!?

...was a game of mine from the aforementioned Le Touquet tournament. My opponent, who was rated around about 2170, whipped out ♕b6 with no shortage of confidence. Of course deep down I realised that 6 ♗xe4 (6 b3? was my limp reply; Hodgson probably wouldn't be seen dead playing such a move. If I had any excuse it was because the game was played at the ridiculous time of 8.30 in the morning(!) but in fact there were three rounds at this horrible time. After 6...♕b4+ 7 ♔f1 I feebly offered a draw, struggling to keep myself from falling asleep. Fortunately for me, he declined and I went on to win anyway.) 6...♕xb2 (6...dxe4?! 7 ♘c3!) 7 ♗xd5 was

critical but, having analysed with computers a great deal, I started getting cynical about whether White would have enough compensation for the exchange after 7...♕xa1 8 ♘f3, realising that the computer would probably give -1.01 in this position (essentially an advantage of a pawn for Black). However in fact the general assessment is unclear, and this sac has been played in a number of games.

3 e4

Morozevich has successfully played 3 ♘d2 in this position. The game can often transpose to the Torre Attack. 3 ♘f3 is the 'pure' Torre Attack, popularised by the former world champion Tigran Petrosian. White can play for a slight nibble.

3...h6 4 ♗xf6 ♕xf6 5 ♘c3

5 c3 d5! 6 ♘d2 c5 gives a French type position that is by no means bad for Black.

5...d6 6 ♕d2 g5 7 0-0-0 ♗g7 8 g3

8...♘c6

8...♗d7!? was in fact Karpov's choice when Topalov played this as White – and the Russian went on to win after 9 f4 ♘c6. Perhaps Topalov was so impressed by White's chances in this game that he chose to try it himself?

9 ♘b5!?

9 ♗b5 ♗d7 10 ♘ge2 0-0-0 (10...♕xf2 looks too bold: 11 ♖df1 ♕g2 12 h3! ♘xd4 13 ♗xd7+ ♔xd7 14 ♖hg1! ♕xh3 15 ♖xf7+) 11 f4 a6 12 ♗xc6 ♗xc6 13 ♕e3 ♔b8 has been played, Black has long term potential with the two bishops, though for the moment White's centre is rather imposing. Unclear seems to be the correct assessment.

9...♕d8

9...♕e7 is an alternative.

10 ♘e2

10 d5 opens up the diagonal for the bishop on g7; Black replies 10...♘e7.

10...a6 11 ♘bc3 b5!

Topalov is always searching for the most active move!

12 ♗g2 ♗b7 13 f4 ♘e7 14 h4 g4

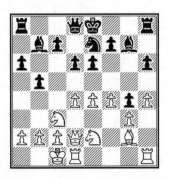

15 h5?!

With this move, Adams centres on the g4 pawn as a target. If he doesn't play h5 Black may very well do so himself, consolidating the pawn on g4. Adams has great positional mastery so it's difficult to criticise his decision. What plans does White have in this position? At some point he would like to advance in the centre to take advantage of his lead in development. 15 e5 clearly won't do, as the bishop is hanging. But what about 15 d5, trying to stick a knight on d4? Then comes 15...b4 16 ♘a4 a5 17 dxe6 fxe6 18 ♘d4 ♕d7 19 b3 ♘c6! 20 ♘xc6 ♗xc6 21 ♘b2 a4 22 ♕xb4 axb3∓ so that won't do either.

15 f5 looks crazy,

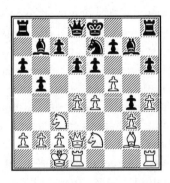

but I want the reader to get into the habit of analysing as many candidate moves as possible;

A) 15...h5 16 fxe6 fxe6 (16...♗h6 17 exf7+ ♔xf7 18 ♘f4) 17 ♘f4 (17 ♔b1!?) 17...♗h6 18 e5 ♗xg2 19 ♕xg2 ♗xf4+ 20 gxf4 d5 and the knight comes to f5;

B) 15...b4 16 ♘a4 exf5 17 ♕xb4 ♗xe4 18 ♗xe4 fxe4 19 ♘f4;

C) 15...exf5 16 ♘f4! fxe4 (16...b4 17 ♘cd5 ♘xd5 18 ♘xd5 ♗xd5 19 exd5) 17 ♘h5 (17 ♗xe4 d5 18 ♗g2 ♕d6 19 ♘h5 ♖g8∓) 17...♔f8 (17...♗f8 18 ♘f6 is an amusing mate!) 18 ♘xg7 ♔xg7 19 ♘xe4 doesn't look totally clear – even though White is a pawn down he has quite natural moves to play – like ♖hf1. So Mickey could have played 15 f5!? but who is brave enough to play such a move against Topalov?

15...b4 16 ♘b1 a5!

Gaining space.

17 ♕e3

17 ♖h4 f5! 18 d5 exd5 19 exf5 ♘xf5 20 ♖xg4 ♕f6 21 c3 bxc3 22 ♘bxc3 c6 23 ♖g6 ♕f7∓

17...0-0

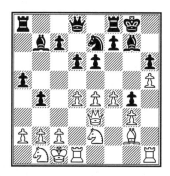

What would you play here as White?

18 ♘d2?

After this, Adams' game gets very difficult! White should have defended the bishop on g2 so that Black's next move wasn't so powerful. It's important to be aware of your opponent's ideas, and maybe Adams just nodded for a moment. 18 ♖hg1! d5 (18...f5 19 exf5 ♗xg2 20 ♕xe6+) 19 ♘d2 dxe4 20 ♗xe4 ♘d5 (20...♘f5 21 ♕d3) 21 ♕f2 and Black is well placed for the task ahead, but White has more freedom to manoeuvre than he ever got in the game.

18...f5! 19 ♖hg1 fxe4 20 ♗xe4

20 ♘xe4 ♘f5 21 ♕f2 a4∓

20...♘f5

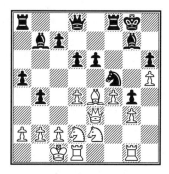

21 ♕b3?!

Somewhat artificial. 21 ♗xf5 exf5 and Black's bishops are likely to be a devastating force – with the bishop coming to e4 the game plays itself.

If 21 ♕d3 ♗a6!-+; but 21 ♕f2! may be best. Then:

A) 21...d5 22 ♗xf5 exf5 (22...♖xf5 23 ♘f1!) 23 ♘b3! with some counterplay;

B) 21...♕c8 22 ♗xb7 ♕xb7 23 ♔b1 ♕d5∓

21...d5 22 ♗xf5 exf5

The black pawns exert a cramping effect on White's position, and even though the pawn on d5 blocks the bishop on b7, it can be relocated to c4 via a6. The white knights are grovelling around on the back ranks and the queen on b3 is at least denying access to a knight trying to reach the c5 square. Also White would like to recycle the e2 knight via c1 to d3 but that leaves the d4 pawn en prise and c3 is always too weakening. In a higher sense White is already lost.

23 ♖ge1 ♖e8 24 ♘f1 ♗a6! 25 ♘g1 ♗c4 26 ♕a4 ♗xf1

The greedy 26...♖xe1!? 27 ♖xe1 ♗xd4 28 ♕c6 ♕f8 was also possible.

27 ♖xf1 ♖e6

28 ♕b3

28 ♖fe1 ♕e8! (28...♖xe1 29 ♖xe1 ♗xd4∓) is a nice little trick forcing a lovely endgame for Black: 29 ♕xe8+ ♖axe8 30 ♖xe6 ♖xe6 and the d4 or g3 pawn will soon drop off.

28...c6! 29 ♖fe1

29 ♕d3 ♕f6! 30 ♖fe1 ♖xe1 31 ♖xe1 ♕xd4.

29...♖xe1 30 ♖xe1 ♗xd4 31 ♘e2 ♕e7 32 ♔d1 ♗f2 33 ♖f1 ♗c5 34 ♕d3 ♖e8 35 ♖e1 ♕e6 36 c3 bxc3 37 bxc3

37...d4!

Topalov never misses an opportunity to open lines and accelerate the winning process.

38 cxd4 ♗b4 39 d5 ♕xd5 40 ♕xd5+ cxd5 41 ♖g1 ♖e3 42 ♘c1 d4 43 ♘b3 a4

Perhaps at this exalted level, giving your opponent the two bishops so early in the game is always going to put you at a disadvantage? This game might give some clues as to why the

Trompowsky has never really taken off at super-grandmaster level. Black's play looked very natural and fluent, and seemingly Mickey Adams did little wrong, but he was unable to generate any counterplay to compensate for the power of Black's bishops.

0-1

Nevertheless we should not be surprised that Topalov, with his very direct approach towards the game, can come unstuck at times. Here we see him in action against 'big daddy' Garry Kasparov himself.

17

V.Topalov – G.Kasparov

Euwe Memorial, Amsterdam 1995

Sicilian Defence

1 e4 c5 2 ♘f3 ♘c6

Kasparov eschews his normal Najdorf, perhaps fearing some special preparation, After all, he had come off worse against Topalov a couple of times in that opening – most notably at the Moscow Olympiad.

3 d4 cxd4 4 ♘xd4 e6 5 ♘c3 d6 6 ♗e3 ♘f6 7 f3 ♗e7 8 g4 0-0 9 ♕d2 a6 10 0-0-0 ♘xd4 11 ♗xd4 b5 12 ♔b1

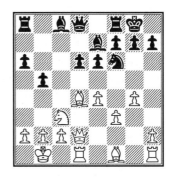

The 'tabiya' for this variation – both sides are committed to attack – White will try to demolish the black kingside defence with deadly pawn thrusts on that side while Black relies more on piece play.

12...♗b7 13 h4 ♖c8

13...♕c7.

14 g5 ♘d7

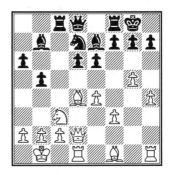

15 ♖g1

15 a3!? was Topalov's improvement when he faced Kasparov just two weeks later, in Novgorod. But he was perhaps regretting that he repeated this line (generally a bad idea against Garry) and lost again;

A) 15...♕c7 was the American (formerly Polish) player Alex Wojtkiewicz's choice when he faced Topalov – however I'm not sure that ♕c7 is always that useful in this line, as in some variations on d8 it will hold up the march of the white h-pawn since the g pawn will be left en prise. After 16 ♖g1 ♔h8 17 h5 e5 18 ♗e3 f5 19 exf5 ♖xf5?! (19...♗xf3!? 20 h6 gxh6) 20 ♘d5! ♗xd5 21 ♕xd5 ♕xc2+ 22 ♔a2 White's control over the light squares and dangerous attacking chances gave him more than enough compensation for a solitary pawn.

B) 15...♘e5

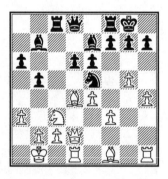

16 ♕e3?! (This allows Black to take the sting out of White's game by exchanging his light squared bishop – a piece that could be very useful in any kingside attack. More accurate it would seem is 16 ♕f2! – also met by 16...♘c4) 16...♘c4 17 ♗xc4 ♖xc4 18 ♖hg1 b4 19 axb4 ♖xb4 20 ♖g2 ♗a8 21 b3 a5 22 h5 ♕c7 23 ♗f6 ♖fb8 24 ♗xe7 ♕xe7 25 ♖d4 e5! 26 ♖xb4 axb4 27 ♘a2 ♕c7 28 ♕d3 ♔f8 29 g6 fxg6 30 hxg6 h6 31 f4 exf4 32 ♖f2 ♔g8 33 ♖xf4 ♕c5 34 ♖f1 ♕b5 35 ♖c1 ♕e5 36 ♕c4+ ♔h8 37 ♖h1 ♗xe4 38 ♕c7 ♖f8 39 ♖xh6+ ♔g8 40 ♘c1 ♗xc2+! 0-1 Topalov – Kasparov, Novgorod 1995.

15...b4 16 ♘e2

16 ♘a4 is of course met by 16...♗c6! 17 b3 ♗xa4 18 bxa4 ♕a5∓ (or 18...♘c5!? 19 ♗xc5 ♖xc5 20 ♗xa6 ♕a5 21 ♗b5 ♖xb5 22 axb5 ♖a8 23 c4 bxc3 24 ♕e2).

16...♘e5! 17 ♖g3 ♘c4

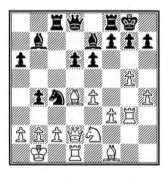

18 ♕c1?!

I always find it difficult to criticise the moves of top GMs as they tend always to have a point behind them. Players like Topalov always play with a plan in mind, even if that plan is bad! They don't play moves 'hoping for the best'. Nevertheless with hindsight we can conclude that Topalov went wrong around here, as he was only to last another 10 moves with White! After all, is his position already so bad that he is bound to lose, even against Kasparov? While

I believe that 99 percent of GMs (including even me, perhaps!) would probably lose this position against Kasparov, it's important to look for improvements. One of the most difficult decisions in chess is where to put the queen, as we saw in the previous game where Adams got into trouble. The queen is a very powerful piece but sometimes its high status works against it, as it can be vulnerable to attack by the enemy pieces. With the text move Topalov still intends to play h5, so he keeps an eye on the g5 pawn. He also wants to protect the c-pawn. Nevertheless the fact that the queen is now on the same file as the black rook on c8 may be significant. 18 ♕e1 retains an attack on the b4 pawn and preserves the square on c1 for the knight. The drawback is that he is not really threatening anything, as now h5 can be simply met by ...♗xg5. Play can continue 18...a5 19 ♘c1 e5 20 ♗f2 ♕c7 (20...a4 21 ♕xb4) 21 h5 a4 (21...♘a3+ 22 bxa3 ♕xc2+ 23 ♔a1 bxa3 24 ♘d3)

A) 22 ♕xb4 ♘a3+! 23 bxa3 (23 ♕xa3 ♕xc2+ 24 ♔a1 ♕xc1+) 23...♕xc2+ 24 ♔a1 ♕xd1-+;

B) 22 g6 ♘a3+ 23 bxa3 ♕xc2+ 24 ♔a1 b3! 25 axb3 axb3 26 ♘xb3 ♕xb3 27 f4 ♕c2 and the white king looks too exposed; 28 ♗d3 ♕a4∓;

18 ♕xb4

This looks the most critical but it would take a brave man to grab such a pawn against Gazza! With the b-file opened, Black will always have good counterchances. Kasparov would most likely play 18...♗a8!? (On 18...♕c7 Black would have the threat of...♘a3 followed by taking on c2. What would you play now? 19 ♕e1 e5 20 ♗f2 ♖b8) 19 ♕e1 (19 b3 d5!) 19...e5 20 ♗f2 (20 ♗c3 ♘e3 21 ♖c1 ♘xf1 22 ♕xf1 d5 with compensation) 20...♖b8 (20...♕c7 21 ♘c1 ♖b8 22 ♘b3 ♖fc8 23 ♖c1) 21 b3 ♕c7 22 ♘c3 ♖fc8 23 ♗xc4 ♕xc4 24 ♖d3 a5 with an attack. So 18 ♕xb4 is not directly losing, but most likely Topalov 'sensibly' concluded that against Kasparov, it wouldn't be wise to take such a pawn...

18...e5!

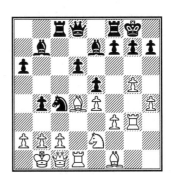

Pushing Topalov back.

19 ♗f2 a5

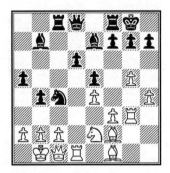

20 ♗g2?

Once more it would be easy to criticise this move, but Topalov again has a point! He wants to play f4 and swing the rook on g3 over to the defence. So to that extent the bishop reinforces e4, as an immediate f4 would be impossible due to ...♗xe4. Nevertheless this move looks 'ugly'. I'm of the opinion that it's a general rule in chess that if a move looks illogical, ugly or unnatural, then in most cases it actually is. Also doesn't that bishop want to go to h3 to attack the rook and possibly later help in the attack on the king? On g2 it looks like a big pawn but what alternatives did he have?

20 h5 looks natural, as that was why he put the queen on c1, so that g5 was defended. However the problem is that a direct attack is unlikely to succeed with so many of White's pieces standing so passively. Nonetheless, without h5

at some point, White's whole set up is completely pointless! Even an unprepared attack can be dangerous if it is not met by accurate defence.

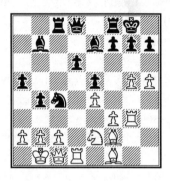

20...a4

A) 21 ♗h3 ♖c6 22 g6 b3! (22...fxg6 23 hxg6 ♗h4? 24 ♗e6+ ♔h8 25 ♖h3!) 23 gxf7+ ♔h8 24 ♘c3 a3! 25 cxb3 axb2! and the queen is rather short of squares.

B) 21 g6 is possible but now it looks as if Black's attack is much quicker as he has a couple of strong moves;

B1) 21...fxg6 22 hxg6 ♗h4! 23 ♗h3 (23 gxh7+ ♔h8 24 ♖g2 ♗xf2 25 ♖xf2 ♗xe4! looks like real problems;) 23...♗xg3

B1a) 24 ♗xc8 ♗xf2 (24...♕xc8) 25 ♗e6+ (25 ♗xb7 ♗e3 26 ♗d5+ ♔h8 27 ♖h1 h6 28 ♕d1 ♘d2+ 29 ♔a1 ♖xf3);

B1b) 24 ♘xg3 ♖xf3 25 ♗e6+ ♔h8 26 ♖h1!;

B2) 21...♗h4 22 ♖g2 (22 ♗h3 ♗xg3 23 ♘xg3 ♖c7 24 gxf7+ ♔h8)

22...fxg6 23 hxg6 ♗xf2 24 ♖xf2 ♗xe4;

B3) 21...b3 22 h6 hxg6 23 hxg7 ♔xg7 and there is no attack – which is why ideally in such lines White would have the queen's rook on g1 so he can leave the other rook on h1.

20 ♗h3! looks the most active.

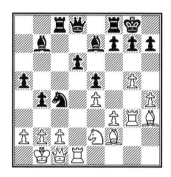

20...♖c7 (20...♖c6 21 f4! and the rook on g3 can defend laterally against the queenside attack) 21 h5 a4 (21...♗a6 22 ♖dg1 ♘a3+ 23 bxa3 ♗xe2 24 g6! fxg6 25 hxg6 gives White a dangerous initiative) 22 g6 (22 ♖dg1) 22...♗h4 (22...b3; 22...fxg6 23 ♗e6+ ♔h8 24 hxg6) 23 gxh7+ ♔h8 24 ♖g2 ♗xf2 25 ♖xf2 b3 26 ♘c3 a3 27 cxb3 axb2 28 ♖xb2! ♘xb2 29 ♕xb2 essentially most of these lines are a mess, with the position teetering on the edge of a precipice. Every move counts in what amounts to a race, and simply playing a move like ♗g2 is far too slow!

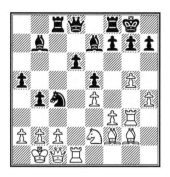

20...♗a6!

Kasparov is alert to any subtle changes in the position. ♗g2 covers e4, but it has the drawback that it leaves the knight on e2 undefended. Right now ...♘a3+ and ♗xe2 is threatened. Topalov cannot allow his queenside pawns to be ruptured like this, so he is forced to play his rook to a less relevant square. 20...a4 21 f4! was probably the variation on which Topalov was concentrating. This is a common problem in calculation – you spend so long looking at one line, which looks dangerous in itself, that you forget to look at other possible moves that your opponent has at his disposal!

21 ♖e1

21 ♘g1 looks horrible of course.

21...a4 22 ♗h3

The right square, but White has lost two tempi!

22...♖c6

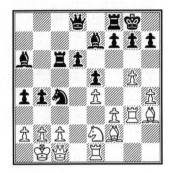

23 ♕d1?!

Walking into Black's next, which is a real 'sucker punch'. Nonetheless it would seem that Black's initiative is already too dangerous; 23 f4! would have forced Kasparov to find some accurate moves. What candidate moves can be identified for Black now? 23...b3, 23...a3, 23...exf4, 23...♕a5! and 23...♕c7!

A) 23...b3 24 axb3 axb3 25 ♖xb3 ♕a5 looks dangerous 26 ♘c3! ♖a8! (26...exf4!?) 27 ♘d5 ♗d8 28 ♘b4! ♗b5 29 c3 and there is no obvious way through;

B) 23...a3?! 24 b3 ♘b2 25 ♕d2 only serves to block Black's attack;

C) 23...exf4 24 ♘xf4 b3 25 axb3 axb3 26 ♖xb3 ♕a5! 27 ♖d1 ♖a8 28 ♗e1!;

D) 23...♕a5! is similar to 23...♕c7 – one glance at the activity of the two armies is enough to see that White faces major problems. Black already has a big threat of ...b3, not to mention...♖b8 at some stage (or ...♖a8 and trying to open the a-file);

E) 23...♕c7! and it is not easy to find a move for White as Black can simply increase the pressure with ...♖fb8 followed by b3 at some stage. Then 24 fxe5 dxe5 or 24 f5 ♖b8 25 f6 ♗f8∓

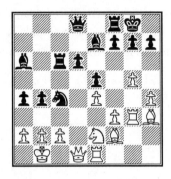

23...d5!

Kasparov goes for the throat.

24 exd5

24 ♕xd5 ♖d6-+

24...♖d6! 25 f4 ♖xd5 26 ♖d3

If 26 ♕c1 ♘d2+ 27 ♔a1 ♘e4 28 ♖g2 ♗xe2.

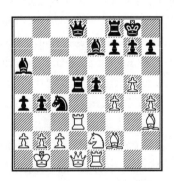

26...♘a3+! 27 bxa3 ♗xd3 28 cxd3 ♖xd3 0-1

Not only is White's king totally exposed, but he is dropping the h3 bishop as well. Garry was always devastating in the Sicilian!

Kasparov was the first player to fully embrace the new computer technology and use it to take his own game to new levels. He realised that training with computers could not only greatly improve your calculating skills, but also be used to unearth new vistas in the opening phase of the game. Kasparov was always the best prepared player in the world anyway, but he would use the computers' astonishing hardware to discover electrifying novelties that he would unleash on a succession of opponents. Who could forget the rook sacrifice that he used to defeat Anand's Open Ruy Lopez in the world championship match in 1995? As Kasparov admitted, a great deal of the analysis for the preparation of that game was done with a computer.

However there is a scary side to this. A bit like the Terminator – computers won't stop, they will keep getting stronger and stronger until theoretically they will solve chess entirely. You make an inaccuracy on move 3 and it announces mate in 106 moves! "You admire it, don't you?" "I admire its purity" (alien) Okay, that day is a long way off, but they have already solved draughts. (although comparing draughts to chess is a bit like comparing noughts and crosses to draughts) Eventually you will get these quantum computers that can look at several quadzillion positions per millisecond, or something daft like

that. Of course it is likely that computers will have realised mankind's pointlessness by the time they solve chess and wipe us all out in a nuclear attack, rather like the scenario in the aforementioned Terminator films, where the only survivors were a few cockroaches and Robert Mugabe. Chess matches and tournaments will simply become a battle of computer power, and will be all the poorer for it.

There's no way around this, not really, as if you try to ban computers it just won't work. Of course this problem doesn't just apply to chess and draughts. In pretty much all games, computers are now superior to humans. I discovered another interesting point about the Deep Blue vs. Kasparov encounter when Benjamin told me that they expected Kasparov to play main line openings in the match (he didn't, and Benjamin thought that was a mistake) and against 1 d4 they had prepared the Noteboom variation of the Slav, 1 d4 d5 2 c4 c6 3 ♘f3 e6 4 ♘c3 dxc4, which, in the main line tends to lead to ridiculously complicated positions in which the computer would be expected to revel. Interesting, I say, because that's just the kind of thing that Kasparov has being doing to his opponents for years, engaging them in a tactical maelstrom where his superior powers of calculation would reign supreme.

Sometimes in chess it's not always about playing the best move. Sometimes it's about making the most complicated move because you want to engineer a situation where you feel superior to your opponent. Against Karpov, Kasparov time and time again whipped up a storm of complications, knowing full well that his opponent would feel less comfortable in a battle of calculation. Karpov, on the other hand, became world champion largely because he was so technically superior to his rivals. He would make the simple move, sometimes taking his games into an endgame which on the face of it seemed to pose no problems, but then his superlative endgame play would win the day.

One player more akin to the Karpov mode, is Kramnik. Although he is regarded as a universal player, his endgame technique is of a special quality. However he's no one trick pony. In his early career he scored a number of dashing wins with devastating attacks, most notably against Kasparov, where he sacrificed a rook to stun the then world champion with Black, and also in the following game. I include the game with fairly light notes – it's all been analysed to death by Kramnik in his great book *My Life and Games* but it's worth seeing if only for entertainment value!

18

V.Topalov – V.Kramnik

Investbank, Belgrade 1995

Sicilian Defence

**1 e4 c5 2 ♘f3 ♘c6 3 d4 cxd4
4 ♘xd4 ♘f6 5 ♘c3 d6 6 ♗c4
♕b6**

7 ♘db5

7 ♘xc6 bxc6 8 0-0 g6 9 e5!? dxe5 10 ♕e2 ♕d4! 11 ♗e3 ♕d6 12 ♖ad1 ♕c7 13 f4 ♗g4 14 ♕f2 e4 (14...♗xd1 15 fxe5 ♕xe5 16 ♗d4 is dangerous for Black) 15 ♖de1 ♗f5 16 h3 h5 and Kramnik was able to secure a comfortable draw in the game Topalov – Kramnik, Novgorod 1996.

7...a6

In another game between these two opponents, Kramnik, perhaps fearing an improvement cooked up in Bulgaria, deviated – 7...♗g4 8 f3 ♗d7 9 ♕e2 a6 10 ♗e3 ♕a5 11 ♘d4 b5 12 ♗b3 e6 13 0-0-0 b4 14 ♘b1

♗e7 with unclear complications in Topalov – Kramnik, Dos Hermanas 1996.

8 ♗e3 ♕a5 9 ♘d4 ♘e5

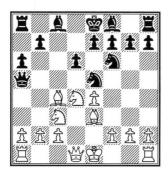

10 ♗d3

10 ♘b3 is essentially the main move. 10...♕c7 11 ♗e2 (11 ♗d3!? is an alternative) 11...e6 12 f4 ♘c4 13 ♗xc4 ♕xc4 14 ♕f3 was Ivanchuk – Kramnik, PCA Intel rapidplay 1995 – a game which resulted in a win for the Ukrainian. Maybe 10 ♘b3 is a safer move? But it was hard to sense the danger...

10...♘eg4!?

10...♘fg4!? had been previously tried by Joel Benjamin and 11 ♕e2?! was the uncritical response of his opponent, Eric Prie. Then Black was more than okay after 11...♘xe3 12 ♕xe3 g6.

11 ♗c1 g6

11...♕b6 can simply be met by 12 0-0.

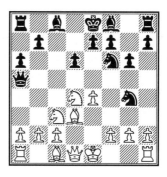

12 ♘b3

Why doesn't White just play 12 h3 to kick away the knight, I hear you ask? 12...♘e5! (12...♕h5 is silly because of 13 ♗e2 ♕h4 14 g3) 13 f4 ♘xd3+ 14 cxd3 ♗g7 and Black is fine.

12...♕b6!

Must keep the pressure on!

13 ♕e2

Kramnik's play is very subtle – the obvious 13 0-0 is met by 13...♗g7 and White has some problems driving the irritating knight away from the centre, since upon h2-h3 it just goes back to e5.

13...♗g7 14 f4

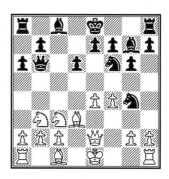

14...♘h5!

Forced, otherwise h3 is played and the knight has to retreat to h6. What I like about this game so much is the way Kramnik incorporates these strange knight moves into a tactical operation to justify his strategic play, i.e. he wants to deny White a comfortable ride and push the knight back.

15 ♘d5 ♕d8 16 ♗d2 e6 17 ♗a5 ♕h4+ 18 g3

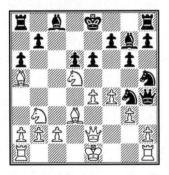

18...♘xg3!

What a mess, and it's about to get messier! From now on I will give very few notes in order not to spoil it for the reader, who will get far more pleasure from working out the fantastic variations for himself!

19 ♘c7+ ♔e7 20 hxg3 ♕xg3+ 21 ♔d1 ♘f2+ 22 ♔d2 ♘xh1 23 ♘xa8 ♕xf4+ 24 ♕e3 ♕h2+ 25 ♕e2 ♕f4+ 26 ♕e3 ♕h2+ 27 ♕e2 ♗h6+ 28 ♔c3 ♕e5+ 29 ♔b4 ♘g3 30 ♕e1 ♗g7 31 ♘b6 d5! 32 ♔a4 ♗d7+ 33 ♘xd7 b5+ 34 ♔b4 ♔xd7 35 ♗b6 ♕xb2?!

35...♘xe4! was given by Kramnik.

36 exd5 ♖c8 37 dxe6+ ♔e8

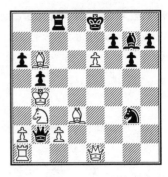

I think this position would terrify most players (in fact the whole game would). Playing White here, I would be afraid that I was missing something.

38 ♗c5?

Kramnik gives a long line here to suggest that White can probably make a draw by 38 ♗xb5+. I think 38 ♗c5 is an interesting move because it is essentially a breakdown in calculation – although entirely understandable after such an exhausting encounter as this. White fails to see a couple of checks – so remember always to consider as many candidate moves as possible!

38...♗c3+!

Topalov must have overlooked this.

39 ♛xc3 a5+ 40 ♔xb5 ♛xc3 0-1

A fantastic attacking jewel by Kramnik and certainly a game to rank alongside the best in the long history of chess. It's a great example of what I mean by imposing your will on your opponent – Kramnik never gave Topalov any time to draw breath as he was forced to make difficult decisions on almost every turn. At no point did Kramnik settle on a safe continuation – for example on move 27 he could simply have repeated – though it takes two to party and without Topalov's equally pugnacious stance I doubt the game would have taken the course that it did. Kramnik simply drove the complication bar up to overload – and was able to find his way through the insanity better than the Bulgarian. In fact here I might speculate that the reason for the bad relations between the two players, which essentially reached its peak during 'toiletgate', may have been due to the drubbing Topalov took from Kramnik in his early career and led to him bearing a grudge... Now just a few words on the 2009 world championship match where Kramnik was soundly defeated by the Indian super-talent Vishy Anand. More of Anand later on, but I have to say that Kramnik gets a bad press. True, Kramnik didn't have such a great match record – a fact pointed out by Kasparov afterwards (Kramnik had previously lost matches to Gelfand, Kamsky and Shirov). However he's an incredible player who in my opinion is simply suffering from some kind of crisis of confidence. After all, if you look at games like this you wonder why he limits his attacking horizons by playing boring Berlin walls and Petroffs – why doesn't he try to mix it up a bit? The pragmatic approach worked against Kasparov, but Anand exposed it as inadequate. Anand had a great team of seconds against Kramnik – though so did Kramnik although maybe the use of Leko was a mistake? Even though Leko is terribly strong, he and Kramnik are very similar in style and sometimes you need someone to take you out of your comfort zone a little. Kramnik has famously bad relations with Shirov, so of course he wasn't an option – but maybe someone like Sutovsky would have been more appropriate? For example, in the World Cup, Kamsky benefited from having Sutovsky as his second, as his inventive, sacrificial style is almost the opposite of his own technical approach. Just speculation though...

Chapter 5

The magic of Moro

Russian Alexander Morozevich first exploded onto the chess scene when, as an unknown teenager, he scored an incredible 9½/10 in the Lloyds Bank Masters in London 1995. At the time (and even now!) this was one of the highest Elo tournament rating performances of all time.

Since then his star has gone from strength to strength, and for a brief period he even hit the no.1 spot in the 'live' chess rankings (a site that monitors Elo ratings from tournament to tournament, whereas FIDE only publishes its list every month or so).

Combining a sharp tactical eye with an inventive repertoire that even reinvigorated antiquated openings such as the Chigorin Defence (1 d4 d5 2 c4 ♘c6!?) Morozevich is probably the most original player among the modern elite grandmasters. With his fearless will to win and sacrificial flair, reminiscent of Tal, Morozevich has built up a large following in the chess world, who are drawn irresistibly to his exhilarating, cavalier style.

19

A.Morozevich – J.Polgar

Donner Memorial,
Amsterdam 1995

Sicilian Defence

1 e4 c5 2 ♘f3 ♘c6 3 ♗b5

Moro prefers to rely on his own huge talent than get too heavily involved in theoretical battles, although in any case this Rossolimo variation is quite well regarded.

3...e6 4 0-0 ♘ge7 5 c3

5 ♖e1 a6 6 ♗f1 is another way to play.

5...a6 6 ♗a4 b5 7 ♗c2 d5

8 e5

8 d4!?, just like the game continuation, has also scored fairly heavily for White; nevertheless

8...cxd4 9 ♘xd4 ♘xd4 10 ♕xd4 ♗b7 doesn't look too bad for Black.

8...d4

8...♘g6 9 d4! reinforces the centre, which Black can only really undermine with the move ...f7-f6. However, as this weakens the squares on his kingside and is likely to make the bishop on c2 an even more powerful beast, Black intends to cut off the e-pawn from its compatriot with the move ...d4.

9 ♗e4! ♗b7

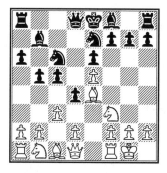

10 cxd4

10 d3 was tried in the game Torre – Fedorowicz, San Francisco 1991. Torre played in relatively few tournaments but spent most of his time in preparation. A very diligent approach, although I'm not sure many people would have the same discipline – or indeed whether this approach is effective. This day and age players like Morozevich and Ivanchuk are very prolific, jetting from tournament to tournament with hardly a break. I'm convinced that the best way to improve at chess is

through experience. There's nothing quite like 'living it'. Only through competing against players at a higher level than yourself can you truly improve – though this must be combined with private study. It is by taking an honest, objective view of your play (and buying this book of course : -)) that you can truly make it to the next level! Incidentally the Torre game continued 10...♘g6 11 ♖e1 ♗e7 12 cxd4 cxd4 13 ♘bd2 0-0 14 ♘b3! (threatening to take on d4) 14...♖b8 15 ♗d2 b4 16 ♖c1 ♕b6 17 h4! (This kind of pawn thrust is very thematic in such positions; White intends to soften up the black kingside by forcing ...g6, after which he will attempt to exchange Black's dark-squared bishop and give mate on g7.) 17...♖fc8 18 h5 ♘f8 (18...♘gxe5? 19 ♘xe5 ♘xe5 20 ♗xb7! ♖xc1 – 20...♕xb7 21 ♖xe5 – 21 ♗xc1) 19 h6! g6 20 ♗g5 ♗xg5 21 ♘xg5 ♘d7 22 ♗xc6! ♗xc6 23 ♕g4 and despite the level material Black resigned because his d-pawn is dropping off and the threats of ♘xe6, and ♕f4 are too much. That's what eight hours a day studying chess does for you!

10...cxd4 11 d3 ♕b6?!

I'm not sure this move helps. Despite the mauling that Fedorowicz received in the Torre game, the immediate 11...♘g6 seems safer, as the queen does very little on b6.

12 ♖e1

Again, as we saw in the Torre game, an important move which makes it very difficult for Black to find an effective way of attacking the e5 pawn.

12...♖c8

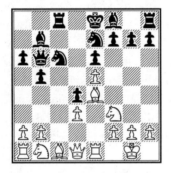

13 a3

What is the point of this move you may well ask? Well, it's simply prophylactic – Black may play ...♘b4, which not only allows him to go ...♘c2 and ...♘bd5, but also to exchange the strong bishop on e4. It's important to ask before every move – what does my opponent intend to play? Of course, in this case, Black intends ...♘b4. Identifying your opponent's plans and threats will help to extinguish the lazy thinking that goes with simply looking at your own ideas. Players like Karpov and Petrosian were masters at prophylactic thinking – and this subject was touched on very effectively in one of the Dvoretsky books, if my memory serves me correctly.

13...h6

What does Judit intend with this move? Is it simply to take away the g5 square from White's pieces? Well no, not exactly. Given the chance she may even play ...g5 and then undermine the knight on f3 with ...g4, after which the e5 pawn really does become weak – so Morozevich defends against this idea as well! On 13...♘g6 might follow 14 h4! ♗e7 15 h5 ♘f8 (15...♘h4 16 ♘xh4 ♗xh4 17 ♕g4±) 16 h6 g6 17 ♗g5!? ♘xe5 18 ♗xe7 ♘xf3+ 19 ♕xf3 ♗xe4 20 ♕f6!

14 h4!

Another prophylactic move! 14 ♘bd2 g5! 15 h3 ♗g7! and Black is ideally poised to counter the e5 pawn.

14...g6 15 ♗f4 ♗g7 16 ♘bd2 0-0 17 ♘f1

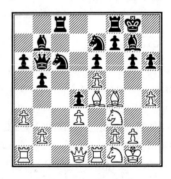

The position resembles a kind of King's Indian Attack with which the legendary Bobby Fischer scored so many routine wins – but surely it won't be so easy to beat Judit? White intends ♘f1-h2-g4 and all the while the bishop on f4 and knight on f3 are keeping a firm grip on the e5 pawn, making any chances of Judit organising counterplay extremely difficult. In fact White already seems to be clearly better.

17...罝fe8 18 ②1h2!

18...♔h8

18...h5 unfortunately has a drawback – it concedes the g5 square 'eternally' to White. 19 g4 (Opening the valves!) 19...hxg4 20 ②xg4 ②f5 21 h5 gxh5 (21...②ce7 22 ②f6+ ♗xf6 23 exf6 ②d5 24 hxg6 fxg6 25 ♗e5 is horrible.) 22 ②f6+ ♗xf6 23 exf6 ♕d8 24 ♗g5 and Black will do very well to avoid being mated. Players like Polgar tend to dismiss moves like h5 on general grounds – their accumulated wisdom and experience tells them that the weaknesses incurred are likely to be decisive.

19 ②g4 ②g8

Polgar's kingside seems to be in sorry state – with the knight, bishop and king tripping over each other. Such situations tend to be ripe for combinations, when Black lacks

'air'. Any check near the king is likely to be mate. Morozevich has what appears to be an overwhelming position but there are many ways to attack – which one is correct?

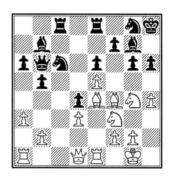

20 ②g5!

As is his wont, Moro goes for the most forceful continuation! 20 ♕d2!? (Not surprisingly this more prosaic move causes Black problems.) 20...♔h7 (20...h5 21 ②gh2±) 21 h5 ②ce7! 22 hxg6+ fxg6 (22...②xg6 23 g3±) 23 g3

A) 23...②d5 24 ♔g2 罝f8 25 ♗xh6! ♗xh6 (25...②xh6 26 罝h1) 26 罝h1±;

B) 23...♗xe4 24 罝xe4 罝f8 25 ♔g2 ②f5 26 罝h1±

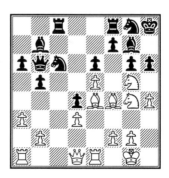

20...♖f8

Black seems to have six possible candidate moves here, all of which Morozevich would have had to calculate when he played 20 ♘g5!: the move played 20...♖f8, 20...hxg5, 20...♖e7, 20...♖c7, 20...♕c7 and 20...♘d8.

Of course 20...hxg5 is the most obvious reply, but not the best. Always calculate your captures and checks first!

A) 21 hxg5 ♘ge7 (21...♘ce7 22 ♕f3! and Black will have to return at least one piece to give his king some breathing space, after which White will still have a raging attack) 22 ♘f6! is a standard idea – White is a piece down, but what is more relevant is that Black's king is in a box. It's very unlikely that he will be able to relieve White's grip and prevent mate. After 22...♗xf6 23 gxf6

A1) 23...♘d5 24 ♕g4! ♘xf4 (24...♔g8 25 ♗xg6! ♘xf4 26 ♗xf7+ shreds the black

kingside.) 25 ♕xf4 ♔g8 26 ♕h6 wins;

A2) 23...♘f5 24 ♕g4 ♔g8 25 ♕h3 ♕c5 whereupon it looks as though Black is going to cover the mate with ...♕f8 after ♕h6, but there is a sting in the tail – 26 g4! – and White regains his piece with an overwhelming position to boot.

B) 20...♖e7 is met by 21 h5!

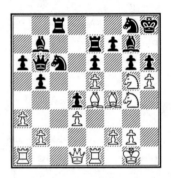

B1) 21...gxh5 22 ♘f6 ♗xf6 (22...♘xf6 23 exf6 ♗xf6 24 ♕xh5+-) 23 ♕xh5!! (23 exf6 ♘xf6 prevents the queen reaching h5 and there is no time to get the bishop to e5 as 24 ♗xc6 ♕xc6 25 ♗e5 ♕xg2 is mate.)

B1a) 23...♗xg5 24 ♗xg5 and ♗f6 is a very nasty threat. Play might continue 24...♔g7 25 ♗f6+ ♘xf6 (25...♔f8 26 ♗h7! ♘xf6 27 exf6 ♖ec7 28 ♕g4 ♔e8 29 ♕g8+ ♔d7 30 ♕xf7+ ♔d8 31 ♕g8+ ♔d7 32 ♕xe6+ ♔d8 33 ♕e8 mate) 26 exf6+ ♔xf6 27 ♕h4+;

B1b) 23...♔g7 24 ♘xf7+ (24 ♕xf7 is a very tempting move, going for a brilliancy, but unfortunately this seems to be refuted by 24...♞d8 25 ♕g6 ♝xe4.) 24...♜xf7 25 ♕xf7 ♕c7! 26 ♕g6 ♝f8 27 ♕xe6±;

C) 21...hxg5 22 ♝xg5 ♞xe5 23 ♞xe5 ♝xe5 24 ♝xe7+-;

D) 20...♞d8 21 ♝xb7 ♕xb7 22 ♞e4 is the prosaic line for White after which Black can't prevent a monstrous fork on d6;

E) 20...♜c7 21 h5 hxg5 22 ♝xg5 and Black has great difficulty covering the f6 square which will be used as launching pad for the final attack;

F) 20...♕c7! at least sets a trap for White;

21 h5?! (21 ♜c1! is simpler; then 21...♕d7 22 ♕f3±) 21...hxg5 22 ♝xg5 ♞xe5! 23 ♝xb7 (23 ♞xe5 ♝xe4 24 ♜xe4 ♝xe5 25 hxg6 fxg6∓ 26 ♕e2 ♝f6) 23...♞xg4 24 ♕xg4 (24 ♝xc8 ♕h2+ 25 ♔f1 ♕h1+ 26 ♔e2 ♕xh5-+). Morozevich probably didn't calculate everything when he played 20 ♞g5 – most likely, similar to Tal before him, he relied on intuition, trusting in the fact that his opponent would find it very hard to defend his king with so

many enemy pieces swarming around – and he was proved correct.)

21 h5!

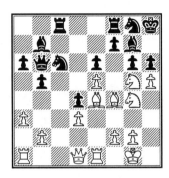

It is important to act as quickly as possible – Moro keeps throwing wood on to the fire

21...♕d8?

This allows a decisive break-through. In many lines ♞f7 will hit the queen on d8 with tempo. 21...hxg5 22 ♝xg5 and ♞f6, hxg6 and h6 are huge threats. Then if 22...♞xe5 23 ♞xe5 ♝xe4 24 ♜xe4 (24 ♞d7 ♕d6 25 ♞xf8 ♝f5) 24...♝xe5 25 hxg6! fxg6 26 ♜xe5 looks winning as the black king is too exposed.

21...♞ce7! is probably best, trying to bolster the squares around his castled position.

A) 22 hxg6 hxg5 23 ♕f3 (23 ♝xg5 fxg6) 23...♞xg6! 24 ♕h3+ ♞h6 25 ♞xh6 ♞xf4 26 ♞xf7+ ♔g8 and Black turns the tables;

B) 22 ♝xb7 ♕xb7 23 ♞e4! ♞f5! 24 ♞gf6 g5 25 ♝h2 ♕e7 26 ♞g4 retains a bind for White, who can keep probing with f4 (pawn breaks are very important!) although mate is still a long way off.

22 hxg6! hxg5

22...fxg6 23 ♘xe6+-

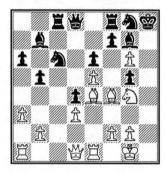

23 ♕f3!

Underlining just how bad it is not to have breathing space for the black king.

23...♗h6

23...fxg6 24 ♕h3+ ♘h6 25 ♘xh6 gxf4 26 ♘f7+ +-

24 ♘xh6 fxg6

24...♘xh6 25 ♕h5 ♔g7 26 ♗xg5+-

25 ♕h3 ♔g7 26 ♘xg8 ♖xf4

26...♖xg8

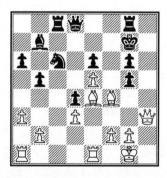

How should White proceed here?

27 ♕xe6 (27 ♗g3? would of course be very limp – 27...♕d7 and Black is still fighting. When attacking you should keep going forward whenever possible!) 27...gxf4 28 ♕xg6+ ♔f8 29 ♕f5+! ♔e8 (29...♔g7 and 29...♔e7 are both met by 30 ♕h7+ winning the bishop on b7 – loose pieces drop off! Another unfortunate drawback of 21...♕d8. When attacking, there's often a prosaic idea that simply recovers material to fall back on) 30 ♕h7! forking two pieces, and winning.

27 ♘f6 ♖h4 28 ♕xe6

Not only is White material ahead but he still has a raging attack – the result is no longer in doubt.

28...♘a5

28...♕h8 29 g3!

29 ♖ac1 ♖c7

White can tidy up with 30 ♖xc7 and 31 ♘e8+. A very flowing, pretty attack by Morozevich whose best games combine the combinational brilliance of a Tal or Kasparov with the forceful positional power of a

Fischer – no greater compliment can be paid.

1-0

Tony Miles, who died at a relatively young age, was another truly original player. The jovial English grandmaster, rather like Morozevich, wasn't by any means a slave to theory. In fact by the standards of the present day pro he was rather lazy and preferred to hone his talents on a regular diet of tournament play rather than an oppressive regime of study. And also like Morozevich, Miles seemed to prefer knights to bishops, perhaps this was a reflection of his own tricky chess style and maverick character – after all, the bishop is quite a straightforward piece whereas the knight is more mysterious and harder to control.

20

A.Miles – A.Morozevich

Lloyds Bank Open 1994

Chiigorin Defence

1 d4 d5

Miles was also fond of an immediate 1...♘c6!?, although he tended to play it against 1 e4 more than against 1 d4. After 2 e4 e5 3 d5 ♘ce7 his opponents would already be forced to meet him on his territory.

2 ♘f3 ♘c6!?

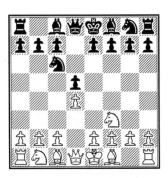

Moro has certainly rekindled interest in the Chigorin Defence, which had previously been considered to give a clear advantage to White. He found many novelties in this fascinating opening, where speedy development is imperative. However more recently he has switched mostly to the Slav Defence against 1 d4, perhaps realising that the Chigorin doesn't really stand up to the steely scrutiny of the 2700+ grandmasters.

3 g3!?

Miles also liked to go his own way and here avoids the complications that arise after 3 c4 ♗g4! 4 cxd5 ♗xf3 5 gxf3 ♕xd5 6 e3 e5 7 ♘c3 ♗b4. However I believe this response is non-critical and Black should now be able to equalise comfortably.

3...g6!?

3...♗f5!? 4 ♗g2 e6 5 0-0 ♘b4!? 6 ♘a3 ♘f6 and on 7 c3 comes the simple retreat 7...♘c6 when the knight on a3 looks a bit silly.

Even better is 3...♗g4! 4 ♗g2 e6 and Black has a very comfortable, typical Chigorin game with ....♗d6, ♘f6 or ♘ge7 etc.

4 ♗g2 ♗g7 5 0-0 e6

6 b3!?

6 c3! was Hans Ree's improvement against Moro in Tilburg. In fact he ended up defeating the Russian after 6...♘ge7 (6...♘f6!?) 7 ♘bd2 f5?! 8 b4! 0-0 9 b5 ♘a5 10 a4 a6 11 ♗a3 axb5 12 axb5 ♗d7 13 ♕b1 b6 14 ♖c1 ♖e8 15 e3 ♘c8 16 ♘e5! ♘d6 17 ♗xd6 cxd6 18 ♘xd7 ♕xd7 19 c4±

6...♘ge7 7 ♗b2 0-0 8 c4

8 ♘bd2 ♘f5 9 e3 a5!?

8...a5!

Grabbing space on the queenside. It's interesting to compare the outcome of this opening with Moro's game against Ree – there he was more or less run over on the queenside.

9 e3

9 a3 would probably have been met by 9...b6, intending ....♗a6, when White always has to worry about Black chucking in the move ...a4, undermining the c4 square. Of course if White himself plays a4 then that gifts Black a very juicy square for his knight.

9...b6!

9...a4 10 cxd5 exd5 11 bxa4!?

10 ♕d2!?

10 ♘bd2 ♗a6 11 a3.

10...♗a6 11 ♖c1 h6!? 12 cxd5 exd5

Black has equalised comfortably and can now look forward to taking over the initiative, as White's set up looks rather pointless and he is struggling for a plan.

13 ♘c3 ♕d7 14 a3 g5!

Grabbing yet more space. Black's position has a very 'together' feel with everything looking fluent and co-ordinated.

15 ♖c2 f6 16 ♖ac1 ♗b7

17 ♘e1!

Miles re-organises his kingside, as the knight was doing very little on f3. Strong players have a good sense of what the Scottish grandmaster and author, Jonathan Rowson, would call 'talking to your pieces'. However, even though he did have some mental health issues in his life, I'm sure Miles didn't take that phrase literally! Essentially it's an invitation to look around and see if any of your pieces can be improved – if that makes sense (it didn't make much sense to me :-)). At the moment the white rooks, queen, bishop on b2 and knight on c3 are quite optimally placed, and so, having talked to them, you then talk to your knight on f3 – assuming he's a good conversationalist.

17...♘d8

Moro also has good relations with his pieces. Here the knight tells him that he wants to re-route to e6 or f7, whilst also giving some breathing space for the pawn on c7 to advance to c5 later on.

18 ♘d3

I must admit I hate positions like this for White – where there is no active plan. If there's nothing going on, if tactics aren't flying about, I feel very uncomfortable. Also if you are playing White against Moro here, you know that at some point he's going to push his kingside pawns and launch an attack, and if you can't get any counterplay it's going to be a long night. Nevertheless White is okay here – Miles only went wrong later on.

18...♖c8 19 a4 ♘f7 20 ♗a3 ♖fe8

21 ♕d1?!

Is this move really necessary? It looks a bit artificial doesn't it? Miles had a habit of writing down a move on his score sheet and covering it up with a heavy wristwatch. That practice has now been banned by FIDE (another one of their totally unnecessary Draconian rules) but Miles would often change his mind, rub out the move and put another in its place. I can imagine that he certainly considered 21 b4! here – after all he plays it on the next move. Then 21...axb4 22 ♘xb4 or 21...♗f8? 22 bxa5 bxa5 23 ♘c5. But 21...♘d6! was surely the reason why Miles rejected the immediate b4 and played ♕d1 instead to take the sting out of this rejoinder. Then after 22 ♘b2! axb4 23 ♗xb4 the game looks very unclear. By organising effective queenside play White would slow Black down on the other wing, but in the game he wasn't able to do this. In fact at the moment White even looks slightly quicker on the queenside. ♗xd6 followed by ♘b5 is threatened, although this may be countered by 23...c6 and if 24 ♗xd6 ♕xd6 25 e4!? ♕b4∞!.

21...♘g6!

Moro of course, is alive to what Miles is threatening. It turns out that 21 ♕d1 was just a bit too prophylactic.

22 b4 ♗f8!

23 ♖a2?

23 ♘b5! would have practically forced a repetition after 23...c6 24 ♘a7! ♖c7 25 ♘b5. Now Moro takes over the initiative and does not let go of it to the end of the game.

23...axb4 24 ♘xb4

24 ♗xb4 c5! 25 ♗a3 cxd4 26 exd4 ♗xa3 27 ♖xa3 ♖c4 28 ♘b2 ♖c7 29 ♘b5 ♖xc1 30 ♕xc1 ♖c8 does look very comfortable for Black.

24...♗xb4!

Moro does not fear giving up the bishop – he wishes to play with his knights!

25 ♗xb4 ♔g7 26 ♕b3 c5!

27 ♗a3

After 27 dxc5 Miles may well have been afraid that Moro would take advantage of his lack of co-ordination by 27...d4! 28 exd4 (28 ♗xb7 ♕xb7 29 exd4 bxc5! 30 dxc5 ♖xc5 and, with ...♘e5 coming, Black has a huge initiative) 28...♗xg2 29 ♔xg2 and now Black has a choice – he can immediately force a draw with

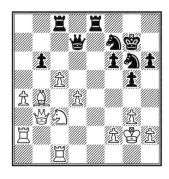

A) 29...♘h4+

A1) 30 ♔h1 ♘f3!? (30...♕h3 31 gxh4 ♕f3+) 31 ♘b5 (31 ♔g2 ♘xd4∓) 31...♘xd4 32 ♘xd4 ♕xd4;

A2) 30 gxh4 ♕g4+ 31 ♔h1 ♕f3+ 32 ♔g1 ♕g4

... or indeed go for more with

B) 29...♕g4! – this power move does indeed look strong as White's weakened light squares are coming back to haunt him – 30 ♕d1 ♘h4+ 31 ♔h1 (31 ♔g1 ♖e1+!) 31...♖e1+!! and mate in two!

27...cxd4 28 exd4

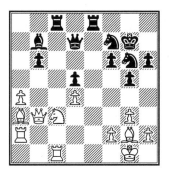

28...♗a6!

Moro exploits the weakness of White's back rank to activate his passive bishop.

29 ♕d1

29 ♕xb6?? ♖xc3! 30 ♕xa6 ♖xc1+ 31 ♗xc1 ♖e1+ -+

29...♗c4 30 ♖b2 ♖c6

Now White really has very little counterplay and can only watch passively as Moro expands on the kingside.

31 ♖cb1 ♕e6 32 h3 f5! 33 a5

A desperate attempt to gain counterplay.

33...bxa5 34 ♖b7 f4!

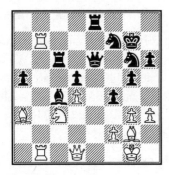

This position now resembles a Dutch gone very wrong for White!

35 ♔h2

35 ♖a7 fxg3 36 fxg3 ♕e3+ -+;

35 ♕f3 fxg3 36 fxg3 ♕e3+! 37 ♕xe3 ♖xe3 looks crushing, e.g. 38 ♗xd5 ♗xd5 39 ♘xd5 ♖xg3+ 40 ♔h2 ♖xa3 41 ♖f1 ♖c2+ 42 ♔g1 ♖g3+ 43 ♔h1 ♖xh3+ 44 ♔g1 ♘gh8-+

35...fxg3+ 36 fxg3 ♕f5

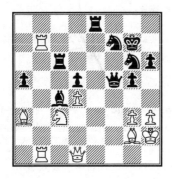

37 ♕d2

37 ♖a7 ♖e3! – that power move again – 38 ♖bb7 ♖f6 39 ♕d2 ♖d3-+

37...h5!

Moro is ruthless. he now intends

...h4 opening up the white king like a ripe banana.

38 ♗c1

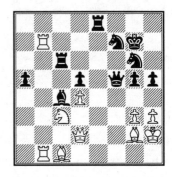

38...♗f1!

Who can forget the famous ...♗b1 that Tal once used to win a game? Moro, in a nod to his great predecessor, intends to exchange off White's last remaining defender.

39 g4

39 ♕xg5 ♕xg5 40 ♗xg5 ♗xg2 41 ♔xg2 ♖xc3.

39...hxg4 40 ♗xd5

40 hxg4 ♕xg4 41 ♗xd5 ♖h8 mate.

40...♖f6 41 ♕xg5 ♕f2+ 42 ♔h1 ♗g2+ 43 ♗xg2 ♖e1+ 44 ♔h2 g3+

It's mate next move. A very smooth game.

0-1

Writing down a move before playing it – and I remember Kasparov doing the same in his match against Short – was originally an old Russian method designed to avoid blunders, as having to check a move before you played it tended to cut out jarring oversights. Nevertheless blunders remain part and parcel of chess. When I talk about calculation I don't just mean being able to see many moves ahead – I also mean the simple routines that you can practice to avoid making silly mistakes and 'one movers'. Moreover if you practice what I preach – which is to examine as many candidate moves as possible and pay an equal amount of attention to your opponent's possibilities – then you are likely to eradicate the kind of mental laziness that can make you susceptible to making horrible blunders.

The importance of the opening

"Win the crowd, and you will win your freedom" could be an epithet attached to the entertaining chess career of Alexander Morozevich. Another one could be "get the openings right, and you will be number one in the world" (Okay, I just made that up, which is probably why it's less catchy.). However I'm a great believer that the opening is by far the most important phase when deciding a game of chess. I've lost track of the number of times that I have lost my way completely in the opening, and gone away from a game with the frustrated feeling of failing to give of my best. This was because I was never in the game in the first place and never had a chance to play. I personally have a great belief in my overall playing ability and feel that is unlikely that I will get outplayed (he says modestly) – provided I can reach the middlegame or the endgame safely. It may seem obvious but the easiest way to deal with the problem of the opening is first and foremost to learn how to play chess properly. Some opening moves and positions are so bizarre that simply learning by rote is not enough, as it is only by broadening our chess knowledge that we can be confident of having the necessary weapons to deal with the complexity of the opening phase. Modern day elite grandmasters tend to be divided into two categories: on the one hand those who will actively seek to gain an advantage in the opening (Fischer, Kasparov, Topalov, etc) and, on the other, players who are content simply 'to get a position' and then outplay their opponents later. Among the latter I would count Karpov, Aronian, Carlsen, etc. And certainly Morozevich also fits into this category as, although his style can be described as very sharp, he is not a great expert on the opening in the same way as Kasparov. However his uniquely imaginative and original style has helped him discover many interesting ideas in the opening – not least in the Chigorin Defence. In the next game we again see Morozevich adopt the Chigorin to devastating effect. In fact Morozevich is one of the world's top ten players and, personally, I would at least like to have White against him. Playing Kramnik you might hope to make a draw against his Petroff or Berlin defences – but Moro tends to go all out for the win regardless of whether he has Black or White.

21

J.Piket – A.Morozevich

Corus, Wijk aan Zee 2001

Chigorin Defence

1 d4 d5 2 c4 ♘c6 3 cxd5 ♕xd5 4 e3 e5 5 ♘c3 ♗b4 6 ♗d2 ♗xc3

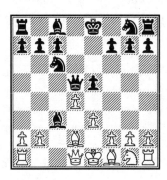

7 bxc3

Morozevich has also managed to mix it up against 7 ♗xc3 (can't he keep it simple?! :-)), e.g. 7...exd4 8 ♘e2 ♗g4 9 f3 0-0-0!? with unclear complications.

7...♘f6 8 f3 0-0

8...e4!? is another sting line – in general here Black will try to use his lead in development to open up the position before White gets the opportunity to exploit his strong centre and two bishops.

9 e4

9 ♗d3 exd4 10 cxd4 ♘xd4!? 11 exd4 ♕xd4 12 ♗e2 ♘d5 13 ♖c1 and here, rather surprisingly and just when it was getting interesting, a draw was agreed in the game Dautov – S.Hansen, German league semi-final – but that's grandmaster chess for you!

9...♕d6

10 d5

10 ♘e2 exd4

A) 11 cxd4 ♘xd4 12 ♗c3 ♘b5 (or 12...♘xe2);

B) 11 ♗f4 ♕a3 12 cxd4 ♘b4!? was the highly unclear continuation of a game played in Madrid between Beliavsky and Yermolinsky – which Yermo went on to win.

10...♘e7 11 c4

11...♘h5!?

11...c6?! with the idea of ...b5, undermining the imposing white centre, is an alternative – but probably not a very good one. I've played this line as White (Incidentally, the variation with 7 bxc3 has also got the Kasparov stamp of approval.) and I can testify from experience that it's surprisingly difficult to keep a grip on Black's counterplay. Best seems 12 ♕b3! b5 13 ♗b4 c5 14 ♗c3±.

There is also 11...♘d7!?, with the idea of re-routing the knight to blockade the c5 square. But, as usual, Moro tries the more dynamic route. He wants to play ...h5 and target White's king in the centre before it has a chance to reach safety. One thing I've noticed when looking at games of the very top players is that when faced with the choice between a safe but slightly passive looking move and an aggressive, albeit risky one, they nearly always choose the latter.

12 ♕b3!?

12 ♘e2 f5 13 ♘c3 (13 exf5 ♘xf5 14 g4? ♘h4∓).

12...c5

This may appear to surrender the centre to White, but in any case ♗b4 was a direct threat. For the time being Moro wants to play only on the kingside.

13 ♘e2 f5

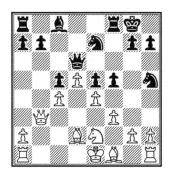

14 ♘c3

14 exf5!? now required checking. After all, a computer would always play this move if it's good! After 14...♘xf5! (14...♘f6 15 g4 e4 16 h3±; 14...♗xf5 15 g4) 15 g4 ♘h4 16 gxh5 ♘xf3+ 17 ♔d1 ♗g4 18 ♔c1 ♗xh5 the consequences of the sacrifice are completely unclear. So, although a computer would go for this line, Piket probably felt that against an attacking player *par excellence* like Morozevich this would be asking for trouble. Black will always have good counter-chances with the opponent's king in the centre. Grandmasters tend to make intuitive judgements based on

their lengthy experience – after all it is impossible to work out over the board all the consequences of such a position.

14...b6 15 ♗d3

15 ♘b5 is met by ♕d8; while 15 exf5 is now simply bad: 15...♘xf5 16 g4 ♘d4-+

15...♘g6!

16 g3!?

White plays a move to contain the threat of ...♘f4 but was that threat really so strong? The text also has the drawback of making kingside castling more difficult, although of course White can always go to the queenside (when assessing a move you should always ask yourself what are its drawbacks as well as its positives.). I would probably have preferred the less pretentious, though not necessarily any stronger, 16 0-0!? ♘gf4 (16...♘hf4 17 ♕c2! ♘xd3 18 ♕xd3) 17 ♕c2 ♕g6 18 ♗xf4 ♘xf4 19 exf5 ♗xf5 20 ♗xf5 ♖xf5 21 ♘e4 ♖af8 22 a4±

16...♕e7

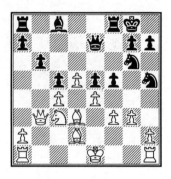

17 exf5

17 0-0 anyway! 17...f4! Black is committed! (17...fxe4 18 ♘xe4±) 18 g4 (18 ♗e1 fxg3 19 hxg3 ♕g5 20 ♔h2 ♘hf4 21 gxf4 ♘xf4 with a winning attack as in any case the bishop on d3 is hanging) 18...♘h4! 19 ♗e1 ♕g5 20 ♔h1

A) 20...♗xg4 21 fxg4 ♕xg4 22 ♕c2 ♘g3+ 23 ♗xg3 fxg3 24 hxg3 ♕xg3 with an attack;

B) 20...♘xf3 21 ♖xf3 (21 gxh5 ♗h3!) 21...♗xg4;

C) 20...♘f6 with the dangerous threat of ...h5.

Alternatively 17 0-0-0!? has the problem that if Black is able to blast open the queenside then the white king would be in trouble – although it's not clear how he achieves this.

17...♗xf5

I think exchanging the light-squared bishops helps Black, as he will no longer have to worry about the power of the two bishops. On the other hand Piket gains the strong e4 square.

18 ♗xf5 ♖xf5

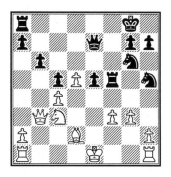

19 ♘e4

I guess Piket dismissed 19 g4 for the same reasons as he did earlier, nevertheless this was still a possibility, e.g. 19...♕h4+ (19...♖xf3 20 gxh5 ♕h4+ transposes) 20 ♔d1

A) 20...♘g3 21 ♖g1 ♕xh2 (21...♖xf3 22 ♖xg3 ♖xg3 23 hxg3 ♕xg4+ 24 ♔c2) 22 ♖xg3;

B) 20...♕f2? 21 gxf5! ♕xf3+ 22 ♔c2;

C) 20...♖xf3 21 gxh5 ♕xh5 22 ♔c1 e4 with a real mess. White may have an extra unit but his remaining pieces are clumsily placed and Black retains an ongoing initiative.

19...♘f6?!

19...♖af8 20 0-0 ♘f6 was a more solid continuation. Then would follow 21 ♕d3±

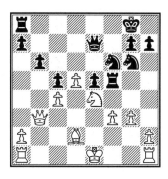

20 ♗g5!?

20 ♕d3! would have given a slight, but enduring advantage for White, e.g. 20...♘xe4 (20...♖f8 21 0-0) 21 ♕xe4 ♖af8 22 0-0 ♕f7 23 ♔g2.

20...♕f8! 21 ♗xf6 gxf6

The problem now is that Black can undermine White's control of e4 with a later ...f5.

22 0-0-0!?

After 22 0-0 ♖h5 23 ♖f2 it is unclear whether White's play on the queenside with a4-a5 is quicker than Black's with ...♔h8, ...f5 and an eventual attack down the g-file with moves such as ...e4 and ...f4. However I would prefer to be Black – mate is mate!

22...♖h5 23 h4

23 d6 might be considered.

23...♖h6

24 h5?

Up to this point, the battle has been waged on a relatively equal footing, but now Piket starts to lose the thread. Nevertheless I'm pretty sure he would have calculated the logical 24 d6!

A) I wonder if Piket feared the direct attempt 24...f5?! but after 25 ♘g5 f4 (25...♕f6 26 ♕d3) there is the strong idea 26 ♘e6! ♕f6 27 d7;

B) 24...♖d8!? 25 ♕d3 f5 26 ♕d5+ ♕f7 27 ♘g5 ♕xd5 28 ♖xd5 ♖d7 and there is still plenty left to be said. Instead he goes for the greedy win of an exchange – but he has failed to calculate the consequences adequately.

24...♘e7

Now d6 is always likely to be a false dawn because of the reply ...♘c6, after which the knight heads for the tremendous square d4.

25 g4 f5! 26 g5 fxe4 27 gxh6 ♕f4+ 28 ♔b1 exf3

How would you assess such a position? After all, not only does White have an exchange to the good, but it would also seem that the d-pawn is rather dangerous. Nevertheless Black does in fact hold all the trumps! The f-pawn will tie down White, preventing him from any undertaking any really active operations, while the black knight becomes a marauding monster, constantly threatening to land a decisive blow on d4 or e3. Now we can see the poverty of Piket's decision to win the exchange – quite simply he must have wrongly assessed this position.

29 ♕d3

29 ♖hf1!? ♖f8 30 ♖d3 e4! 31 ♖g1+ ♔f7!; or 29 d6 ♘c6 and the knight is on its way to d4.

29...♘f5 30 ♖de1 ♘d6! 31 ♖hg1+ ♔h8 32 ♖g7 ♕xh6 33 ♖d7 ♖f8

Now White has no real answer to the combined might of Black's connected passed pawns.

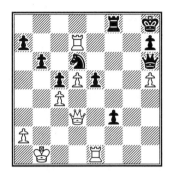

34 ♕c3 ♕f6 35 h6 f2 36 ♖f1 ♕f5+ 37 ♔a1

37 ♕c2 ♕xd7.

37...♘e4

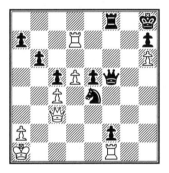

38 ♕d3?

38 ♕b2! looked a better chance. Even when you are on the verge of defeat, a chance will often present itself to pose problems for your opponent – so long as you are alert! Then follows 38...♕xd7 39 ♕xe5+ ♘f6 40 ♖xf2 ♕f7 but after 41 ♔b2, for example, Black will have some difficulties unravelling. In fact it's not at all clear how he can do so, as the h-pawn makes that task problematical.

38...♕xd7

Now it really is all over.

39 ♕xe4 ♕f5 40 ♖xf2?

A final mistake, but ...e4 was coming anyway.

40...♕xf2

I believe it was Larsen who said "all long variations are incorrect" and the problem isn't just that you might overlook moves during the calculation of a long line, but your judgement of the resulting position might be faulty! Here Piket made a decision to grab the exchange, but as it turned out it was the wrong one and it ultimately cost him the game.

0-1

In the next game, I analysed a lot of the lines with a computer, probably because the kind of situation that arises in the game, with sacrifices and tactics flying about, is one that a computer is particularly strong in analysing. So, having been rude to computers before in this book, I can now be officially classed a hypocrite.

22

A.Morozevich – L.Van Wely

Corus, Wijk aan Zee 2000

Sicilian Defence

1 e4 c5 2 ♘f3 d6 3 d4 cxd4 4 ♘xd4 ♘f6 5 ♘c3 a6 6 ♗e3

Nowadays this is the preferred move of choice against the Najdorf in super-grandmaster circles and has taken over in popularity from 6 ♗g5, 6 ♗e2 and 6 ♗c4. White plays an 'English' attack, so called because it was honed into a dangerous attacking weapon in the 1980s by the new breed of English grandmasters, Nigel Short, Murray Chandler and John Nunn. In fact when I play the Najdorf in Internet games I rarely have to face anything else.

6...e6

7 f3

7 g4!? introduces the feared Perenyi attack, which is possible after 7...e5 8 ♘f5 g6 9 ♕f3!? with White sacrificing a knight in an attempt to generate unanswerable threats in the centre. On the other hand, I myself have played 7...d5 against French grandmaster Etienne Bacrot. Though I managed to hold on for a draw, White should be slightly better after 8 g5 ♘xe4 9 ♘xe4 dxe4 10 ♕g4.

7...b5 8 g4 h6 9 ♕d2 ♘bd7 10 0-0-0 ♗b7 11 ♗d3 ♘e5 12 ♖he1 ♖c8

12...b4 is the main alternative, upon which White normally responds 13 ♘a4 keeping an eye on the b6 square. Then again, 12...♕a5!? 13 ♘b3 ♕c7 has been tried by Boris Gelfand – possibly the leading theoretical expert in the Najdorf around today.

13 ♔b1 ♘fd7 14 f4 ♘c4

14...♘xg4 is considered risky – White can continue simply 15 ♗g1!? with compensation or 15 e5 dxe5 16 ♘xe6 fxe6 17 ♗g6+ ♔e7 18 fxe5 ♘gxe5 19 ♗g5+ hxg5 20 ♕xg5+ ♘f6 21 ♖xd8+-

15 ♕e2

15 ♗xc4?! would be a positional error – it is more dangerous to retain the light squared bishop. After 15...♖xc4 16 f5 e5 17 ♘f3 ♕a8! 18 b3 ♖xe4 19 ♘xe4 ♗xe4 Black had excellent compensation in Korneev – Topalov, Spanish team championship 1999.

15...♘xe3 16 ♕xe3

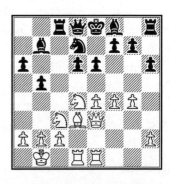

16...g5?

Van Wely, who had something of an ongoing theoretical duel in this variation at Wijk aan Zee 2000, tried to improve in the later rounds with 16...♛b6!? but after the move played in the game what would you do as White? Black has a strategical idea – he wants to gain total control over the dark squares – take on f4 followed by ...♘e5 after which it would be almost impossible for White to launch an attack! ...g5 is a standard idea in the Sicilian – unfortunately for Van Wely, in this particular situation it simply doesn't work! It just weakens the king too much.

However Van Wely's improvement 16...♛b6!? has a very logical basis – in some lines Black will play ...e5, exchange queens and take the sting out of White's attack. Indeed, against Anand he made an easy draw.

A) 17 f5?! e5 18 ♘b3 ♛xe3 19 ♖xe3 ♘c5.

B) 17 ♘d5 was Timman's improvement a few rounds later – ♘d5 is a very thematic sacrifice in the Sicilian. After 17...exd5 (17...♛c5!? 18 b4 ♛a7 19 ♘xe6? ♛xe3 20 ♘ec7+ ♚d8 21 ♖xe3 ♖xc7) 18 exd5+ ♚d8 19 ♗xb5! axb5 20 ♛e8+ ♚c7 21 ♛xf7 he was in a position to recover a piece, the knight on d7. Although at this stage the outcome of the battle was still

unclear, Timman later went on to win.

17 e5!

Of course! Forced, but strong. When you play the main line of the Sicilian as White you should be prepared to make sacrifices! 17 f5?! won't really do (Black is handed the e5 square on a plate) 17...♛e7!? (17...e5∞) 18 ♗xb5 axb5 19 ♘dxb5 ♛f6 20 ♘xd6+ (20 ♖xd6 ♛e5∞) 20...♗xd6 21 ♖xd6 ♛e5 22 ♖ed1 ♘f6 and Black seems to be holding on.

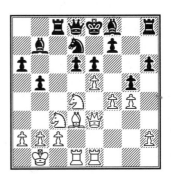

17...gxf4?!

A lot of players would be afraid to play a move like 17 e5, fearing a miscalculation or being simply unwilling to make a sacrifice. But main line Sicilians aren't for the faint-hearted. In such positions top players think more in concrete terms – relying heavily on the calculation of long tactical lines rather than on generalisations such as how much an individual piece is worth to me. Grandmasters such as Morozevich and Shirov have no problem sacrificing material, they look at pieces in terms of achieving the greater goal, rather than having any real value in themselves. It's a similar situation when top poker players say they are not really thinking about the money in the pot – they just have the guts to put in all their chips if the situation demands it! What about 17...dxe5 18 fxe5! (18 ♘xe6 should be calculated, but there does not appear to be any obvious way in after 18...fxe6 19 ♗g6+ ♔e7. Although a diligent reader may well be able to find something here for White – I haven't been able to)

A) 18...♗c5 19 ♗e4! ♗xe4 20 ♘xe4±;

B) 18...♕c7 looks safe, but White can get through by sheer brute force: 19 ♘xe6! fxe6 20 ♗g6+ ♔d8 (20...♔e7 21 ♕f2! is immensely powerful: 21...♘xe5 22 ♖xe5 ♕xe5 23 ♕f7 mate) 21 ♖xd7+ ♕xd7 22 ♕b6+ ♖c7 (22...♔e7 23 ♖f1!) 23 ♖d1 ♕xd1+ 24 ♘xd1;

C) 18...♕b6 seems relatively best – Black tries to activate the queen – which is vulnerable to all sorts of nasty tricks on d8 – and prevents a sacrifice on e6 (where he can simply exchange queens.) 19 ♗e4! b4 (19...♗xe4 20 ♘xe4±) 20 ♘a4 ♕c7 and there is still plenty of fight left, although White's strong grip on the centre and potential for exploiting the rather unsafe black king on the kingside makes him favourite;

D) Upon 18...♗g7, which candidate moves would you consider for White? 19 ♘(d)xb5, 19 ♘xe6, 19 ♗e4!?, 19 ♘f5!, – that's a lot to look at!

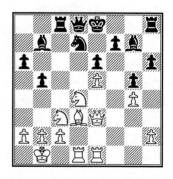

D1) 19 ♘dxb5 axb5 20 ♗xb5 ♖c7 21 ♕b6 ♗c8;

D2) 19 ♘xe6 fxe6 20 ♗g6+ ♔e7 21 ♘xb5 axb5 22 ♕a3+ ♖c5 (22...♘c5!? 23 ♖xd8 ♖hxd8) 23 ♖xd7+ ♕xd7 24 ♕xc5+ ♔d8 isn't totally clear, but Black is defending;

D3) 19 ♗e4!? ♗xe4 20 ♘xe4 0-0 21 ♘f3;

D4) 19 ♘f5! is a very strong rejoinder! 19...♗xe5 (19...exf5 20 ♗xf5 ♗c6 21 e6+-; 19...0-0? 20 ♘d6 ♖c7 21 ♘xb7 ♖xb7 22 ♕e4) 20 ♗xb5 axb5 21 ♖xd7! ♕xd7 (21...♔xd7 22 ♖d1+ ♗d5 23 ♘xd5) 22 ♕xe5; 17...b4? 18 ♘xe6 fxe6 19 ♗g6+ ♔e7 20 exd6+ ♔f6 21 ♕xe6+. So it seems that after 19 ♘f5 Black is in trouble. I'm not surprised that Van Wely rejected this line – at best it's unfathomable, at worst he's losing.

18 ♕xf4

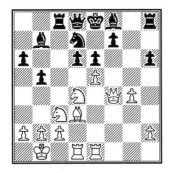

18...dxe5

18...♕g5 was a worthy alternative. Then I know what I would like to do if I were Black – exchange queens as quickly as possible! Unfortunately even that simple objective isn't feasible – White has the relatively straightforward continuation (well, simple for this position anyway) 19 ♕xg5! hxg5 20 exd6 and if 20...♖xh2? (if 20...♗xd6 21 ♘xe6 fxe6 22 ♖xe6+ ♗e7 23 ♖de1) there is...

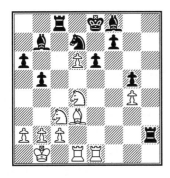

21 ♖xe6+!!

A crushing blow which dismantles the king's defences, even in the endgame! 21...♔d8 22 ♖de1! and

Black will be forced to give up buckets of material to prevent mate.

Finally 18...♘xe5? allows 19 ♘xe6! fxe6 20 ♖xe5 dxe5 21 ♗g6+ ♔e7 22 ♕f7 mate.

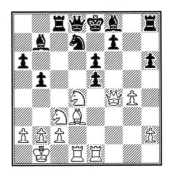

19 ♘xe6!

There's no going back now!

19...♕e7 20 ♕d2!

The 'straightforward' 20 ♘xf8? exf4 21 ♖xe7+ ♔xe7 22 ♘xd7 ♔xd7 23 ♗f5+ ♔e7 24 ♗xc8 ♖xc8 will, of course, not do.

20...fxe6

20...♕xe6 21 ♗f5+−

21 ♗g6+ ♔d8

How to increase the pressure further?

22 ♖f1!

White has a rampaging initiative.

22...♖xc3

Forced, otherwise the rook comes to f7 and it's all over, e.g. 22...♗c6 23 ♖f7 wins too much material.

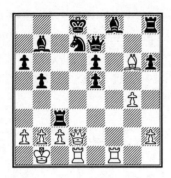

23 ♕xc3

23 bxc3? is met by 23...♗d5! Now, however, despite the almost level material (actually Black has a slight advantage in that respect) Black cannot seriously hope to survive. Not only is his king stumbling around in the centre as if in a drunken stupor, but he has yet to develop the rest of his kingside, whereas all White's pieces are taking part in the final assault.

23...♕c5

23...♗d5 24 ♕a5+ ♔c8 25 ♕xa6+ strips the king's defences even further.

23...b4 24 ♕xe5 ♗g7 25 ♕b8+ ♗c8 26 ♕b6 mate;

23...♗c8 24 ♖f7 transposes to the game.

24 ♖f7 ♗c8

24...♗c6 25 ♕a5+ ♔c8 26 ♕xa6+ wins.

25 ♕d2 ♕a7

25...♕d4 26 ♕a5+;

25...♕c7 26 ♕f2! (we see this recurring idea time and time again) 26...♗e7 27 ♖xe7 ♔xe7 28 ♕f7+ ♔d8 29 ♕f6 mate

Now how would you finish off? Moro opens yet another front.

26 g5! b4

After 26...h5 27 ♗xh5 Black is move-bound, and if 27...♖xh5 28 ♖xf8+ ♔c7 29 ♕d6+ ♔b7 30 ♖f7 ♔a8 31 g6.

27 gxh6 ♗xh6 28 ♕xb4 ♗g5 29 ♕g4

Another crushing attack from Moro, and it all stems from the dubious decision by Van Wely to play the very risky 16...g5?, exposing his king at a time when his opponent is ideally placed to launch an attack. When playing the Sicilian, I tend to find that even dubious sacrifices by White are difficult to defend against – especially when your king is floating around in the centre.

1-0

Hard work

Recently a survey was published which suggested that genius really is more perspiration than inspiration. The report suggested that to become a master in your chosen field, a minimum of 10,000 hours would be required practising your craft. God only knows how they stumbled upon such a precise figure, but apparently it applies to piano players, golfers, footballers and chess players (to name but a few).

Personally I think such a huge number of hours is a massive exaggeration, and assuming one has a gift for chess in the first place, a much smaller figure should suffice. How many hours people put into studying and practising is up to themselves and depends on their character. If you have the sort of personality that primarily enjoys playing, then you should concentrate on that, although it is important to remember that without study and analysis of your own games, real improvement is probably not possible. In fact I've often wondered who are these people who claim to study for hours on end. In England, the grandmasters are notoriously lazy, and don't let chess study get in the way of an honest visit to the local pub or betting shop, nor indeed an episode of *Hollyoaks*. Each culture is different, and in countries such as China and Russia there is a much greater work ethic, which is probably why these nations consistently produce much stronger players than we do. After all, if you live in Russia then you are unlikely to have the alternative of a highly paid career in finance like most young English chess players (unless your surname happens to be Abramovich). I recall when the Indian player Sasikiran was asked in an interview how much time he spends studying chess, he replied 12 hours a day. I don't know if this was an attempt to intimidate any future opponents, as I'd be very sceptical that he would do that much on a day to day basis. Regularly studying chess 12 hours a day would most likely cause you to morph into a chess piece. It would also be counter-productive as you would soon become very stale with too much chess – which is an art and a science as well as a game and overexposure could easily lead to a creative drought.

I'm sure that despite his profound talent, Morozevich works fairly hard, otherwise it would be impossible for him to keep up with the latest chess developments – essential if he is to continue performing at the level he does. His opponent in the next game is also a very hard worker – Mikhail Gurevich – who once worked as a second for Kasparov (apparently he said this was all very nice apart from the fact that Kasparov wanted to analyse everything up to mate!).

23

A.Morozevich – M.Gurevich

FIDE World Championship
Knockout, Moscow 2001

French Defence

1 e4 e6

Gurevich has been playing the French Defence since Morozevich was in short trousers. I remember preparing for his French in Cappelle a few years back – fortunately he didn't play it as the line I had in mind was rubbish!

2 d4 d5 3 ♘c3 ♘f6 4 e5 ♘fd7 5 ♘ce2 c5 6 c3 cxd4 7 cxd4 f6 8 f4 fxe5 9 fxe5

9...♕h4+

9...♗b4+ is an alternative. In this line, White attempts to construct a strong centre – if he gets the opportunity to play the moves ♘f3, ♗e3, ♔f2, h4, ♘f4 and ♗d3 without anything really nasty happening then he generally stands well. On the other hand Black will generally try to blast open the centre with some kind of piece sacrifice (as he has no pawn breaks) before White gets the chance to get organised. The game J.Polgar – G.Hernandez, Merida 2000 took a very similar course to our main game; 10 ♔f2 0-0+ 11 ♘f3 ♘c6 12 a3 ♘dxe5?! 13 axb4 ♕h4+ 14 ♔g1 ♘xf3+ 15 gxf3 ♖xf3 16 ♘g3 ♘xd4 17 ♗g2 ♖f7 18 ♗e3 ♘f5 19 ♘xf5 ♖xf5 20 b5 ♗d7 21 b6 a6 22 ♕d4 ♕h5 23 h3! and Judit was able to consolidate and win fairly easily with the extra piece.

10 ♘g3 ♗b4+ 11 ♔f2 0-0+ 12 ♘f3 ♘c6 13 ♗e3

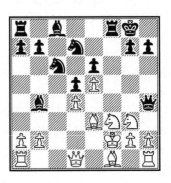

What candidate moves would you identify here as Black? Retreating with 13...♕e7 looks too passive. Nor will 13...♘b6 cut the mustard – Black needs to maintain pressure on the centre. That leaves 13...♗a5 and the move played in the game, 13...♘dxe5.

13...♘dxe5?

Radical don't you think? Although this kind of sacrifice is standard for such a position, I wouldn't recommend playing this line with either colour if you are not confident in your ability to calculate (although I'm assuming all readers will be razor sharp calculators after finishing this book) – as tactics are flying about and evaluations here will be based more on concrete analysis than general considerations. What alternatives did Gurevich have? In the later game Nataf – P.H.Nielsen, European Championship, Istanbul 2003, the Danish player made the more circumspect retreat 13...♗a5! with the intention of moving the bishop (which to a certain extent was out of the game on b4) to b6 in order to pressurise the centre, and only then weigh up the possibility of a sacrifice. That game continued 14 ♔g1 ♖xf3! (14...♗b6?? 15 ♘xh4) 15 gxf3 ♗b6 16 f4 g5! 17 ♕h5 (17 fxg5 ♘dxe5 with an attack) 17...♕xh5 18 ♘xh5 gxf4 19 ♘xf4 ♘dxe5 20 ♗h3 ♘xd4 21 ♔f2?! ♘c4! 22 ♗xd4 ♗xd4+ 23 ♔e2 ♔f7 and although at this point Black was doing very well, White managed to hold on for a draw. The pawns on d4 and e5 are all very well and good, but there's always a danger they'll simply drop off... 13...♘cxe5 certainly won't do – it is the black knight on c6 that is more active after the sacrifice.

14 dxe5 ♘xe5 15 ♔g1

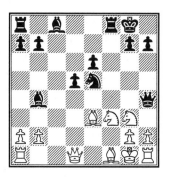

15...♕f6

15...♘xf3+ was an obvious alternative. Then 16 gxf3 ♗d6 17 ♕d4! ♗xg3 18 hxg3 ♕xg3+ 19 ♗g2 and though Black is doing well from a material point of view, positionally this is not the case at all. White has a potential attack down the g and h files, for example. Then again, 15...♘g4?? is a move that Black would like to play – but unfortunately the queen is en prise!

16 ♕d4!

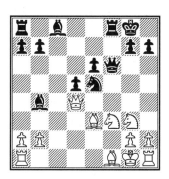

16...♗d6

On the face of it 16...♘xf3+ 17 gxf3 ♕xd4 (17...♕xf3 18 ♗e2+–) 18 ♗xd4 ♖xf3 would appear to be acceptable for Black, who does have three pawns for the piece. Unfortunately for him the activity of the opponent's pieces is likely to be the decisive factor here and White has easy play after 19 ♔g2 ♖f7 20 ♗d3 ♗d6 21 ♖ae1 followed by ♖hg1, ♔h1, ♘h5 etc. Instead Gurevich wisely endeavours to forgo the queen exchange in order to maintain the tension as long as possible. Meanwhile Morozevich must create counterplay to distract Black before his initiative reaches unmanageable levels.

17 ♗e2 ♗d7!

17...♘xf3+? 18 ♗xf3±

18 ♖c1!

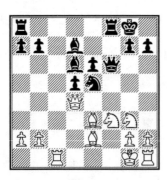

What is the idea behind this move? We have already seen how important it is, before each move, to ask yourself "what is my opponent intending to do". In this case, Black's plan is clear: he will simply play ...♖c8, so first of all Morozevich ensures this will lead to an exchange of pieces that will reduce Black's initiative. Also in some lines Black can play ...b6, but

now he has to reason that a later ...♗c5 will lead to an exchange sacrifice enabling White to gain control over the dark squares.

18...b6

18...♖ac8 19 ♔f2! ♘xf3 20 ♕xf6! (20 ♗xf3 ♗e5 21 ♕xa7 d4 22 ♗d2 ♗c6 23 ♖xc6 is better for White, but much less clear) 20...gxf6 21 ♗xf3±

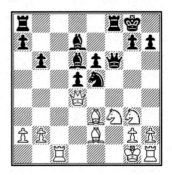

19 a3!

Moro effectively calls Gurevich's bluff. "You're not going to play ...♗c5, I'll just take it". 19 ♔f2 ♗c5! 20 ♖xc5 bxc5 21 ♕xc5 ♘g4+ 22 ♔g1 ♕xb2 looks dangerous only for White; while 19 b4 ♘xf3+ 20 ♗xf3 (20 gxf3!?) 20...♕xd4 21 ♗xd4 ♗xb4 22 ♔f2 ♗d6 allows Black good holding chances at least.

19...♘xf3+

19...♗c5 20 ♖xc5 ♘xf3+ 21 ♗xf3 bxc5 22 ♕xf6 ♖xf6 23 ♗xc5 and White's game plays itself, with moves like ♔f2, b4, ♗d4 and ♘e2 coming in quick order.

But how would you meet 19...♖ac8 ?

After all, Black now has a direct threat of ...♖xc1 followed by ...♗c5, winning. So White continues 20 ♖xc8! (20 ♔f2? ♗c5!∓; 20 b4?? is even worse because of 20...♖xc1+ 21 ♗xc1 ♘xf3+–+) 20...♖xc8 (20...♗xc8 21 b4 and it's not clear how Black should continue as White will simply follow with ♔f2) 21 b4 ♖c2 22 ♔f2! and with ♖c1 coming, Black again does not appear to have full compensation.

20 gxf3!

20 ♗xf3 looks more natural, but in fact Moro wants a hidey hole for his king on g2, otherwise it's very difficult to connect rooks, as the *luft* move h3 will hang the knight on g3.

20...♗e5 21 ♕d2 ♗xb2

Gurevich goes after this pawn, but it's fairly irrelevant. What's more relevant is that White is beginning to consolidate where he can proceed to use his extra piece to help mount an attack.

22 ♖c7 ♖f7

22...♗e8 23 ♔g2 ♗xa3 24 ♖a1!

♗d6 (24...♕xa1 25 ♗d4 turns the tables) 25 ♖axa7 ♖xa7 26 ♖xa7±

23 ♔g2 ♗xa3

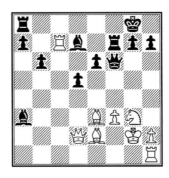

Without the capture of this pawn Black's whole play would be redundant, but now he hopes that with four pawns for the piece he will enjoy enough compensation. But unfortunately for him no simple trade to an endgame is forthcoming, and the extra piece enables White to create more than irritating threats. Still, four pawns is four pawns, and at this stage the game is relatively unclear – but I would rather have the extra piece!

24 ♖f1

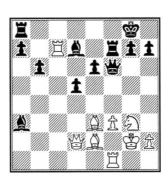

24...♗d6?

A critical position. It would seem that Gurevich overlooked the strength of White's next which forces a favourable exchange. 24...♕d8!? (not 24...a5? 25 ♗xb6) seemed a better try, avoiding the tactical rejoinder in the game and keeping it as complicated as possible. 25 ♖c2 (25 ♗f4!? is also possible, retaining the powerful rook: then 25...♗e8 26 ♖xf7 ♗xf7 27 ♗e5 ♗d6 28 f4±) 25...♗d6?! (25...♖c8! with the idea of ...♗c5 keeps the outlook unclear.) 26 f4! (If 26 ♗g5 ♗e7. White intends to break up the e6-d5 pawn chain.) 26...g6 27 ♗g4 a5 28 ♘e4! ♗e7 29 ♘g5 ♗xg5 30 fxg5 ♖xf1 31 ♔xf1 and the weakness of the dark squares is decisive.

25 ♗g5! ♗b4

No use are 25...♕e5? 26 f4; or 25...♕g6 26 ♗d3+-

26 ♕xb4

26 ♕e3 ♕b2.

26...♕xg5 27 ♕d6

It may seem surprising that Gurevich lets the a-pawn go so easily, after which at best he faces an uphill struggle to achieve a draw and without having any counter-chances. However the main alternative 27...♕e7 has quite a straightforward drawback; 28 ♕xe7! ♖xe7 29 ♗b5! ♖d8 30 ♖xa7 and White will win the b-pawn, after which it simply becomes a matter of technique.

28 ♖xa7

Now with the b-pawn also likely to drop it is unlikely that Black will be able to save the game.

28...♗c8 29 ♕xb6 ♖xa7 30 ♕xa7 e5

Seemingly forced, otherwise White will establish a bind with f4 then get to work with his extra piece.

31 ♕c7 ♗e6 32 ♖b1! h5 33 ♖b7 ♖e8

33...h4 34 ♕e7! ♕xe7 35 ♖xe7 hxg3 (35...♗f7 36 ♘f5) 36 ♖xe6 gxh2 37 ♖xe5 d4 38 ♗d3+-

34 h4!

Moro allows no respite.

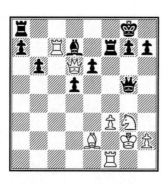

27...♖d8

34...♕g6

34...♕h6 35 ♘xh5!

35 ♗d3 e4 36 fxe4 dxe4 37 ♗xe4+- ♕h6 38 ♕c3 ♗g4 39 ♗f3 ♗xf3+ 40 ♕xf3 ♕g6 41 ♕d5+ ♔f8 42 ♖b2 ♖e6 43 ♕d8+ ♖e8

43...♕e8 44 ♕xe8+ ♖xe8 45 ♘xh5.

44 ♖f2+ ♔g8 45 ♕d5+ ♔h8 46 ♖f5! ♖e2+ 47 ♔f1 ♖e6 48 ♘e4 ♕e8 49 ♕xe6 1-0

A pleasing finish. The ability to judge a position resulting from a sacrifice is one of the most difficult challenges in chess – perhaps Gurevich's judgement let him down on this occasion as Black never seemed to have enough compensation for the piece. Material sacrifices by Tal and Shirov were normally made to exploit a temporary lack of co-ordination in their opponents' forces. In this game White had no such problems and Moro showed great control in gradually quenching Black's initiative.

24

C.Lutz – A.Morozevich

Biel 2003

French Defence

1 e4 e6 2 d4 d5 3 ♘c3 ♘f6 4 ♗g5 dxe4 5 ♘xe4 ♗e7 6 ♗xf6 gxf6

Morozevich actually reinvented this tricky line, where the dynamic positions that arise perfectly compliment his imaginative, counterattacking style. Previously it was thought that saddling yourself with doubled pawns so early in the game would be asking for trouble, but chess theory has advanced so much in the last few years... Nowadays players have woken up to the idea that doubled pawns can be as much a strength as a weakness, as in this case where they form a strong barrier, controlling the important e5, g5, f5 and d5 squares.

7 ♘f3 a6 8 c4 f5 9 ♘c3 ♗f6 10 ♕d2 c5 11 d5 0-0 12 0-0-0

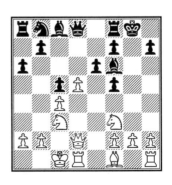

12...♗g7

12...e5, immediately trying to gain counterplay in the centre, has been played a couple of times but with variable success. Shirov has championed this line for White but the general verdict remains unclear. Shirov – Topalov, Sarajevo, 2000 was a stunning success for Shirov after 13 h4 b5 14 d6 (It's very dangerous for White to open the queenside by 14 cxb5 axb5.) 14...♘c6 (The young Azerbaijani grandmaster, Teimour Radjabov, later improved here with 14...♗e6! against Bruno Belotti, in Valle d'Aosta 2001. One of the ideas is that the bishop will not run into d7 with tempo. 15 ♘d5 ♗xd5 16 ♕xd5 ♘d7 17 ♘d2 ♗g7! 18 ♖h3 ♕f6 19 cxb5 ♖ab8 20 ♕c6 e4! (This kind of position closely resembles those found in the Sveshnikov Sicilian.) 21 ♖c3 ♕d8 22 ♖c2 axb5

and Radjabov had dangerous counterplay against the white king (note how little progress White has made on the other wing) and went on to win. 15 d7! ♗b7 16 ♕d6 e4 17 ♘d5! ♗g7 18 ♘g5 ♘d4 19 ♘e7+ ♔h8 20 ♖h3! and Shirov

went on to win in brilliant style. This game can be found in the second collection of Shirov's best games, *Fire on Board, Part 2*, which is a must-read for anyone trying to improve their attacking skills.

13 ♔b1?!

13 h4!? was Shirov's choice against Morozevich in Astana 2001. I'm not convinced that ♔b1 is necessary. That game went 13...exd5 14 ♘xd5 ♘c6 15 h5 h6 16 ♖h3 f4 17 ♖h4 ♘b4?! 18 ♘xb4 ♕xd2+ 19 ♖xd2 cxb4 20 ♖xf4 ♗e6 21 ♘d4 ♗xd4 22 ♖dxd4 ♖ac8 23 b3 and Shirov went on to convert the extra pawn despite stout defence. However Lutz deviates first – of course he would have been aware of that game and was presumably afraid of an improvement. Nevertheless in any case it was dangerous to play this line against Moro – who must have studied it intensely after his loss to Shirov. There's nothing more motivating than a chastening defeat!

13...exd5 14 ♘xd5

14 cxd5?! would allow Black to lash out on the queenside with 14...b5!

14...♘c6

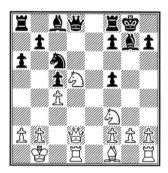

Black's kingside pawn structure resembles one of Salvador Dali's creations – after a few too many glasses of chianti. However there are plenty of dynamic opportunities waiting to be unleashed in his position, with the dark squared bishop on g7 continually on the look out to strike at the white king.

15 h4 b5 16 h5

Grandmasters would be wary of the pawn grab 16 cxb5 axb5 17 ♗xb5 on principle – as it opens up the game in Black's favour. In fact I doubt if Lutz even really examined the possibility as it just looks too risky. Play might continue 17...♘d4! 18 ♘xd4 (18 ♗c4 ♗e6 19 ♘e3 f4!) 18...♕xd5 (18...cxd4 19 ♘f4) 19 ♘b3 ♕e4+! 20 ♕d3 (20 ♗d3 ♕a4 is overpowering) 20...♗e6 21 ♕xe4 fxe4 and with both of the black bishops raking the queenside, he clearly has more than enough for a solitary pawn.

16...h6 17 ♖h3 f4

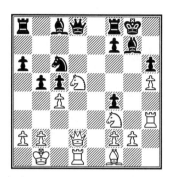

Now we have almost the exact position as that which occurred in the Shirov-Moro game – the only change being the moves ♔b1 thrown in for White and ...b5 for Black. But does this make a big difference?

18 ♕xf4?

Most likely Lutz considered these lines too dangerous for him. As I've mentioned previously, grandmasters will use their experience to dismiss a move on intuitive grounds – and in this case lines where White has to play b3 to shore up his king seem unpalatable in view of the bishop on g7. I've lost track of the number of times I have played strong grandmasters and they make a reply quickly in what seems a complicated position; it's like they have a sixth sense of which positions are playable and which are not. Although this intuition can only be cultivated through many hours of study and practice, it does also develop confidence. However as

Lutz fails to gain enough compensation in the game, 18 ♖h4 should have been preferred. The question then is would Moro have then come up with an improvement on ...♘b4? Let's put ourselves in Lutz's shoes. What went through his mind in this position? (assuming that this was not still part of his preparation) It's important that the white rook doesn't have access to the g4 square, so

A) 18...♖b8!? "Now he's threatening ...bxc4 and ...♖xb2, I need a good answer to this." 19 b3 (19 cxb5 axb5 20 ♖xf4)

A1) 19...♗f5+ is possible, then:

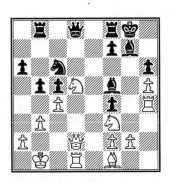

A1a) 20 ♗d3 bxc4! looks scary (On 20...♗xd3+ 21 ♕xd3 bxc4 22 ♕xc4 ♘a5 23 ♕xc5) 21 ♗xf5 cxb3 there is 22 a4! (22 axb3 ♖xb3+ 23 ♔c1 ♘d4 with very serious counterplay) Does it stop here? No! 22...♘d4! 23 ♗e4 (23 ♘xd4? ♕xd5!) 23...♘c2!! 24 ♕c1 (24 ♘c3 ♘a3+ 25 ♔b2 ♘c4+) 24...♕a5!

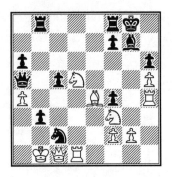

with overwhelming threats.

A1b) 20 ♔c1 What attacking ideas does Black have now? I like 20...♘b4, and if he takes, then ...♕f6!. But can he ignore ...♘b4 and simply take on f4 with the rook?

A1b1) 20...♘b4

A1b11) 21 ♘xb4? ♕f6!! 22 ♘d3 (22 ♘d4 cxd4 23 ♖xf4 d3!) 22...♕a1+ 23 ♔c2 ♕b2 mate;

A1b12) 21 ♖xf4! ♕a5!? 22 ♖xf5 ♘xa2+ 23 ♔b1 (23 ♔c2 ♘b4+ 24 ♘xb4 cxb4) 23...♘b4 24 ♘e5! "So it doesn't look as if ...♘b4 quite works";

A1b2) 20...♘d4;

A2) On 19...bxc4 20 ♗xc4

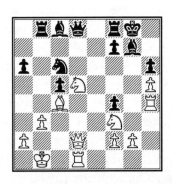

… he has

A2a) 20...♘a5! "This is the real problem, just simple moves"

A2a1) 21 ♕xf4 ♘xc4 22 ♕xc4 (22 ♕xb8 ♗f5+! 23 ♔c1 ♗b2 mate) 22...♗f5+ 23 ♔c1 ♕a5;

A2a2) 21 ♖xf4 ♘xc4 22 ♖xc4 ♗f5+ 23 ♔c1 ♖e8 with a very dangerous initiative for just a pawn, as White's king is permanently stuck in the centre.

A2b) 20...♗f5+! "and I have to go to the ugly square c1" but is 21 ♔c1 (not 21 ♗d3 ♕xd5) playable?

A2b1) 21...♘b4 that old idea again: 22 ♖xf4 (22 ♕xf4!? ♘xa2+ 23 ♔d2 ♗e6 looks a complete mess; while 22 ♘xb4 ♕f6! is very similar to the previous line: 23 ♗d3 cxb4 24 ♗xf5 ♖fc8+!) 22...♕a5 23 ♖xf5 (23 ♘xb4 ♕a3+ -+) 23...♘xa2+ 24 ♔c2 (or 24 ♔b1) "and I don't see where the attack is going".

A2b2) 21...♗e4 22 ♖xf4 (22 ♕xf4 ♗xf3 23 gxf3 ♘e5∞) 22...♗xf3 23 ♖xf3 ♘d4 24 ♖g3 ♔h8;

B) 18...bxc4! 19 ♗xc4 (19 ♖xf4?! ♖b8; 19 ♕xf4 ♖b8 20 ♘c3 ♕a5!) 19...♖b8 transposes to the main lines of 18...♖b8 without giving White the additional possiblity of 19...cxb5 20 b3 (20 ♘c3 ♗xc3!);

C) 18...♗f5+ 19 ♗d3 ♗xd3+ 20 ♕xd3 won't do. Even after 20...♖b8 White has 21 ♖g4 when 21...bxc4 22 ♕c3 kills the 'attack' dead in its tracks, while White turns

his attention to the black king.

18...♗xh3 19 gxh3 ♔h8

So Lutz has sacrificed the exchange. What compensation does he have? Well, if he can play ♗d3 and ♕f5 it'll be a snap mate on the light squares. The problem he faces is time – he never gets enough of it to carry out these ideas. Black will keep making threats to distract White from building up his own attack, until the extra exchange is felt more and more.

20 ♖d2

20 ♗d3 looks like a worthy reply. How would you meet this move? 20...bxc4! Of course! Then 21 ♕xc4 ♖b8 22 b3 (On 22 ♖d2 simplest is 22...♘d4! cutting off the queen's retreat to d4.) and I go back to what I said before about White not wanting to play this move under any circumstances: 22...♘a5! 23 ♕e4 (23 ♕xc5 ♖c8! and the knight drops on d5) 23...f5 24 ♕e6 c4 25 ♘f4 (25 ♗xf5 cxb3) 25...cxd3 26 ♘g6+ ♔h7-+;

20...bxc4 21 ♗xc4 ♖b8!

Now it is clear that Black is on top as White is hard pressed to find any counterplay.

22 a3

The problem with 22 ♕f5 is that Black has 22...♕c8! (A 'safety net' move, i.e. one that is without risk. If you have calculated other lines and have come to no clear assessment, then you can fall back on a safety net.) 23 ♕xc8 ♖fxc8 24 ♗xa6 ♖d8 and Black is probably winning the endgame as ...♗xb2 is already a threat. Play might continue 25 b3 ♘d4! 26 ♘xd4 ♖xd5 27 ♘f3 ♖xh5∓

It should be noted that 22...♘e7? fails to 23 ♘xe7 ♖xb2+ 24 ♔c1! (It's easy to overlook this move when calculating 22...♘e7. On the other hand, not 24 ♖xb2 ♕d1 mate) 24...♖xd2 25 ♘xd2 ♕xe7 26 ♗d3.

22...♘a5!

Lutz has no time to draw breath!

23 ♗a2

White's plan of playing ♗d3 and ♕f5 has clearly failed, but no better was 23 ♗f1 because of the counter-sacrifice 23...♖xb2+!! as after 24 ♖xb2 ♕xd5 the white king is stripped bare.

In fact 23...♘b3 should also suffice: 24 ♖d1 (24 ♖d3 c4 25 ♕xc4 ♘a5-+) 24...♘d4!

A) 25 ♘e3 ♖xb2+ 26 ♔xb2 ♘xf3+ (26...♕b6+!? 27 ♔c1 ♖b8 28 ♔d2 ♕a5+ 29 ♔d3 ♕xa3+ 30 ♔e4 ♖e8+ 31 ♔d5 ♕b3+ is an amusing king hunt);

B) 25 ♘c3 ♕a5! and a quick kill is on the cards.

23...♖b7!

Intending ...♕b8, barrelling up pressure against b2.

24 ♕a4

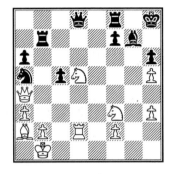

24...♕c8

With this move Black takes advantage of White's lack of co-ordination to threaten ...♕f5. Yet 24...♕b8! is perhaps an even cleaner kill. Black is having a lot of fun in this position as 25 ♕xa5? fails to 25...♖xb2+ 26 ♔c1 ♖xa2! 27 ♖xa2 ♕b3-+. So White is forced to weaken his king's position even further with 25 b4. A lot of players wouldn't even look at such a move but it's White's only chance even if 25...cxb4 26 axb4 ♖b5 still seems to be winning for Black (but not 26...♗c3? 27 ♕xa5 ♗xb4 28 ♘xb4 ♖xb4+ 29 ♔a1 which is unclear).

25 ♘e3

25 ♕xa5 ♕f5+ 26 ♔c1 ♕xf3-+

25...♖b5

Now a crude pile up on the b-file is threatened (along with a lot of other nasty things) by 25...♕b7 and 26...♖fb8. There is no defence.

26 ♕e4

26 ♗c4 ♘xc4 27 ♕xc4 (27 ♘xc4 ♕f5+) 27...♕xh3.

26...♕b8 27 ♘d1 ♘b3 28 ♗xb3 ♖xb3 29 ♔a2 c4 30 ♘d4 ♖d8!

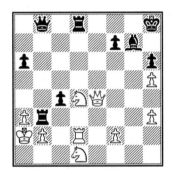

Note how, seemingly by magic, Morozevich seems to include all his pieces in the attack at some stage.

31 ♔a1

31 ♘c6 ♖xd2 32 ♘xb8 ♖dxb2+ 33 ♘xb2 ♖xb2+ 34 ♔a1 ♖e2+.

31...♖d3 0-1

Another terrific counterattacking game by Moro.

Chapter 6

Vishy Anand – Speed Superstar

Viswanathan Anand, from Chennai in India, is a chess phenomenon. He first gave notice of his extraordinary talent when he almost defeated Anatoly Karpov in their World Championship Candidates match in 1991, despite having only a fraction of his opponent's match experience. With his lightning quick sight of the board and remarkable tactical flair, Vishy would often blitz his opponents whilst himself using very little time on the clock. In fact it was often the case that his opponents would be a state of bewilderment as they got crushed by an opponent who needed as little as five minutes thinking time. Though this was practically unheard of in the polite circles of grandmaster play, Vishy's super-fast play wasn't born of arrogance as he is known to be one of the most likeable and affable of the top players. It was simply the case that Anand had a superior talent, and what came easily to him took much longer, or not to all, to others. I first saw Anand in 1995 at the PCA Intel Grand Prix in London. During his semi-final match with Alexey Dreev, I was struck by the feeling that this was a player with a gift and talent for chess that I had never seen before. Remarkably he went on to lose that match, but I suppose that's the random element of rapidplay for you. However, in the following game against the same opponent, he makes no such mistake.

25

A.Dreev – V.Anand

Candidates match, Madras 1991

Queen's Indian Defence

1 d4 ♘f6 2 c4 e6 3 ♘f3 b6 4 ♘c3 ♗b7 5 a3 d5 6 cxd5 ♘xd5 7 ♕c2

Dreev is an expert in the Petrosian variation of the Queen's Indian, and as is often the case, it was Garry Kasparov who came up with many new ideas in this system for White.

7...♘xc3 8 bxc3 ♗e7 9 e3 ♘d7 10 ♗d3 c5 11 0-0 ♖c8 12 ♕e2 0-0 13 e4 ♕c7 14 ♖e1 ♖fd8

The lines of battle are drawn. White has more space and control of the centre, and the possibility of playing on both sides of the board. One idea, utilising the rook on a1, is simply to play a4-a5-axb6, softening up Black's queenside. Another standard idea is ♗b2, giving extra support to the d4 pawn. Black, on the other hand, has a very solid position with no real weaknesses and straightforward development. He will try to restrain the white centre and hope to be given targets later on.

15 ♗d2

In light of what I just said, 15 a4!? may be more accurate. After all, there is no threat of taking on d4 as upon 15...cxd4 16 cxd4 ♕c3 17 ♗d2 kicks the annoying queen away. There is also 15 ♗b2!? but it is in Black's favour that he has not yet committed himself to cxd4, as then d4-d5 might later become a threat – since the bishop would be targeting g7. However this idea is fairly pointless if the bishop is blocked by the pawn on c3. I seem to remember

Kasparov winning a famous game against Portisch in this variation, where he put the bishop on b2 and later broke through with d5. Dreev possibly feared a later ...♘f8-♘g6, threatening ...♘f4, which will force the slightly weakening move g3. In such positions, where there is no immediate clash of the opposing forces, identifying candidate moves is not so much about noticing hidden tactics but rather about overall understanding and an intuitive feel for the opening – since at this stage it is impossible to see the difference between having the bishop on b2 and on d2.

15...e5!

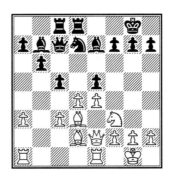

Anand, not noted for his love of passive defence, immediately counterattacks in the centre. What candidate moves for White can be identified now?

16 d5?!

Black had a genuine threat of taking twice on d4, so to that end something like 16 a4? cxd4 17 cxd4 exd4 18 ♘xd4 ♘e5 really won't do.

16 ♖ac1!? (or 16 ♖ec1!? so the rook on a1 defends a3) 16...♕b8?! (16...exd4 17 cxd4 ♕b8 18 d5 ♗f6 19 ♖ab1± ; 16...cxd4! 17 cxd4 ♕b8 18 d5∞) can then be met by 17 d5! as c4 is no longer possible.

16...c4

Forced, otherwise White will play c4 himself and support the centre, after which he can build up his game at his leisure. The problem White now faces is that both bishops are fairly passive; if you take away the c4 and c3 pawns here you would get a much better version for White, as the light-squared bishop would have more freedom of movement – for example it can go to the queenside.

17 ♗c2 ♗a6

Just in case, Anand prevents any idea of ♗a4, as then there is ...b5. Anand has also a high-level positional feel, and here he borrows from Nimzowitsch, over-protecting the c4 pawn, which in turn frees the queen and rook on c8 for subsequent active operations.

18 ♗e3 ♗c5! 19 ♘h4 g6

Now it is hard for White to think up an active plan. Playing on the kingside with g3 and f4 always entails a large element of risk, since his king is stationed over there and may be vulnerable to a counterattack. Nevertheless, this may have been an improvement on the game

20 ♕g4?!

This pseudo-active move doesn't really achieve anything. When you can't do anything in particular with your pieces you should think about pushing your pawns! I'm sure Karpov would have played here 20 g3!, slightly improving his position, followed by ♔g2 (or even ♘g2!?) or ♖f1, followed later by f4 etc. g3 accomplishes two goals – it gives *luft* for the king, and also provides more options for the knight on h4.

20...♔h8!

A typically strong, 'Karpovian' prophylactic king move from Anand.

21 ♗g5

It was not too late to revert to the correct plan with 21 g3!. It soon becomes all too apparent that White cannot breach Black's defence by 'brute force'.

21...f6 22 ♗h6 ♖g8 23 ♖ad1

23 ♕e6 ♖ce8 24 ♕f7? ♖e7.

23...♗d6 24 ♗a4?! ♘c5 25 ♗c6

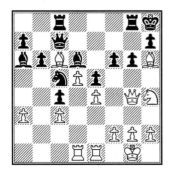

25...♗b7!

Grandmasters often think in terms of which pieces to exchange, or conversely to keep on the board, etc. The finest masters of this art tend to be those with the best positional feel for the game. White wants to weaken the light squares, but I'm not convinced that this exchange helps him as Black's bishop was fairly passive on a6. It also hands the black knight a virtually permanent jumping off point on d3.

26 ♕f3

26 ♗xb7 ♕xb7 27 ♖e3 ♘d3! 28 ♖f3 ♕e7 29 ♖h3 (29 ♕e6 ♕xe6 30 dxe6 ♗e7) 29...♕f7 and there is no way through.

26...♕e7

26...♗e7? would of course be a blunder: 27 d6! ♕xc6 (27...♗xd6 28 ♕xf6+ +-) 28 dxe7±

27 ♗xb7 ♘xb7 28 ♕h3

What's clear is that White has run out of active ideas and can only watch passively as Black improves his position.

28...♖c7!

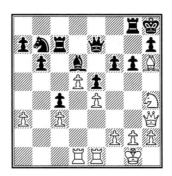

Again very Karpovian. Anatoly Karpov was a master of playing little moves to quietly improve his position.

29 f4?

Aware of the danger of just passively awaiting his fate, Dreev lashes out – but this simply accelerates his defeat. But then it wasn't clear what he could do about the threat of taking on a3, as 29 a4 ♘c5 (29...♖c5!? intending ...♖c5 and ...♘c5, gulping the a pawn, was another option, e.g. 30 ♗e3 ♖a5 31 ♖a1 ♗c5!) 30 ♖a1 ♘d3 31 ♖e3 ♗c5 32 ♖f3 a6!? and Black is in control. The line up of white pieces on the h-file now looks pretty pointless.

29...exf4 30 e5 ♗xe5 31 ♗xf4

31 ♘f3 ♕c5+ 32 ♔h1 ♗xc3-+

31...♕c5+ 32 ♗e3 ♕d6 33 ♗d4

33 ♘f3 ♗xc3.

33...♗xd4+ 34 ♖xd4 ♘c5 35 ♖xc4 ♕xd5

Not only is Black a pawn to the good, but his pawn structure is vastly superior. The rest is simply an exercise in technique for Anand.

36 ♖d4 ♕f7 37 ♘f3 ♖e7 38 ♖f1 ♕e6! 39 ♕h4 ♖ge8 40 h3 ♔g8

Again, small improvements. 'Just in case' Black avoids any variations where White takes on f6 with check and prepares to move the king towards the centre for any endgame.

41 ♖e1 ♕f7 42 ♖f1 ♖e4 43 ♕h6 ♕g7 44 ♕c1 ♖e2 45 ♖d6 ♘e4 46 ♖d3 ♘c5 47 ♖d6 ♕e7! 48 ♕d1 ♕e3+ 49 ♔h2 ♕f4+ 50 ♔g1 ♕g3 51 ♕d5+ ♔h8 52 ♘d4 ♖xg2+

Winning another pawn, and the game.

53 ♕xg2 ♕xd6-+ 54 ♕f3 f5 55 ♖d1 ♕e5 56 ♘c6 ♕e3+ 57 ♔g2 ♕g5+ 58 ♔f1 ♘e4 59 ♕d3 ♕f4+ 0-1

In 2009 Anand defeated Kramnik to become the 'undisputed' world champion (Kramnik holding the non-FIDE version after defeating Kasparov) and any cursory examination of the games in that match might suggest to the casual observer that Kramnik is some sort of patzer who can barely move the pieces, while Anand is by far the strongest chess player ever. However it's not as simple as that, and there's probably not much between the two, only that a match can often become one-sided when one player collapses psychologically as the other guy gets on top. In fact Kramnik has since bounced back with some fine tournament results and no doubt will be a force at the very highest level for many years to come. Anand has always been very dangerous with the white pieces and I recall the Russian grandmaster Vladimir Epishin telling me that while Anand is generally happy to take a draw with Black against strong grandmasters, like most Russians he is quite capable of winning 'to order' when he has the advantage of the first move...

26

V.Anand – I.Rogers

Interzonal, Manila 1990

French Defence

1 e4 e6 2 d4 d5 3 e5 b6 4 ♗b5+

The idea of this move is to displace the black bishop, so that ...♗a6 is not possible. Black is cramped, so exchanging bishops is in his favour – not to mention the fact that his queen's bishop is generally considered to be bad in the French, as it is blocked by the pawns on e6 and d5.

4...♗d7

After 4...c6 5 ♗a4 White avoids the exchange of bishops and can follow later with c3 and ♗c2. Meanwhile White can meet 5...♗a6 with 6 ♘e2.

5 ♗d3 c5 6 c3 ♘c6 7 ♘f3 f6?!

7...cxd4 8 cxd4 ♗b4+ 9 ♗d2± ; but 7...f5!? has its points.

8 0-0 fxe5 9 dxe5 ♕c7 10 ♖e1 ♘h6 11 c4 d4 12 ♘a3 a6 13 ♗e4

13...0-0-0!

Of course it looks extremely risky putting your king in the line of fire against someone like Anand, especially when Black has already weakened his queenside with the moves ...b6 and ...a6. But White was threatening ♕c2 in any case, exerting pressure on h7. So we have to ask ourselves, what prompted Rogers into castling queenside? What was he afraid of?

If 13...♘f7 14 ♗f4 ♗e7 15 ♘c2 g6 (15...0-0 16 ♕d3 g6 17 ♗xg6 hxg6 18 ♕xg6+ ♔h8 19 ♖e4 with an attack.) 16 b4 with the initiative;

13...g6?!

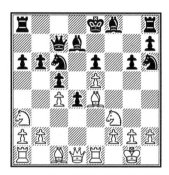

...is the move Black would like to play but unfortunately it has a tactical flaw. If permitted, Black will play ...♗g7, 0-0 and ...♘f7 (or ...♘f5 if the white queen goes to c2) which of course allows White the additional possibility of ♘b5, but this is not so dangerous in itself (though it may be if combined with other ideas). White now has any number of candidate moves: 14 ♕d3, 14 ♕c2 14 ♗f4, 14 ♗g5, 14 ♘c2, 14 b4 and 14 ♘g5 14 h4 – that's a lot to look at!

A) 14 ♗f4 ♗g7 15 b4 0-0∓;

B) 14 ♕d3 ♘f7! (14...♘f5 15 g4) 15 h4 ♗g7∞;

C) 14 ♕c2 ♘f7 is similar (although ♕c2 is slightly inaccurate as the knight may want to go to that square);

D) 14 ♗f4 ♗g7 15 ♕d2 ♘f7 16 h4 0-0 17 h5 ♘e7!? 18 ♗xa8

♖xa8 is an interesting sacrifice, Black has easy play with ...♗c6, ...♖f8 and ...♘f5, etc.

E) 14 ♗g5 ♗g7 15 ♗f6? (15 ♕d2) 15...♗xf6 16 exf6 0-0 17 ♕d2 ♘g4;

F) 14 ♘c2 ♗g7 15 b4 0-0 16 b5 axb5 17 cxb5 ♘e7 18 ♗xa8 ♖xa8 and with two monsters on c5 and d4, Black has more than enough for the exchange;

G) 14 b4! is surely the move that Rogers feared as White creates an immediate threat of b5. Then if 14...cxb4 15 ♘b5! (15 ♘c2! is also good, e.g. 15...♗g7 16 ♘cxd4 0-0 17 ♗xc6 ♗xc6 18 ♘xe6.) 15...axb5 (15...♕b8 16 ♗xh6 ♗xh6 17 ♘d6+ with an attack.) 16 cxb5 ♗g7 17 bxc6 ♗xc6 18 ♕c2 ♖c8 19 ♗xc6+ ♕xc6 20 ♕xc6+ ♖xc6 21 ♘xd4 looks very strong as e6 drops;

H) 14 ♘g5!? (This would not be possible after Black castles queenside, as then the e5 pawn is simply dropping to the knight on c6.) 14...♗g7 15 ♘b5!? axb5 16 cxb5 with a dangerous initiative.

14 ♘c2!

Now White threatens b4 – which is necessary if he wants to rip the black king asunder.

14...♘f7 15 ♗f4 ♗e7 16 b4! g5! 17 ♗g3

17...g4

Not a bad move in itself but Black may have had a stronger option with 17...cxb4! Although this seems to open the game in White's favour, things aren't so clear...

A) 18 ♘fxd4 ♘cxe5 19 ♕h5 ♗d6∞ (19...♘xc4 20 ♕xf7);

B) 18 ♗xc6 ♗xc6 19 ♘fxd4 (19 ♘cxd4 g4) 19...h5! with strong counterplay (19...♗c5?! 20 ♕g4) 20 h3 ♗c5;

C) 18 ♘cxd4

C1) 18...g4!? 19 ♘h4 (19 ♗xc6 ♗xc6 20 ♘xe6 ♖xd1; 19 ♕a4 ♘b8);

C2) 18...♘xd4 19 ♘xd4 ♗c5 20 ♘b3 h5 21 ♕f3 ♖df8.

The problem in such positions, when both White and Black have a variety of options on each move, is seeing your way through the morass of complications – and so choosing the best line isn't at all easy.

18 ♘d2

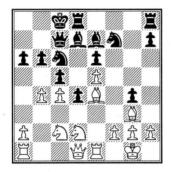

18...♘cxe5?

Rogers cannot resist the temptation and grabs the e-pawn – but at the least opportune moment! Best was 18...h5! when, if White continues as in the game with 19 a4, well, for one thing, there is simply 19...cxb4 20 a5 ♘xa5 21 ♘xd4 ♗c5 (21...h4 22 ♗f4 ♗c5 23 ♘2b3 ♘xb3 24 ♘xb3 a5 25 ♕xg4±) 22 ♘4b3 ♘xb3 23 ♘xb3 a5 24 ♗h4 and it's a bit of a mess – although Black's kingside play has been brought to a halt he is still a pawn to the good. Black can play 24...♘xe5! for example.

On the other hand 18...cxb4 is met by 19 ♕xg4! when White gets rid of an annoying pawn and is able to continue with his attack: 19...h5 (19...♘cxe5 20 ♕h5±) 20 ♕e2! (20 ♕g7? ♖df8 and her majesty is in danger of being trapped) 20...h4 21 ♗f4.

After the move played in the game, however, Anand is given the chance that he has been waiting for

– to attack the black king!

19 a4! cxb4

On 19...a5 follows 20 bxa5 bxa5 21 ♘a3! and ♘b5 is coming with a huge positional advantage.

And 19...h5 is met by 20 a5 h4 21 ♗xe5 ♘xe5 22 axb6 ♕xb6 23 bxc5 ♗xc5 24 ♖b1.

20 a5!

No point stopping now!

20...bxa5 21 ♘xd4

21...♗c5

Practically forced. After 21...h5 what would you do now as White? 22 c5! Attack! 22...♗xc5 23 ♕e2 and the black king is prised open in a very nasty way. 23...♕b6

A) 24 ♘c4!? ♗xc4 25 ♕xc4 ♗b5 26 ♕xe6+ ♕xe6 27 ♘xe6 ♗b6 28 ♖ac1+ ♔d7 29 ♘xd8 (29 ♗f5) 29...♖xd8? 30 ♗f5 mate;

B) 24 ♖ec1 ♔b8 25 ♖xc5 ♕xc5 26 ♕xa6 ♕a7 (26...♗c8 27 ♕a8+ ♔c7 28 ♘2b3) 27 ♕d6+ ♕c7

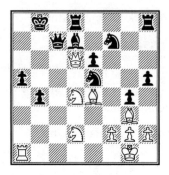

28 ♕xb4+!!

22 ♘4b3! a4 23 ♘xc5 ♕xc5 24 ♗c2!

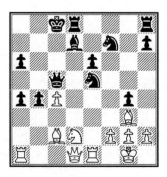

While at first sight it would seem as if White has just given his opponent two connected passed pawns, in fact the exposed nature of Black's king is the decisive factor. White has many threats: ♗xa4, ♘e4 etc.

24...a5

24...b3!? is an obvious try that falls short. 25 ♗xb3! is the problem – the a-file is opened after which the heavy pieces flood in. 25...axb3 26 ♘xb3 ♕c7 (otherwise the knight on e5 drops off)

A) 27 ♕d4 ♗a4;

B) 27 ♖xa6 ♗b5 (27...♗c6 28 ♕a1)

B1) 28 cxb5?! ♖xd1 29 ♖xd1 ♕b7 (29...♕c2 30 ♖c1 ♕xc1+ 31 ♘xc1 ♖d8 32 ♖a8+ ♔d7 33 ♖xd8+ ♔xd8 34 ♘e2 is a winning endgame for White.) and Black should be able to defend;

B2) 28 ♕a1 ♗xa6 29 ♕xa6+ ♕b7 30 ♕xe6+ ♕d7 31 ♕a6+ ♕b7 32 ♕e6+;

C) 27 ♕e2! and White regains the piece with an overwhelming advantage.

Finally there is 24...a3 25 ♖xe5! ♘xe5 26 ♘e4! ♕a5 (26...♕b6 27 ♘d6+) 27 ♘d6+ ♔b8 28 ♘f7 – a line that reveals the latent power of the bishop on g3.

25 ♘e4?

Although he is still winning after this move, Anand missed an immediate kill here with 25 ♖xe5!! (The silicon monster finds this instantly of course.) which would have been a fitting conclusion to an excellently played attack. After 25...♘xe5 26 ♘e4 the knight on e5 drops. There is a lesson here: when you see a line that seems to be winning, don't play it straight away – look around for something that might be even stronger. It's very easy to get nervous when you have a winning position, then rush things and end up blowing the win completely.

25...♕c7 26 ♗xa4

Despite Anand's inaccuracy, Rogers' king is too exposed to expect to survive in the long run.

26...♗c6 27 ♕c2 ♗b7

27...♖d4 28 ♘g5 ♖xc4 29 ♕b2! ♗xa4 30 ♘xf7 ♕xf7 31 ♕xe5+-

28 c5 ♖d5

28...♗xe4 29 ♕xe4 ♖d5 30 ♗b3.

29 ♗b3 ♖hd8

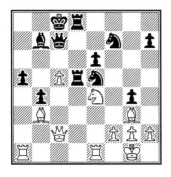

Now there are a lot of wins. 30 ♕a2, 30 ♗xd5 and 30 ♘d6+, to name a few. Anand prefers simply to build up his attacking force.

30 ♖ac1 ♕c6 31 ♗a4 ♕c7 32 ♘d6+ ♖8xd6 33 cxd6 ♕xc2 34 ♖xc2+ ♔b8

34...♔d8 35 ♗h4+

35 ♗b3

Everything falls apart.

35...♖xd6? 36 ♖xe5

A nice attack by Anand, even if he spoiled it slightly by missing 25 ♖xe5!! (Though I have no idea of the times used for this game, I doubt Anand took more than a millisecond to play 25 ♘e4, so probably had no time to look for alternatives!)

1-0

Psychology in chess

How important is psychology in chess? Very important. We've already seen how a player can limit himself through negative psychology. Discussing the subject of Anand, I wonder what was the primary reason he had such a terrible record against Kasparov – apart from the obvious, that Kasparov is a terrifyingly gifted chessplayer. In terms of the rating difference between them and the fact that Anand had a much worse record than Kramnik had against Gazza, some explanation is needed. I think it comes down to basic psychology. To put it bleakly, Anand was out-psyched by Kasparov (who incidentally had an even better record against Shirov for more or less the same reasons). Kasparov was a Mike Tyson, a bully of the chess board who simply didn't have a reverse button, and many a wounded prey were intimidated by that. He would back up his moves on the board – which he infused with a kind of demonic quality – with machismo strutting off it and an intimidating stare and presence. A nice guy like Anand had great difficulty handling this and once Kasparov got on top psychologically he wouldn't let go. In fact I think it's no fluke that this best part of Anand's career has coincided with Kasparov's retirement – it must have been a mental drain to continually have this one guy get in the way of your ultimate success – or to quote Yeats, "to tread on your dreams". But getting back to general psychology – how does a player best react to a defeat? After all I sometimes feel more pain after a loss than I ever would feel joy from a victory – losing can really ravage the soul. In chess there is no hiding place – you lose at football, you can blame your team mates, in poker the cards. It is my belief that during a tournament a player should always try to adopt a positive psychology – it's too easy to get dragged down if you do the opposite, to get devoured by your demons. If you start moaning, start complaining, start losing interest – then everything is a negative spiral. Jonathan Rowson

once gave me some useful advice: when you see your pairing for the next tournament game, the first thought going through your head is the most important. If you think in a negative way "God, I hate playing him" etc then it's more than likely to trigger a whole host of negative thoughts, which will lead to your eventual defeat. Similarly – the opposite is true!

27

V.Anand – G.Serper

PCA World Championship, Groningen 1993

Sicilian Defence

1 e4 c5 2 ♘f3 d6 3 d4 cxd4 4 ♘xd4 ♘f6 5 ♘c3 ♘c6 6 ♗g5 e6 7 ♕d2 a6 8 0-0-0 h6

8...♗d7 is an alternative. After 9 f3 h6 10 ♗e3 h5!? can be played, to prevent g4.

9 ♗e3 ♗e7 10 f3 ♘xd4 11 ♗xd4 b5 12 ♔b1 ♖b8

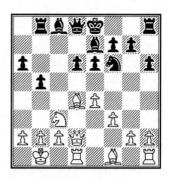

13 ♕e3

Remarkably, White has no less than 8(!) other tries in this position: 13 ♗a7, 13 c5, 13 ♗xf6, 13 ♕f2, 13 ♕e1, 13 g4, 13 h4, and 13 ♗d3.

13 ♗a7 is probably the main move. Then on 13...♖b7 comes 14 ♗e3 – the idea being that not only does White slightly misplace the rook on b7 (the bishop may wish to go there) but he also gets out of the way of a possible ...e5 by Black, hitting the bishop later on. 14...♕c7 15 g4 ♘d7 16 ♘e2! (A standard re-routing in this line; the knight on c3 isn't doing much, so heads for greener pastures on g3 or d4.) 16...♖b8 17 ♘g3 ♘e5 18 ♗e2 ♘c4 19 ♗xc4 ♕xc4 (19...bxc4 20 ♗d4 e5 21 ♗c3) 20 ♘h5! ♖g8 21 ♖hg1 and White was better in the game Bologan – Obodcuk, Poikovsky 2003.

13 e5?! dxe5 14 ♗xe5 ♕xd2 15 ♖xd2 ♖a8 and Black is fine in the ending;

13 ♗xf6 ♗xf6! was the continuation of the game Anand – Kramnik, Amber blindfold/rapidplay 1996. Black is not afraid of giving up the d-pawn as the time he gains in return is more than sufficient compensation. 14 ♕xd6 ♕xd6 15 ♖xd6 ♔e7 16 ♖d1 ♗xc3 17 bxc3 e5! 18 ♔b2 ♗e6 19 ♗d3 ♖hc8 20 ♖a1 ♖c5 and Kramnik had more than enough for the pawn and went on to win.

Serper, a bit of an expert in this line, had to face 13 ♕f2 on an earlier occasion. After 13...♕a5 14 h4 b4 15 ♘e2 e5 16 ♗a7 ♖b7 17 ♘c1 ♗e6 18 ♘b3 ♕c7 he held on for a draw against Hjartarsson in the World Team Championships, Lucerne 1993.

13...b4 14 ♘a4 ♕c7 15 ♗a7

15 b3 was Kasparov's choice against Kramnik at the Moscow PCA rapid 1996. After 15...0-0 16 ♗d3 e5 17 ♗b2 ♗d7 18 ♗xa6 ♖a8 19 ♕e2 ♗xa4 20 bxa4 ♘d7! Kramnik achieved a comfortable draw.

15...♖b7 16 ♗b6!

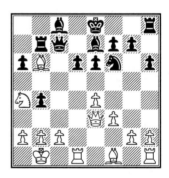

Anand's opening is quite subtle. He displaces the queen so that it will have to move again to make possible a later ...♗d7, gaining a move for White.

16...♕c6

It looks as if Serper misses a trick here with 16...♕b8!? but in fact Anand has everything under control;

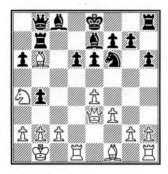

A) 17 ♗a5 looks as if it renews the threat of taking on a6. However Black continues 17...♗d7 18 b3 ♗xa4! (18...♗b5!?) 19 bxa4 0-0 and the bishop is out of play on a5, while 20 ♗xa6? does not work because of the simple 20...♖a7;

B) 17 ♗xa6? ♖xb6! 18 ♗xc8 (18 ♕xb6 ♕xb6 19 ♘xb6 ♗xa6∓) 18...♖c6 and the bishop is trapped.

C) 17 b3! ♗d7 (17...♘d7 18 ♗d4 e5 19 ♗b2 ♖c7 20 ♗c4)

C1) 18 ♗xa6 ♗xa4 19 ♗xb7 ♗b5! and the bishop on b7 is trapped – was this what Serper missed?

C1a) 20 a4 bxa3 21 c4 ♗xc4 (21...♕xb7 22 cxb5 ♘d7 23 ♗d4 e5 24 ♗c3 ♕xb5 25 ♔a2 ♘c5 26 ♖b1 0-0 with compensation) 22 bxc4 ♕xb7 23 ♔a2 0-0 24 ♗d4 ♕c6 is a bit of a mess but again the white king is exposed;

C1b) 20 c4 bxc3 21 a4 ♕xb7 22 axb5 ♘d7 23 ♗d4 ♕xb5 24 ♕xc3 e5 25 ♗e3 0-0 and the white king is somewhat exposed;

C2) 18 ♗d4! ♗xa4 (18...♕a8? is very passive – for one thing there is ♘b6. There is also 18...♗b5. Black doesn't capture the knight on a4 as it holds up his queenside counterplay. 19 g4!? and White will play h4, g5 etc, when his kingside play is more relevant.) 19 bxa4 0-0 (19...e5 20 ♗b2 a5 21 ♗b5+ ♘d7 22 g4 0-0 23 h4±) 20 ♗xa6± when the bishop will return to b5, if need be, to hold the a4 pawn. White has easy play here with g4, h4, and g5, which can be conducted on auto-pilot.

17 b3

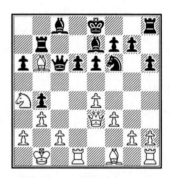

17...0-0

17...♘d7 18 ♗d4; while 17...e5 is an attempt to strand the b6 bishop in enemy territory. However it fails tactically to 18 ♗xa6! ♖xb6 (18...♖b8 19 ♗xc8 ♖xc8 20 ♕e2) 19 ♗xc8 ♖b8 20 ♗h3 (Now it looks as if the bishop is out of play on h3, but in fact it does a good job of controlling the c8 square, thereby preventing Black from getting any play on the c-file.) 20...0-0 21 c4! (Trying for a bind on d5.) 21...bxc3 (21...♖a8 22 ♕b6!) 22 ♘xc3±

18 ♗d4 e5 19 ♗b2

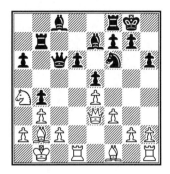

19...♗d7?!

Better is 19...♗e6! with the idea of breaking out with ...d5. It would seem that the plan of hitting the knight on a4 backfires in the game – so perhaps Black should try something a bit more active? Nevertheless it appears that this will not solve his problems either: 20 h4 (20 g4!? ♖c8 21 ♗d3 d5 22 exd5 ♗xd5 creates counterplay – the weak f3 pawn is one reason why Anand delayed playing g4.) 20...d5 (20...♕c7 21 g4 d5 22 exd5 ♘xd5 23 ♕xe5; 20...♖c8 21 ♗d3 ♘h5!; 20...h5!? slows down White's plan of g4, which is why g4 first may be more accurate.) 21 exd5 ♘xd5 22 ♕xe5 ♗f6 23 ♕e4 ♗xb2 24 ♔xb2 and, with ♗d3 coming, Black is struggling to prove he has any compensation.

20 h4?!

20 g4! is actually more accurate, as it prevents the idea of h5.

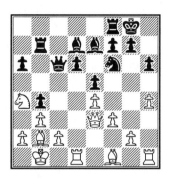

20...♕c7?!

Perhaps something radical needs to be done to stop the white attack in its tracks, e.g. 20...h5!?. It's sometimes these subtle little points that can make the difference between victory and defeat. You should try to put as many obstacles in your opponent's path as possible! But even in this case White can initiate an attack if he shows a bit of imagination and isn't afraid to sacrifice: 21 ♗d3 ♕c7 22 g4! hxg4 23 fxg4 (23 h5 ♗xa4 24 h6 g6 25 h7+ ♔h8 26 bxa4 gxf3 and it is not clear how White should continue the attack.) 23...♘xg4 (23...♕a5 24 g5 ♘h5 25 ♗c4) 24 ♕e2 ♘f6 25 ♖dg1 and White has huge pressure for only a mere pawn. 20...♘h5!? 21 ♗c4 ♗e6!

21 g4

Now all the ideas of ...♘h5, and h5 have been extinguished. White's attack on the kingside plays itself. The question is whether Black can generate enough counterplay on the queenside?

21...♗xa4 22 bxa4 ♘d7 23 ♗xa6

23 g5 h5 24 ♗xa6 ♖a7 25 ♗c4
♘b6 26 ♗b3 g6.

23...♖a7 24 ♗c4 ♘b6

24...♕xc4 25 ♕xa7.

25 ♗b3

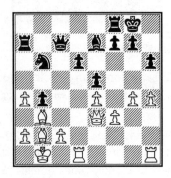

25...♕c5?

This seems a bit slow. 25...♘xa4!
looks critical. 26 g5 ♘xb2 27 ♔xb2
♔h7 (27...♕c3+ 28 ♕xc3 bxc3+
29 ♔xc3 and the a-pawn is going to
be hard to stop in the endgame.)
28 gxh6 gxh6 and it is far from clear
how White can breach the black
kingside, if he can at all.
Nevertheless 29 ♖d3 should still
give a positional advantage for
White, as he has a bind on the white
squares.

**26 ♕e1 ♘xa4 27 ♖d5! ♘c3+
28 ♗xc3 ♕xc3 29 ♕e2!**

Avoiding the exchange as Anand
wants a quick mate! Now, of course,
g5 is threatened.

29...♖fa8?

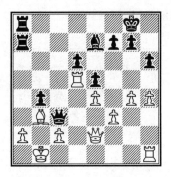

It turns out that this is the final
mistake, as Black 'undefends' f7,
which means that later on ...♔h7 is
not possible.

30 g5! hxg5

Opening the h-file is tantamount to
a form of hara-kiri but Black's
position was beyond repair in any
case; 30...♔h7 31 ♖d3! and f7
drops, which is why the rook would
have been best left on f8.

31 hxg5 ♗xg5 32 ♖xd6

♕h2 is now a threat.

32...♗f4 33 ♕g2 ♕c7

33...♔f8 34 ♖d3 ♕c7 35 ♖h8+
♔e7 36 ♕xg7+–

34 ♖g6

Yet another powerful display by
the Indian, but this game was
notable for the way Serper missed
many interesting possibilities to
slow down White's attack; for
example the ...♘h5 idea earlier on;
and possibly...h5 as well.

1-0

Weaknesses in the castled position and how to exploit them

In the previous game against Serper, we saw how Anand was able to take advantage of just one weakness in the black kingside – the pawn on h6. In the following game Anand faces his old rival Gata Kamsky. This game is also significant in that respect, since Anand ruthlessly targets Kamsky's weakened queenside. Soon after this match, which Anand surprisingly lost after being ahead by a couple of points, the two players' careers headed in different directions. Anand went on to challenge Kasparov for the world crown, while Kamsky, who in his youth was tipped as a future world champion, retired from competitive chess to concentrate on a medical career. Only quite recently did he made a comeback and proceeded to defeat Shirov in the final of the World Cup to earn the right to play a match with Topalov.

28

G.Kamsky – V.Anand

Candidates match,
Sanghi Nagar 1994

Queen's Indian Defence

1 d4 ♘f6 2 c4 e6 3 ♘f3 b6 4 a3 ♗b7 5 ♘c3 d5 6 cxd5 ♘xd5 7 ♗d2 ♗e7 8 ♕c2 0-0 9 e4 ♘xc3 10 ♗xc3

A departure from the Dreev game where White played the somewhat less critical e3. Kamsky is an aggressive 1 d4 player and elects to go for a sharp attack.

10...♘d7 11 0-0-0?!

As the course of this game indicates that castling queenside is in fact extremely risky – the sedate 11 ♖d1! is preferable.

11...c6!

This was a novelty at the time. As always, Anand displays great insight into the position. Being familiar with this line, I once employed it in a rapidplay game – and with success. 11...c6 looks slow (surely Black should be playing ...c5?) but whereas ...c5 allows White to play d5, creating a strong d-pawn, ...c6 restrains the white centre, and more importantly lays the foundations for a counterattack on the queenside with ...b5, ...a5, and ...b4! Of course this whole idea would be ridiculous if the white pawn was still on a2 – but on a3 it forms the basis for Black's counterattack. Such apparently insignificant differences can be decisive!

12 h4 b5!

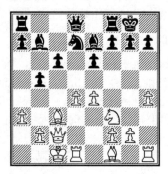

13 ♖h3?!

They say an attack on the wing should be met by an attack in the centre – but what about an attack on the other wing? 13 ♔b1 was tried by the Swedish player Pia Cramling against Z.Almasi, Horgen 1995. However it didn't work out very well for her; 13...a5 14 ♗e1 (14 d5!? was the game Tregubov – R.Akesson, Cap d'Agde 1994, but that turned out well for Black as well: 14...cxd5 15 ♘g5 dxe4 16 ♗xb5 ♗d5 17 ♘xe4 ♕c7 18 ♘g5 ♘f6 and Akesson was probably winning later, although the game ended in a draw.) 14...b4 15 a4 ♖c8 16 ♘g5 c5 17 d5 ♗xg5 18 hxg5 exd5 19 exd5 g6 20 ♗b5 ♘b6 21 d6 c4! and Black's queenside pawns were already looking ominously poised.

13...a5!

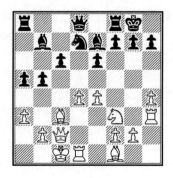

14 d5?!

This move already has an air of desperation about it, but how else to meet the threat of ...b4? It seems to me that White players have yet to solve the problem of this line (if indeed there is a solution).

14 ♔b1 b4 looks horrible for White: 15 axb4 axb4 16 ♗e1 ♕a5 Surely chess can't be this easy?

Also not 14 e5?! b4 15 ♘g5 g6 16 ♗d2 bxa3 17 bxa3 c5! and the queenside will be opened forthwith.

Better is 14 ♗e1

A) 14...♕b6!? 15 ♔b1 b4 16 a4 b3!? 17 ♕c3 c5 18 d5 exd5 19 exd5 ♗f6 20 ♕c1 (20 ♕c4 ♗a6) 20...♗a6 21 ♗c3 ♗xf1 22 ♖xf1 ♖fb8;

B) 14...b4 15 a4 ♖c8 is similar to the Cramling – Almasi game. 16 ♔b1 c5 17 d5 exd5 18 exd5 c4 (or perhaps 18...♘b6) 19 ♗xc4 (19 d6 ♗f6 20 ♘g5 g6) 19...♘b6 20 b3 Could you play such a move against Anand? 20...♕c7 21 ♘g5 (21 ♘d2 ♗xd5∓) 21...g6 22 d6 ♗xd6 23 h5! ♘xc4 24 bxc4 ♗xg2 25 ♖h4.

14...cxd5 15 ♗xb5 ♘f6!

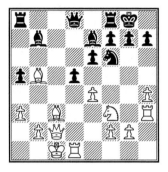

Black already has great control over the centre, not to mention his easy play on the queenside. In a higher sense, it might already be said that Black is winning!

16 ♘g5

Of course, this is Kamsky's idea. However, given how well co-ordinated the black forces are, not surprisingly Anand has prepared a strong rejoinder.

If 16 exd5 ♘xd5 17 ♘g5 ♗xg5+ (17...g6!?) 18 hxg5 ♕xg5+ 19 ♗d2 ♕g6 20 ♗d3 f5–+;

16 e5 is answered by ♘e4.

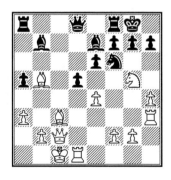

16...♕b6!?

How to refute 16...g6!? was probably the question that Kamsky was concerning himself with in the game. But, as is the problem when you have lost control, your opponent has any number of decent options: 17 e5 (17 ♕a4 ♖c8) 17...♘h5 18 ♕d2 – although perhaps here he could try 18...♕b6.

17 exd5 ♖ac8 18 ♗d7

18 dxe6 ♕xb5 19 exf7+ ♔h8.

18...♗xd5 19 ♗xc8 ♖xc8

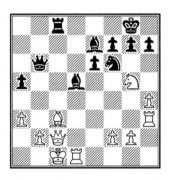

Anand doesn't even have a pawn for the exchange, but this position is very simple to play for Black. On the other hand White's extra exchange consists of a rather haggard rook on h3. Already the white queenside is looking rather sparsely defended, and threats loom at every turn. In desperation Kamsky lashes out.

20 ♖xd5

20 ♖e1 h6 21 ♘f3 ♗c5 and Black enjoys superb compensation, as all his pieces are combining perfectly. 22 ♗xf6 (22 ♗d4 ♗b3!; 22 ♖e2 ♗c4 23 ♖d2 ♘d5) may be an

attempt to bail out to a tenable endgame but 22...gxf6! (22...♗e3+ 23 ♖xe3 ♖xc2+ 24 ♔xc2) is the refutation: 23 ♖g3+ ♔f8 24 ♔b1 ♖c6! and the combined power of the black forces will soon overwhelm White.

20...exd5 21 ♕f5 ♕a6! 22 ♔d2 g6 23 ♕e5 ♖e8 24 ♖e3?

After 24 ♖d3!? Black enjoys a very comfortable existence, with the candidate moves ...h6 and ...♕c4 springing to mind, but at least this would have avoided the loss of the queen...

24...d4 25 ♗xd4 ♗b4+ 26 axb4 ♖xe5 27 ♖xe5

27...♕c4

Now it's simply a technical exercise.

28 ♘f3 ♕xb4+ 29 ♔d3 a4 30 ♘d2 ♕b7 31 f3 ♕a8 32 ♘c4 ♘d5 33 ♘d6 ♘f4+ 34 ♔d2 ♘e6 35 ♗c3 ♕d8

Now the h-pawn drops and it really is all over. Even Kamsky's legendary powers of resistance can't save him here.

36 ♖d5 ♕xh4 37 ♘e4 ♔f8 38 ♗b4+ ♔g7 39 ♖d7 g5 40 ♗c3+ ♔g6 41 ♔e3 h5 42 ♖a7 ♕h2 43 ♔f2 ♕b8 44 ♖a6 ♕c8 45 ♖a5 h4 46 ♘f6 a3 47 ♖xa3 ♕c5+ 48 ♔f1 ♕b5+ 49 ♔g1 ♕e2 50 ♘g4 ♘f4 51 ♘f2 h3 52 ♖a8 h2+ 53 ♔xh2 ♕xf2 0-1

What I found impressive about this game is how effortlessly Anand was able to get a winning position with Black against a very solid grandmaster like Kamsky. In fact, after the strong 11...c6!, it already looks as if White is struggling to equalise!

Anand's opponent in the following game, Alexander Khalifman, the former FIDE world champion, has described Anand as a genius. This may have something to do with the fact that he has been on the wrong end of some chessboard drubbings from the Indian star.

29

V.Anand – A.Khalifman

Las Palmas 1993

Pirc Defence

1 e4 d6 2 d4 g6 3 ♘c3 ♗g7 4 ♗e3 a6!?

This 'modern' move order is extremely popular nowadays, Black intends the flexible ...b5, ...♗b7, ...♘d7. In some lines he will delay the development of the king's knight until he knows better what White's intentions are. It is interesting that Kasparov considered these Pirc and Modern systems to be bordering on dubious. According to the great man, the only really correct ways of meeting 1 e4 are the Sicilan, and 1...e5 – everything else concedes too much space. The French and the Caro are semi-dubious, as they give up some central control, but the Pirc and the Alekhine (1...♘f6) for example, are giving up too much space. Food for thought!

5 ♕d2 b5 6 a4

In similar positions I have played 6 h4!? and if Black plays 6...h5 then 7 ♘f3 and the knight can head for g5, when the only way to remove it is to play the further weakening move ... f6.

6...b4 7 ♘d1 a5 8 c3 bxc3 9 bxc3

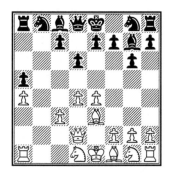

9...♘f6

9...c6 enabled English grandmaster Julian Hodgson to produce one of his imaginative attacking masterpieces against V.Koshy in the British Championship, Dundee 1993, with the game going 10 f3 ♗a6 11 ♗xa6 ♘xa6 12 h4 d5 13 e5 f6?! 14 f4 h5? 15 exf6 exf6 16 f5! gxf5 17 ♘h3 ♘e7 18 0-0 ♘c7 19 ♘f4 ♔f7 20 ♕e2 ♘e8 21 ♗c1! (The bishop re-routes to a more fruitful diagonal.) 21...♕d7 22 ♗a3 ♘c8 23 c4 ♘b6 24 ♖b1!

and Koshy resigned, as 24...♘xc4 allows a pretty finish – 25 ♖b7!! It's a shame that Hodgson has retired from competitive play – he now concentrates on more lucrative chess coaching. There simply isn't enough money in playing these days!

10 f3

10...c6

10...0-0 was the continuation of the rapidplay game Hamdouchi – Azmaiparashivili, Cap d'Agde 1998: 11 ♗d3 ♗a6 12 ♗xa6 ♘xa6?! (12...♖xa6 may have been an improvement – the queen's knight may be better deployed later on the b6 square; on a6 or b4 it doesn't seem to do much.) 13 ♘e2 e5 14 0-0 exd4 15 cxd4 ♘b4 16 ♗h6

♗xh6 17 ♕xh6 c5 18 ♘e3! ♖e8 19 ♘g3 ♔h8 20 dxc5 d5 21 ♖ad1 ♕c7 22 ♘gf5! and Hamdouchi was giving an almost text-book example of how to attack against the Pirc and won a few moves later. I too enjoy playing against such openings – it always seems to me that after the exchange of the dark-squared bishops with ♗e3-h6, the white king will always be much safer than its counterpart – due to the weakened dark squares on Black's kingside.

11 ♗h6 0-0 12 h4!

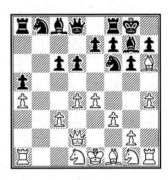

12...e5

12...♗a6!? 13 ♗xa6 ♖xa6 14 ♘e2 ♘bd7 15 h5! ♘b6 (15...♘xh5?? 16 ♖xh5 gxh5 17 ♕g5 is a standard trap) 16 hxg6 fxg6 17 ♗xg7 ♔xg7 18 ♕h6+ ♔g8 (18...♔f7 19 g4!?) 19 ♘f4 and White is getting on top, as there is already a threat of ♘xg6.

12...d5 13 ♗xg7 ♔xg7 14 e5 ♘h5 15 ♘e2 f5 16 ♘f2 f4 17 ♘d3;

12...♗xh6 13 ♕xh6 ♘h5 14 g4 ♘g7 (14...♘g3 15 ♖h3 ♘xf1 16 h5! g5 17 ♕xg5+ ♔h8 18 ♔xf1) 15 h5 gxh5 16 gxh5±

13 h5 ♖e8

What about the greedy try 13...♘xh5 ? How should White then react? 14 ♘e2! (14 ♗xg7 ♔xg7 15 ♘e2 ♕f6!; 14 ♖xh5 gxh5 doesn't work of course, as the black queen covers the g5 square.) 14...♕f6 (14...f5 15 ♗xg7 ♔xg7 16 exf5! ♗xf5 17 g4 nets a piece) 15 ♗g5 ♕e6 16 g4 ♘f6 17 ♘e3! and all sorts of gruesome ideas with ♘f5 are threatened as the queen is poorly placed on e6.

14 hxg6 fxg6

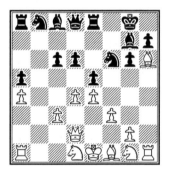

Khalifman must have felt he was defending here. Admittedly White is a long way from delivering mate as his minor pieces are still on the first rank. But the weaknesses Black has incurred on the kingside are already looking critical. 14...hxg6 15 ♗xg7 loses on the spot of course.

15 ♗xg7 ♔xg7 16 ♘f2!

Black is finding it difficult to gain counterplay – his only chance is somehow to lash out in the centre.

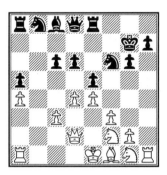

16...♖a7

Somewhat passive. A more confrontational try would have been 16...d5!? but can such a counter-attack succeed when Black's own king is still under fire? Indeed, how should White respond? It would seem there are a few candidate moves – 17 ♗d3, 17 dxe5, 17 ♕h6+, and 17 ♘e2.

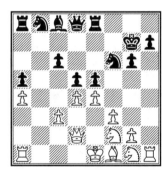

A) 17 ♗d3 exd4 18 cxd4 dxe4 19 fxe4 ♕xd4 is simply bad;

B) 17 dxe5 ♖xe5

B1) 18 ♕h6+ ♔g8 19 f4 ♖h5 (19...♖e7 20 e5 with the advantage as ♗d3 is threatened) 20 ♖xh5 ♘xh5 and with the white rook gone, there is no clear culmination of the attack;

B2) 18 ♘d3 ♗e7 19 e5 ♘bd7 20 ♕h6+ ♔g8 21 f4 ♘e4;

C) 17 ♕h6+ ♔g8 18 dxe5 ♖xe5;

D) 17 ♘e2!?, reinforcing the centre, may be best: then 17...dxe4 18 fxe4 exd4 19 cxd4! and 19...♘xe4? is not an option because of 20 ♕h6+. Put simply, Khalifman did not choose to play ...d5 as this would have opened the position still further – a risky proposition when his king lacks cover.

17 ♖b1! ♗e6?!

17...♗a6 18 ♗xa6 ♘xa6 19 ♘e2 and there is little question of White's advantage after 19...exd4 20 cxd4 (20 ♕xd4 ♘c5) 20...♘b4 21 ♔f1. However this would at least have avoided the passivity of the game continuation.

18 dxe5!

After this capture, Black's game is robbed of much of its dynamism. The pawn structure is cast in White's favour, as the pawns on e4, f3 and g2 are superior to those on e5, g6 and f7.

18...dxe5 19 ♕h6+ ♔g8 20 ♘gh3

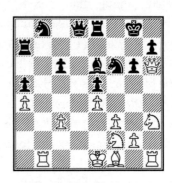

Can such a knight go unmolested?

20...♕e7

Unfortunately, the removal of the potentially marauding beast by 20...♗xh3 also has its complications: 21 ♘xh3 ♕e7 22 ♗c4+ ♔h8 23 ♘g5

A) 23...♖f8 24 ♖xb8! ♖xb8 25 ♘f7+ ♕xf7 (25...♔g8 26 ♘xe5+ ♔h8 27 ♘xg6 mate is a cute finish) 26 ♗xf7 ♖xf7 27 0-0 and the extra material will soon decide matters.

B) 23...♕c5 24 ♕xg6! ♕xc4 25 ♕xf6+ ♔g8 26 ♔f2 ♕xc3 27 ♖xh7! ♕c2+ 28 ♔g3 batters down the king's defences.

21 ♘g5 ♗a2

21...♘h5 22 ♖xh5! gxh5 23 ♘xe6 wins material.

22 ♖b2 ♕a3

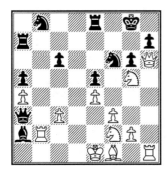

This is Khalifman's idea. With the queen sally he hopes to prove that the delay in the white king's flight to safety has its drawbacks after all. However, not surprisingly, there is a tactical refutation!

23 ♖xa2! ♕xa2 24 ♘xh7!

Dismembering the last lines of defence.

24...♘xh7

24...♖xh7 25 ♕xg6+ ♖g7 26 ♕xf6 ♕b1+ (If 26...♘d7 27 ♕xc6 with the threat of ♗c4, which is hard to meet.) 27 ♘d1 ♘d7 28 ♗c4+

25 ♕xg6+ ♔f8 26 ♖xh7 ♖xh7 27 ♕xh7

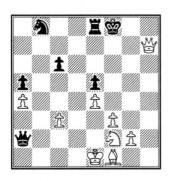

Now, despite being an exchange to the good, the black king has been stripped of all its cover and is defenceless against a barrage of queen checks. To that end Khalifman eschews active defence and decides to retreat his queen.

27...♕g8

27...♕b1+ 28 ♘d1 ♖d8 29 ♕h8+ ♔e7 30 ♕xe5+ ♔f8 31 ♕f6+ ♔e8 32 ♗e2! and there is not much for Black to do...

28 ♕h4 ♘d7

28...♕g7 29 ♘g4 ♘d7 30 ♗c4 ♖b8 31 ♕h5 and White is likely to infiltrate quickly on the light squares.

29 ♘g4 ♕b3 30 ♕h6+ ♔e7 31 ♕xc6 ♕b1+ 32 ♔f2 ♕b2+ 33 ♗e2 ♖b8

34 ♘xe5! 1-0

As 34...♘xe5 35 ♕c5+ ♔e6 36 ♕d5+ wins further material, Khalifman decided he had seen enough. In this game we saw Anand's speciality – a raw attack on the enemy king!

Chapter 7

Bobby, the two K's and Les Enfants Terribles

Bobby Fischer... The name alone evokes a mythical figure of yesteryear. When I first got into chess, Bobby Fischer was the one player who fascinated me. He was always described as 'legendary' and I felt that if I looked up this word in the dictionary it would simply say 'Bobby Fischer'. Here was a man who turned his back on chess, after achieving previously unattained heights – destroying Taimanov and Larsen 6-0 – before routing Petrosian and Spassky. At the time his rating of 2785 was by far the highest in the history of chess – it was not until seventeen years later that this record was broken – by Kasparov. You could make an argument that with inflation (chess inflation brought about by more chess players being added to the Elo rating system, and the inherent anomaly with the k factor) such a rating would be equivalent to 2850+ today. What a tragedy his retirement was! Kasparov speculated that his retreat from public life was the superhuman complex that he had created – that the incredibly high standards he had set for himself couldn't possibly be repeated, and

that he feared the consequences if they weren't. He may well be right, but no one will ever know the real answer. My own guess would be that after winning the world championship title he lost his motivation. As for myself – well it's nice to be a strong player, though of course I still have some further goals. I would like to be 2600. That's my own personal Everest (although I might find myself in the death zone – and slowly dying at that level due to a lack of talent). For 2600 players, it's going to be 2700. For 2700s, it'll have to be world champion. But basically Fischer had no more heights to conquer. He was the world champion, he had crushed everyone around. Kasparov had the extraordinary motivation to be able to keep going at that level for twenty years, but perhaps he's an exception rather than the rule – and even he dropped out eventually to concentrate on politics. In the end Bobby did make a short comeback, but not surprisingly, after twenty years in the wilderness, his chess was in terminal decline – rather like his mental health. Still I shall never forget the excitement I felt when I saw the headline on the front page of the *Daily Telegraph*, after game 1 of the comeback match – Bobby had demolished Spassky in a brilliant game, like those twenty years had never passed and we had been sent back in a time machine. The genius was back! But sadly such flashes of brilliance were few and far between – although one other notable exception was seen in the following game.

30

R.Fischer – B.Spassky

St Stefan/Belgrade 1992

Sicilian Defence

1 e4 c5 2 ♘f3 ♘c6 3 ♗b5 g6 4 ♗xc6 bxc6 5 0-0 ♗g7 6 ♖e1 e5

In the next game in which he played Black, Spassky deviated here with 6...f6!? 7 c3 ♘h6 8 d4 cxd4 9 cxd4 0-0 10 ♘c3 d6 11 ♕a4 ♕b6 12 ♘d2 ♘f7 13 ♘c4 ♕a6 and was able to achieve a fairly comfortable draw.

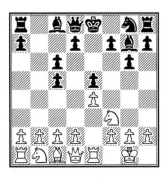

7 b4!

Was this over the board inspiration by Fischer or a novelty he had been storing up for 20 years, hidden in one of his dusty old notebooks? I'd favour the former. White sacrifices a pawn in wing gambit style – in order to take advantage of the weakened dark squares on the a3-f8 diagonal, now that the bishop has been posted on g7. Normal theory here was (and still is) 7 c3 ♘e7 8 d4 cxd4 9 cxd4 exd4 10 ♘xd4 0-0 11 ♘c3 ♖b8 with good counterplay for Black, who enjoys the long-term advantage of the two bishops.

7...cxb4 8 a3

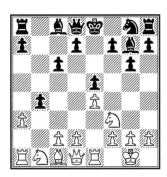

8...c5!?

Perhaps wisely, drawing on his vast experience of decades of top level international play, Spassky declines to capture on a3, which would accelerate the development of White's queenside. For example: 8...bxa3 9 ♘xa3 (9 ♗xa3!? d6 10 d4 exd4 11 ♘xd4 ♘e7) 9...d6 10 d4 exd4 11 e5! dxe5 12 ♘xe5 ♗e6 13 ♕f3 ♘e7 (13...♕d5 14 ♕xd5 cxd5 15 ♘b5) 14 ♘xf7! ♗xf7 15 ♗g5 0-0 16 ♗xe7 ♕d7 17 ♗xf8

♖xf8 18 ♕d3 turned out well for White in the game K.Klundt – R.Hubner, Bayern 1997.

On the other hand 8...b3 9 cxb3 ♘e7 10 ♗b2 d6 11 d4! obliges Black to play the unwieldy 11...f6 (11...exd4 12 ♗xd4 ♗xd4 13 ♕xd4 0-0 14 ♘c3 looks horrible.) if he doesn't want to get blown away on the dark squares.

9 axb4 cxb4 10 d4!

Viciously blasting open the centre before Black is able to get his king into safety.

10...exd4

10...♘e7 11 dxe5 0-0 12 ♗g5 seems unpleasant.

11 ♗b2

11...d6

Spassky wants to take the sting out of a possible e5 advance.

11...a5!? 12 ♗xd4 ♘f6 13 e5!

A) 13...♘d5 14 e6! 0-0 (14...♗xd4 15 ♕xd4 ♘f6 16 e7) 15 ♗xg7;

B) 13...♘h5 14 g4 ♘f4;

11...♘f6!? is a quite logical and sensible attempt to get the king to safety as quickly as possible – I'm sure if Spassky had known what was in store for him in the game, he would have made this his top priority:

A) 12 ♗xd4! (better than 12 ♕xd4) 12...0-0 (12...a5 13 e5) 13 e5 ♘d5 (13...♘e8 14 ♗c5 d6 15 ♗xb4) 14 ♗c5 ♘e7 – and now White has a pleasant choice between 15 ♗xe7 ♕xe7 16 ♕d5 ♖b8 17 ♖xa7 with a slight advantage and 15 ♗xb4 ♗b7 16 ♘c3 which is also fairly promising.

12 ♘xd4

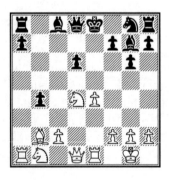

12...♕d7?

Spassky is thrown by Fischer's imaginative opening play! This comes back to the point that when a move looks ugly and unnatural, then it usually is. What other candidate moves did Black have available here? It's not too difficult to see what his intention was with ...♕d7 – he wants to prevent ♘b5. But the move is slow and lacking in dynamism.

12...♘e7! seems fairly logical – then 13 c3 (13 ♘d2?! 0-0 14 ♘c4 a5 15 ♘b5 ♗xb2 16 ♘xb2 d5 17 e5 ♘f5!) 13...bxc3 14 ♗xc3 0-0 15 ♘b5 ♗e5!;

12...♕b6!? looks like a more dynamic square than d7 but 13 c3! (13 ♘d2? ♗xd4 14 ♘c4 ♗xf2+ 15 ♔h1 ♕c5 16 ♘xd6+ ♔e7 and the tactics aren't really working for White) 13...bxc3 14 ♗xc3

A) 14...♘e7 runs into a similar problem to the game – White has the powerful thrust 15 ♘f5! ♗xc3 16 ♘xc3! (16 ♘xd6+ ♕xd6 17 ♕xd6 ♗xa1 is less clear) 16...gxf5 17 exf5!;

B) 14...♘f6 15 e5! and again we can conclude that Black is suffering with his king in the middle. So Spassky's last chance for equality was indeed 12...♘e7 – now he runs into trouble.

13 ♘d2

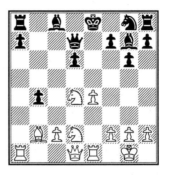

13...♗b7

Bobby smells blood ... the attempt to evacuate the king immediately runs into a simple fork. Also bad is 13...♘e7 14 ♘c4 0-0 15 ♘b6!; while 13...♘f6 14 ♘c4! 0-0 15 ♘b6 axb6 16 ♖xa8 and 13...♗e5 14 ♘c4 ♗b7 15 ♖a5! f6 16 ♘b5 lead to a huge initiative for White – it is clear that ...♗e5 is taking one liberty too many with development.

14 ♘c4! ♘h6

Here simple moves like 15 e5 or 15 ♕d2 look quite promising, but twenty years out of competitive play had not dulled Fischer's tactical flair... 14...♘e7 15 ♘f5! ♗xb2 16 ♘fxd6+ ♔f8 17 ♘xb2 and the highly unpleasant ♕d4 is threatened,

while 17...♖d8?? is a blunder of
material – 18 ♘xb7!

15 ♘f5!

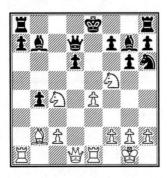

Played in the style of Morphy, or
indeed of the young Fischer!

15...♗xb2

Seemingly forced. If 15...gxf5
16 ♗xg7; 15...♘xf5 16 exf5+ ♔f8
17 f6 (It is not wise to allow the
creation of such a strong pawn.)
17...♖h6 18 ♕xd6+ ♕xd6 19 ♘xd6
♗d5 (19...♗c6 20 ♖e7) 20 ♖xa7!

16 ♘cxd6+ ♔f8 17 ♘xh6 f6

17...♗xa1!? 18 ♕xa1 ♕xd6
(18...♔e7 19 ♕e5+ ♕e6 20 ♘df5+
gxf5 21 ♘xf5+ ♔d7 22 ♖d1+ is
crushing.) 19 ♕xh8+ ♔e7 and the
exposed state of the black king
should decide the game in White's
favour. 20 ♕xh7 (20 ♕g7 ♕f4 21 g3
♕f6 22 ♘g8+) 20...♖f8 21 ♕g7±

18 ♘df7! ♕xd1

18...♕e6 19 ♘xh8 ♔g7 20 ♘8f7
and the two knights save each other.

19 ♖axd1 ♔e7 20 ♘xh8 ♖xh8

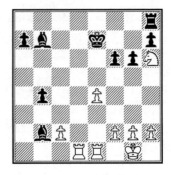

Now what is the most efficient
way for White to convert his
material advantage?

21 ♘f5+!

Good technique is about good
tactics! It is amusing to see how the
knights have kept leaping back and
forth from this square, torturing
Spassky.

21...gxf5

21...♔e6 22 ♖d6+ ♔e5 23 ♖d7
♗c6 24 ♖e7+ ♔f4 25 g3+ ♔g4
26 ♘e3+ ♔h5 (26...♔f3 27 h3! and
the black king is caught in a net)
27 ♖xa7 ♗xe4 28 ♘c4!

22 exf5+ ♗e5

22...♔f8 23 ♖d8+ ♔g7 24 ♖e7+
♔h6 25 ♖xh8 is immediately
decisive.

23 f4 ♖c8 24 fxe5 ♖xc2 25 e6

Now Fischer needs only to display his endgame technique, which has always been regarded as exemplary.

25...♗c6

25...♗c8 26 ♖c1 ♖xc1 27 ♖xc1+-

**26 ♖c1! ♖xc1 27 ♖xc1 ♔d6
28 ♖d1+ ♔e5**

28...♔c5 29 e7 doesn't help, as now White is threatening ♖c1; also bad is 28...♔e7 29 ♖a1 b3 30 ♖xa7+ ♔d6 31 ♖a3 ♗e4 32 ♖xb3 ♗xf5 33 ♖b6+ +-

29 e7

29...a5

29...b3 30 ♖e1+! ♔d6 (30...♔d4 31 ♖b1 ♔c3) 31 e8=♕ (31 ♖e6+ ♔d5 32 ♖xc6 is also probably winning but is far less practical: 32...b2 33 e8=♕ b1=♕+ 34 ♔f2 ♕b2+ 35 ♔e3 ♕d4+ 36 ♔f3 ♕d1+ 37 ♔f2 ♕d2+ 38 ♔g3 ♕g5+ 39 ♔f3 ♕xf5+ 40 ♔e3 ♕g5+ 41 ♔d3) 31...♗xe8 32 ♖xe8 ♔c5 33 ♖a8.

30 ♖c1 ♗d7 31 ♖c5+

Now Fischer removes one of the two dangerous pawns, and the end is

in sight.

31...♔d4

31...♔d6 32 ♖xa5 ♔xe7 33 ♔f2 b3 34 ♖a3 b2 35 ♖b3 ♗xf5 36 ♖xb2 and White must be winning this endgame.

32 ♖xa5

White can afford to give up the rook for the b-pawn, as the white king rampages into the black position, stealing pawns in its wake.

**32...b3 33 ♖a7 ♗e8 34 ♖b7 ♔c3
35 ♔f2 b2 36 ♔e3 ♗f7 37 g4 ♔c2
38 ♔d4 b1=♕ 39 ♖xb1 ♔xb1
40 ♔c5 ♔c2 41 ♔d6**

The f-pawn will decide. Such brilliance from Fischer! Sadly the great champion has now passed away, and I would hope that his memory is not sullied by some of the regrettable utterances he made in his later years – clearly the result of a paranoid personality. He deserves to be remembered for the remarkable gifts he brought to the chess world.

1-0

King Garry

Garry Kasparov is quite simply the greatest player in the history of chess. Like other great champions, such as Muhammad Ali in boxing and Tiger Woods in golf, Garry transcended chess in a way that we had never seen before. What kept him at the top so long was a fearsome desire to succeed – it seemed to me that Kasparov had a terrible fear of failure. He is also a very emotional man and would have made a terrible poker player – at the board he was like an open book. But by channelling that emotion and anger he was able to dominate chess for 15 years until retiring to concentrate on politics. With so many strong players around now, it is very doubtful if anyone else will ever come along who will be as dominant as Garry was – and who will have the same motivation. Garry was driven in a way that, for example, Kramnik isn't – Kramnik was able to peak for his match with Kasparov, but maybe he doesn't have quite the inner desire to continually be No.1, or to sacrifice everything in his life towards that goal, that Kasparov had. Of course Kasparov will find Russian politics much harder to conquer than the chess world – there he will come across far more obstacles. Just to give you some impression of what he is up against in trying to take on Putin... watching a documentary recently, I was stunned to see that they close off a busy thoroughfare in Moscow for an hour each day just so that Putin can drive through to the Kremlin. Changing the face of the Russian political scene will take many generations, if it is even possible at all – but one has to admire Garry for even trying.

31

G.Kasparov – V.Anand

Tal Memorial, Riga 1995

Evans Gambit

1 e4 e5 2 ♘f3 ♘c6 3 ♗c4 ♗c5 4 b4

Garry breathed new life into the Evans Gambit, with the resulting open positions suiting his highly attuned tactical brain.

4...♗xb4 5 c3 ♗e7 6 d4 ♘a5 7 ♗e2 exd4 8 ♕xd4 ♘f6 9 e5 ♘c6 10 ♕h4 ♘d5 11 ♕g3

Forcing a kingside weakness.

11...g6

With the knight on d5, the position almost resembles the Alekhine Defence (1 e4 ♘f6). If 11...0-0 12 ♗h6 wins the exchange.

12 0-0

12...♘b6

Anand moves the knight out of the firing line. How should White meet 12...d6 ?

A) 13 c4 ♘db4 14 ♘c3 dxe5 15 ♘xe5 ♘xe5 (15...♗h4 16 ♘xc6 ♘xc6) 16 ♕xe5 0-0 17 ♗h6 ♗f6;

B) 13 ♖d1! ♗e6 14 c4 ♘db4 15 ♘c3.

13 c4

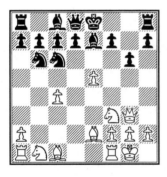

What is the idea behind this move? Well, it gains space – and more importantly the b1 knight is heading for the juicy outpost on d5. Less accurate players may have preferred 13 ♘bd2 but not only would that temporarily block the d-file, taking the sting out of ♖d1, but deny Garry his planned ideal set-up.

13...d6

Anand hopes to 'refute' Garry's ultra-aggressive play by putting the question to the centre. However it was not so easy to refute Kasparov's opening preparation! What about 13...0-0 – an attempt to move the king to safety and delay action in the centre? Kasparov would have reacted with 14 ♗h6! ♖e8 15 ♘c3

A) 15...♗f8 16 ♗xf8 ♖xf8 17 ♘d5! taking advantage of the weakness on f6;

B) 15...d6 16 ♖ad1 ♘d7 (16...♗f5 17 c5! ♘c8 18 cxd6 cxd6 19 ♗f4) 17 exd6 ♗xd6 18 ♗f4 ♗xf4 19 ♕xf4 may be critical. There is 19...♕f6! (19...♘ce5 20 ♘xe5 ♖xe5 21 ♕xe5) 20 ♕d2 But how to keep the knight out of d5? 20...♘de5 21 ♘d5 ♘xf3+ 22 ♗xf3 ♕d6 23 c5! ♕xc5 24 ♘f6+ is a nice demonstration of White's dominance in the centre.

C) 15...d5!? looks very risky but at least sets a trap; 16 ♖ad1 but not 16 cxd5 ♘xd5 17 ♖ad1?? ♘xc3 which would be most unfortunate.

C1) 16...♗e6 17 cxd5 ♘xd5

C1a) 18 ♘e4!?;

C1b) 18 ♘xd5 ♗xd5 19 ♗c4 (19 ♖d2!? ♗b4 20 ♖d3 ♘e7 21 ♖fd1 c6 22 ♕f4 ♗f5!) 19...♗xc4 20 ♖xd8 ♖axd8 with compensation;

C1c) 18 ♖xd5! ♗xd5 19 ♖d1 and then 19...♘b4 looks forced, but there is 20 a3! and White is winning.

C2) 16...d4 17 ♘b5 ♗c5 18 ♗g5 ♕d7 19 ♗f6 (19 e6 ♖xe6 20 ♘xc7 ♖xe2 21 ♘xa8 ♘xa8);

D) 15...f6 16 ♗d3! ♔h8

D1) 17 ♗xg6 hxg6 (17...♖g8) 18 ♕xg6 (18 ♘h4 ♖g8) 18...♖g8 19 ♕h5 ♕e8 20 ♕h3 d6 21 e6 ♕g6!;

D2) 17 ♖fe1 ♗b4 (17...fxe5 18 ♘xe5 ♘xe5 19 ♕xe5+ +-) 18 exf6! ♗xc3 (18...♖xe1+ 19 ♖xe1 ♗xc3 20 ♗xg6 ♗xe1 21 ♗f7 and mate is not far off) 19 ♗xg6 (19 ♗g7+ ♔g8 20 f7+ ♔xf7 21 ♗xc3 and White has a raging attack.) 19...♗xe1 (19...♖xe1+ 20 ♖xe1 ♗xe1 21 ♗f7) 20 ♗g7+ ♔g8 21 ♕h4 hxg6 22 ♕h8+ ♔f7 23 ♘g5 mate is a nice finish.

14 ♖d1!

14 exd6 ♗xd6 would not be in the spirit of the opening – Kasparov is playing for restraint of Black's counterplay – 15 ♗f4 (15 ♕h4 ♕xh4 16 ♘xh4 ♗e5 would not do of course) 15...♕f6! 16 ♗xd6 ♕xa1 17 ♘bd2 ♕xa2 and the situation is completely unclear. 18 ♗c5 (18 ♗xc7 0-0) 18...♘a4!

14...♘d7

This is the idea. Anand plans to capture on e5, knowing full well that Kasparov will not want to take on d6, as this frees the black position.

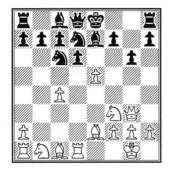

15 ♗h6!

All hands on deck!

15 exd6 ♗xd6

A) 16 ♖xd6 cxd6 17 ♕xd6 ♘de5! (17...♕f6 18 ♕xf6 ♘xf6 19 ♗b2 ♔e7 20 ♗a3+ ♔d8 21 ♘c3; or 17...♕e7 18 ♕d2 0-0 19 ♗a3 ♕f6 20 ♘c3 ♖e8 21 ♖d1 with some compensation for the exchange);

B) 16 ♗f4

B1) 16...♗xf4 17 ♕xf4 ♕f6!? and though it looks as if Black is out of difficulties White can still pose some irritating problems with 18 ♕e3+! ♕e7 19 ♕h6 ♘de5 (19...♕f8 20 ♕f4) 20 ♘c3 ♗e6 21 ♘d5!;

B2) 16...♕f6 17 ♗xd6 ♕xa1 is a gamble – it is unclear whether White has enough for the exchange. 18 ♗a3 ♕xa2 19 ♕xc7 looks like a bit of a mess. But of course Kasparov wants more!

15...♘cxe5 16 ♘xe5 ♘xe5

It looks as if Black has won a central pawn, and an important one at that – but Garry shows great insight into the position. Catching the king in the centre, he plans to launch an attack before Black has an opportunity to consolidate.

17 ♘c3

The computer, of course, afraid of the material deficit White is facing (after 17 ♘c3 it gives Black having a decisive advantage!) wants to restore the balance somewhat with the greedy 17 ♗g7?! when after 17...♗f6! it judges the position to be about level. But, as I said, Garry is looking for more. 18 ♗xh8 ♗xh8 and Black has two pawns for the exchange, and what's more his pieces co-ordinate perfectly – and unlike in the game Black's king is in no danger and play can continue 19 ♘c3 ♗e6 20 c5 d5!

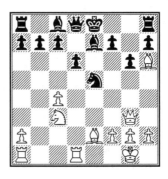

17...f6?

Just in case, Anand tries to take the sting out of any ♗g7 idea by White. However the drawback is that this leads to further weaknesses! Black had any number of alternative candidate moves to analyse – 17...♘d7, 17...♗h4, 17...♗f8, 17...♗f6, 17...♗d7, 17...♖g8, 17...♗e6 and 17...c6, but would any of them have solved his problems and drastically altered the assessment of the position?

17...♘d7!

...looks more logical than most tries, as it prevents one of White's main ideas, c5. How could White then rustle up some compensation? Black intends ...♘c5, ...♗e6 and ...♕d7, after which White would struggle to claim any compensation. White needs to act quickly!

A) 18 ♗f3?! White has in mind ♖e1, or possibly ♖b1. Black continues 18...♘c5 19 ♖e1 ♗e6;

B) 18 ♗g7 ♖g8 19 ♗d4 cuts down Black's options. 19...♗f6 20 ♗xf6! (20 ♘e4 ♗xd4 21 ♖xd4 ♘f6;

20 ♘d5 ♗xd4 21 ♖xd4 ♘f6) 20...♕xf6 (20...♘xf6 21 c5 d5 22 ♘b5! hands White a large advantage) 21 ♘d5 ♕d8 22 c5 (22 ♖e1 ♘c5! and there is no dangerous discovered check, though White still has a useful initiative after 23 ♕c3) 22...♘xc5 23 ♕c3 ♗e6 24 ♘f6+ ♔f8 25 ♘xh7+ ♔e7 and again the black king is caught in the centre – but can White take advantage?

C) 18 ♘d5

C1) 18...♗f6 19 ♕e3+ ♗e7 20 c5 c6 (20...♘xc5?? 21 ♘f6 mate; 20...dxc5? 21 ♗g7 ♖g8 22 ♗f6 scoops a large amount of material) 21 cxd6 cxd5 22 ♗b5!;

C2) 18...♘b6 19 ♕c3 ♖g8 20 ♖e1 ♗e6 21 ♖ad1 keeps up the pressure, e.g. 21...c6 22 ♘xe7 ♕xe7 23 ♕g3!?;

17...♗h4?! 18 ♕e3 ♗e6 19 c5 ♗f6 20 cxd6 cxd6 21 ♘e4 ♗e7 22 ♗g7!;

17...♗f8 is bad, as after 18 ♗xf8 ♖xf8 (18...♔xf8? 19 ♕xe5!) 19 c5 ♗e6 20 cxd6 cxd6 21 ♘e4 White has a huge attack;

17...♗f6?! 18 c5! ♗e6 19 cxd6 cxd6

A) 20 ♘e4 d5 21 ♗b5+ (21 ♘xf6+ ♕xf6 22 ♗b5+ ♘c6 23 ♗xc6+ bxc6 24 ♕d6 ♖c8) 21...♘c6 (21...♘d7 22 ♘d6+ ♔e7 23 ♕a3! with powerful threats) 22 ♘d6+ ♔e7 23 ♘xb7 ♕b6 24 ♕a3+!;

B) 20 ♘b5 d5 21 ♕a3 (21 ♖ac1 ♖c8 22 ♖xc8 ♗xc8 23 ♖xd5! is an unpleasant twist in the tail);

Other moves also have their problems:

17...♗d7 18 ♗g7

A) 18...♖g8 19 ♗xe5 dxe5 20 ♗g4! ♗d6 (20...f5 21 ♗xf5!)

21 ♗xd7+ ♕xd7 22 c5 wins a piece.

B) 18...♗f6 19 ♗xf6 ♕xf6 20 ♘d5 ♕d8 21 f4! ♘c6 22 ♕c3 yet again hits on the f6 weakness;

17...♖g8 has the drawback that Black is practically committing the king to the centre.

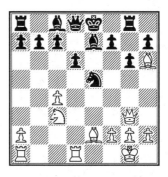

Then 18 c5 ♗e6 (18...♗d7 19 cxd6 cxd6 20 f4!? removing the strong knight from the centre: 20...♘c6 21 ♖ab1! It's important to use all the pieces! 21...♖b8 22 ♕e3 ♗e6 23 ♗f3 ♔d7 leads to unclear complications after 24 ♗g5!) 19 cxd6 cxd6 20 ♗b5+ ♘c6 21 ♗f4 d5;

17...♗e6.

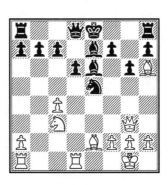

In some ways this seems like the most natural move. 18 ♖ab1 ♖b8

19 c5 ♘d7 20 cxd6 ♗xd6 21 ♖xd6! cxd6 22 ♘e4 ♕a5 23 ♕xd6 and the threats are growing. Given the complexity of these variations, and the fact there seems no easy way out, it's not surprising that Anand wished to give his king some breathing space on f7.

18 c5

18...♘f7

18...♗d7!? with the idea of placing the bishop on the invulnerable square c6. 19 cxd6

A) 19...♗xd6?! 20 ♘e4 ♕e7 21 ♖xd6 (21 ♘xd6+ cxd6 22 ♕a3 ♗c6 is fairly unclear) 21...cxd6 22 ♖d1 ♘f7 23 ♕e3;

B) 19...cxd6 20 ♘b5! (20 f4? ♘f7; 20 ♘d5 ♗c6) 20...♗c6 (20...♕b6 21 ♗e3 ♕a5 22 ♘xd6+; 20...♗xb5 21 ♗xb5+ ♘c6 22 ♕b3 with an attack on the light squares) 21 ♕b3! ♘f7 22 ♗e3 and White has established dominance in the centre – and 22...0-0 is met by 23 ♗h6! ♖e8 24 ♗c4 d5 25 ♖xd5!

19 cxd6

Now, however, all of Kasparov's moves are easy to see – but to see how Anand will ultimately escape the stranglehold of White's initiative is nowhere near so easy!

19...cxd6

20 ♕e3!

Tightening the screw. Anand has had enough of the irritating bishop and decides to chop it off.

20...♘xh6

20...f5 21 ♘d5! is similar to the game, only with the difference that f5?! doesn't in any way help Black.

21 ♕xh6

Now there is an obvious threat of ♕g7.

21...♗f8!?

It's natural to want to move the bishop off the passive looking e7 square. But if Anand had seen what was coming he may have left it there! 21...♔f7!? 22 ♗c4+ ♗e6

This looks like suicide, as the black king is forced into the centre (and I would imagine that Kasparov's eyebrows would have risen if this had been played in the game) – but how would you meet this defence? 23 ♗xe6+ ♔xe6 24 ♘d5! (24 ♕e3+ ♔f7 25 ♘d5 ♕d7 26 ♕b3 ♔g7; 24 ♕g7 ♕f8) 24...♔f7 25 ♕h3! intending a killer switch with ♕b3, which there seems to be little that Black can do to prevent.

22 ♕e3+ ♔f7 23 ♘d5

23...♗e6

What other defensive ideas were possible? What if I just move the king to g7? Then 24 ♖ac1!.

23...h5!? has the idea of trying to redevelop the beleaguered dark-squared bishop;

A) 24 ♕b3 ♔g7 (24...♗e6 25 ♕xb7±) 25 ♖ac1 looks quite nasty as the beast on d5 totally dominates the position;

B) 24 ♖ac1 ♗h6! 25 f4! ♗d7 (25...♖e8 26 ♕f2 ♖xe2 27 ♕xe2 ♗g4 28 ♕b5!) 26 ♕b3 ♖b8 27 ♘xf6+!

24 ♘f4 ♕e7

24...♕d7 was no better; 25 ♗b5! ♕xb5 26 ♕xe6+ ♔g7 27 ♘d5 ♕a4 28 ♕xf6+ ♔g8 29 ♕e6+ ♔g7 30 ♖ac1 and the king is hunted to its doom.

25 ♖e1! 1-0

Since 25...♕d7 is met by the extremely painful shot 26 ♗b5, Anand decided he had seen enough. A tidy miniature by Kasparov, played in the style of Tal and thus appropriate for his own memorial tournament – the sacrifice of material for a vague attack, but one that poses very difficult problems for the opponent to solve.

Anatoly the Boa Constrictor

Facing Karpov in his prime must have been an insufferable task for any chess player. Karpov simply did not allow his opponents the slightest glimpse of counterplay and strangled them in a suffocating strategic bind. Karpov was a master of prophylaxis, but it would be a mistake to call him a defensive player, as was, for example, Petrosian. In fact Karpov had a very aggressive approach, it was just that he went about it in a very different way from others – to use an analogy with mountaineering, there are two classic ways of tackling a Himalayan peak (of course I've adopted both). On the one hand, you can adopt the siege style, which is to lay siege to the mountain with a succession of camps and porters, in order to grind the mountain into submission, which is what most modern day mountaineers will do; or you can employ the alpine technique to climb even a peak like Everest, which involves the use of very few camps and little equipment – and takes days rather than weeks. I'm sure if Karpov was a mountaineer he would favour the siege approach, whereas Kasparov would be with the alpine climbers. Karpov would seek out the tiniest weakness in his opponent's strategy – the tiniest weakness in their position – and capitalise on it with his ruthless strategic skill.

32

A.Karpov – V.Milov

Credit Suisse, Biel 1997

Queen's Gambit Accepted

1 d4 d5 2 c4 dxc4 3 e4 ♘c6

Other replies worthy of note are 3...♘f6; 3...c5 and; 3...e5.

4 ♘f3

4 ♗e3 ♘f6 5 f3 (5 ♘c3 e5 6 d5 ♘a5 7 ♕a4+ ♗d7! 8 ♕xa5 a6 9 ♘d1 ♘xe4) 5...e5 6 d5 ♘e7 and the knight heads for g6.

4...♗g4 5 d5 ♘e5 6 ♗f4 ♘g6 7 ♗e3

7 ♗g3!? is also possible, for example 7...e5 8 ♗xc4 ♗d6 9 ♗b5+ ♗d7 10 ♕b3 ♘f6 11 ♘c3 0-0 12 ♗xd7 ♕xd7 13 0-0±

7...♘f6 8 ♘c3

8...e5

8...e6!? is an interesting alternative to the game continuation. It should be met by 9 ♕a4+! (9 ♗xc4 exd5 10 exd5 [10 ♘xd5 ♘xe4] 10...♗d6 with a comfortable game for Black.) 9...♕d7 10 ♕xd7+ ♔xd7 (10...♘xd7 led to an advantage for endgame maestro Vasily Smyslov against Fontaine, in Cannes 1996, after 11 ♗xc4 exd5 12 ♘xd5 ♗d6 13 ♘d4!?; also possible is 13 0-0-0!?) 10...♔xd7 11 ♘g5! (11 ♗xc4 exd5 12 exd5 ♗xf3 13 gxf3 a6 seemed comfortable for Black in M.Gurevich – Ivanchuk, Reggio Emilia 1992, with the game later ending in a draw.) 11...exd5 12 ♘xf7 ♖g8 13 f3 ♗e6 14 ♘g5 c6 15 0-0-0 h6 16 ♘xe6 ♔xe6 17 ♗d4! ♗d6 18 ♗xf6 gxf6 19 exd5+ cxd5 20 ♖xd5 ♘e5 21 g3 and Karpov had regained his pawn and obtained an endgame advantage with control of the light squares and the better pawn structure against Lautier, Amber blindfold/rapidplay 1997

9 ♗xc4 a6 10 0-0 ♗d6 11 ♗e2

A standard position for this opening has arisen. White has slightly more space and room for manoeuvre and will try to probe for weaknesses on Black's queenside.

On the other hand Black's position is very compact and solid, and for the moment Karpov lacks any real targets.

11...0-0 12 ♘d2!

White is intending the manoeuvre ♘b3-a5, which will discourage Black from playing ...b5 since then the c6 square becomes weak.

12...♗d7

12...♗xe2 13 ♕xe2 would not only give White more freedom of movement but also more control over the light squares; in particular the f5 square will make a nice jumping off point for a white knight. Play might continue 13...♘f4 14 ♕f3 (14 ♗xf4 exf4 15 ♘f3) 14...♕d7 15 g3.

13 ♖c1 ♕e7 14 a3

14...b5

What other ideas does Black have here? How should he place his pieces? Or does he just have to wait passively as it is unlikely that he can improve his position? I would argue that ...b5 leads to weaknesses in the black position that Karpov will later be able to exploit. Perhaps better is 14...♘f4 15 ♘b3 b6 (15...c6 16 ♘a5 cxd5 17 exd5 ♗c8 18 ♘c4 looks comfortable for White) 16 ♗f3 g5!? (A radical way to initiate counterplay on the kingside.) 17 g3 ♘h3+ 18 ♔g2 g4 19 ♗e2 h5 20 f3 gxf3+ 21 ♗xf3 ♘g4!?; 14...♖fe8 15 ♘b3 h6 16 ♘a5 ♗c8 17 b4±

15 ♘b3 ♘f4 16 ♗f3

16 ♗xf4? exf4 and Black has a potentially raging attack with ...g5-g4 etc.

16...♔h8

Perhaps he should play an immediate 16...g5.

17 ♘a2!

Karpov has a masterly ability to reorganise his army to take advantage of any soft spots in the enemy position – an ability that in this game he exploits to the full. Here he targets the b4 square. You could also make a case for 17 ♘a5 but on c3 the knight blocks the c-file, and does little besides defending the e-pawn.

17...g5 18 ♘c5 ♖g8

18...g4!? 19 ♗e2 h5 20 ♘b4 ♘h7.

19 ♘b4 ♖g6

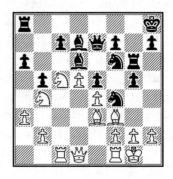

20 ♕c2!

Of course, White is unlikely to be distracted by a fairly meaningless a-pawn – the action is in the centre and on the kingside. Nevertheless the 'greedy' 20 ♘cxa6 came into consideration. Then 20...g4 21 ♗e2

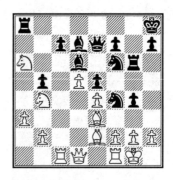

A) 21...♘xe2+ 22 ♕xe2 ♘xe4 23 ♘xc7

A1) 23...♖ag8 24 ♘xb5 ♕h4 (24...♗xb4 25 axb4 ♕xb4 26 ♘c3) 25 ♘xd6 ♖xd6;

A2) 23...♖c8 24 ♘xb5 ♖xc1 25 ♗xc1±;

B) 21...♘xe4 22 ♘xc7 ♖c8
(22...♖ag8 23 ♗xf4 exf4 24 ♕d4+)
Now we understand why Karpov did
not enter this line – Black's knights
are menacingly poised around his
king. 23 ♘xb5 ♖xc1 24 ♗xc1 g3!
(Such an advance is not surprising
with all of Black's army aimed at the
white king. Instead 24...♘h3+ can
be met by 25 gxh3 gxh3+ 26 ♔h1
♖g2 27 ♘xd6 ♕xd6 28 ♕e1)
25 hxg3 ♘xg3 26 fxg3 (26 ♗xf4
exf4 is extremely dangerous)
26...♗c5+ 27 ♖f2 ♘h3+ 28 gxh3
♖xg3+ 29 ♔f1 ♕h4.

20...g4 21 ♗e2 ♖ag8

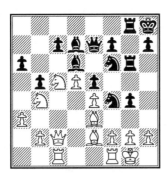

Now it looks as if White's poor
kingside will soon get overwhelmed,
but Karpov has seen a weakness in
the black position – namely the e5
pawn – and if that falls, then the
diagonal to the black king will be
opened.

22 ♖fd1?

Once again Karpov declines to
capture the a-pawn, which would
slow down his own counterattack in
the centre. However 22 ♘bxa6!?
seems to work better in this position.

A) 22...♘h3+ 23 gxh3 gxh3+
24 ♔h1;

B) 22...g3 23 fxg3 ♘xe2+
24 ♕xe2 ♘g4 25 ♘xd7;

C) 22...♖h6 23 ♘xc7 ♗xc7
(23...♘6h5 24 ♘xd7) 24 ♘xd7
♘xe2+ 25 ♕xe2 ♕xd7 26 ♗xh6;

D) 22...♘6h5 23 ♘xd7 ♕xd7
24 ♖fe1 and Black is struggling to
find a way through on the kingside,
as 24...♘h3+ 25 gxh3 gxh3+
26 ♔h1 is a dead end.

In view of the next note 22 ♖fe1!?
was worth considering.

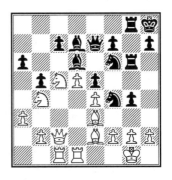

22...♘6h5?

The idea of playing the rook to d1
would not be to be everyone's taste
as once Black captures the bishop on
e2, the queen will be lined up on the

same diagonal as the rook – which will give Black additional tactical possibilities. Perhaps Milov should have preferred 22...♞xe2+! 23 ♕xe2 g3! 24 hxg3 (24 fxg3 ♗g4 25 ♕d3 ♗xd1 26 ♞c6 ♕f8 27 ♕xd1 ♞g4∓) 24...♗g4 when White is forced to weaken his kingside, whereas if the rook was on e1 he could simply move his queen.

25 f3

A) 25...♗xf3!? is the caveman approach, however White is not without defensive resources: 26 gxf3 (26 ♕xf3 ♖xg3 27 ♕f2 ♖xg2+ 28 ♕xg2 ♖xg2+ 29 ♔xg2 ♞g4!) 26...♖xg3+ 27 ♔f1 ♞h5 28 ♞bd3 ♕h4 29 ♔e1!;

B) 25...♗c8! 26 ♗f2 ♞h5 27 g4 ♞f4 28 ♕c2 h5 and now 29 ♞cd3 hxg4 (29...♞xd3 30 ♞xd3 hxg4 31 f4 exf4 32 e5 g3 33 ♗d4) 30 ♞xf4 exf4 31 ♗d4+ ♔h7∓ gives Black a dangerous attack down the g-file.

23 g3!

Karpov, of course, is not one to give an opponent a second chance, and quickly kills any idea of the black bishop coming to g4.

23...♗c8

23...♞h3+ is the forthright continuation. But then 24 ♔h1 ♞5f4 25 gxf4 (Safer is 25 ♗f1!? ♖h6 26 ♞xd7 ♕xd7 27 gxf4) 25...exf4 26 ♗d4+ f6 27 ♞xd7 ♕xd7 28 ♞xa6 g3 29 ♗f1! and 29...g2+ 30 ♗xg2 ♖xg2 31 ♗xf6+ ♕g7 32 ♗xg7+ ♖8xg7 33 f3 ♞f2+ 34 ♕xf2 ♖xf2 35 ♖g1 leads to a better endgame for White.

24 ♞c6

24 gxf4 g3! rudely opens up the white king; 25 hxg3 ♞xg3 26 fxg3 ♖xg3+ 27 ♔f1 ♕h4 with a crushing attack. Now Karpov is able to avoid any trouble from the menacingly placed knights and introduce some threats of his own.

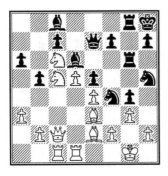

24...♕g5!?

Milov is not prepared to accept the slightly worse position that would arise after, say, 24...♘xe2+ 25 ♕xe2 ♕f6 26 ♘d3± and instead goes 'all in'.

25 ♗f1! ♖h6 26 ♕c3 ♘f6

This is the idea. Now ♕h5 is coming – and mate. Right? Well, not quite. Karpov has seen deeper into the position...

27 ♘d3 ♕h5 28 h4!

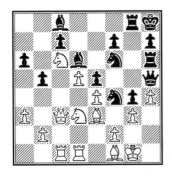

28...gxh3??

28...♘xe4! was forced.

A) 29 ♕c2 ♘g5! 30 ♘dxe5 ♘f3+ 31 ♘xf3 gxf3 32 ♘e7 ♕xh4!;

B) 29 ♕e1 ♘g5 30 ♘dxe5 ♘f3+ (30...♘gh3+ 31 ♗xh3 ♘xh3+ 32 ♔g2 and 32...♗xe5 33 ♘xe5 ♕xe5 loses to 34 ♗d4) 31 ♘xf3 gxf3 32 ♘e7 ♕xh4 33 ♗d4+ f6∓;

C) 29 ♘xf4 ♕f5 30 ♕c2 (30 ♘d4 ♕f6 31 ♕c2 exf4 32 ♕xe4 fxe3 33 ♕xe3 ♖h5 34 ♗g2 looks slightly better for White due to his better pawn structure.) 30...exf4 31 ♗d4+ ♘f6 32 ♕c3 ♔g7 is pretty unclear.

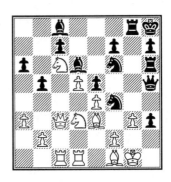

29 ♘dxe5!

Now the whole Black edifice comes tumbling down like a house of cards...

29...♖g7 30 ♗xf4 ♘xe4 31 ♕e3 ♕f5 32 ♗xh6 h2+ 33 ♔xh2 ♘xf2 34 ♗xg7+ ♔xg7 35 ♖d4

In this game Karpov resembled a cobra luring on his prey, waiting for the right moment to strike.

1-0

Magnus and Les Enfants Terribles

The new wave of extremely gifted young chess players is headed by a player tipped as the next world champion: Magnus Carlsen from Norway. Magnus is regarded in the West as the natural successor to Bobby Fischer – someone capable of matching the powerful chess culture of the East. Magnus is primarily a grinder – in fact his endgame play is already at a fabulous level and his ability to win seemingly unwinnable endgames has played a big part in propelling him to the number one spot in the world rating list, unheard of for an 18 year old. Nevertheless, as is usual with most top players these days, Magnus's style is universal and he is equally at home in complicated, unfathomable tactical battles.

33

M.Carlsen – E.Inarkiev

FIDE Grand Prix, Baku 2008

King's Indian Defence

**1 d4 ♘f6 2 ♘f3 g6 3 ♗g5 ♗g7
4 ♘bd2 0-0 5 c3**

Here Magnus chooses an apparently innocuous opening – showing his willingness to defer the fight, if necessary, until the middlegame.

5...h6

5...d6 6 e4 c5 7 dxc5 dxc5 8 ♗e2!?, posting the bishop on a less aggressive square, was the Russian/German player Arthur Yusupov's choice when encountering Garry Kasparov in the Tal Memorial, Riga 1995. Whether Yusupov played this opening with the intention of obtaining a draw, is unclear. However in any case he was gradually ground down after 8...♘c6 9 0-0 ♕c7 10 ♕c2 ♖d8 11 ♖fe1 h6 12 ♗h4 ♘h5! 13 ♘c4 ♗e6 14 ♘e3 ♘f4 15 ♗f1 ♘e5 16 ♘xe5 ♗xe5 17 ♘c4 ♗xc4 18 ♗xc4 b5! 19 ♗f1 (19 ♗xb5 c4! creates annoying counterplay) 19...c4 and Garry had a positional advantage.

**6 ♗h4 d6 7 e4 c5 8 dxc5 dxc5
9 ♗c4!**

Magnus plays the bishop to a more active square, which poses greater problems than if it's stuck on e2.

9...♘c6 10 0-0 ♘h5 11 ♕e2

11...♕c7

White does not fear 11...♘f4 because of 12 ♕e3 g5 13 ♘xg5!? (Of course, the simple 13 ♗g3!? e5 14 ♖fd1 with an advantage, is also possible.) 13...hxg5 14 ♗xg5 ♘e6 (14...♘g6 15 f4!) 15 ♗h4. Normally two pawns would be considered insufficient for a piece, but given the time and attacking potential that White gains, we can confidently say that he enjoys more than enough compensation.

12 ♖fe1

12 a4!?, to take the sting out of ...♘a5, may have been more accurate.

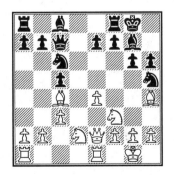

12...♘a5

Of course, here Black has many

possibilities, but which one to choose? As well as the move in the game, ...♘e5, ...♘f4, ...g5, ...b6, ...a6 ...e6 and ...♖d8 were all ideas. However sometimes it's a case of thinking, we have reached the middlegame, it is time to make a plan. Where do I want to place my pieces? Which pieces do I want to exchange, and which would be better to keep on?

12...g5!?

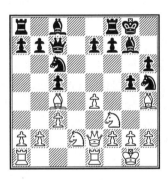

...is an attempt to gain the 'advantage' of the two bishops. The drawback of this move of course, is that it rather weakens the kingside and in particular the f5 and h5 squares, where White may be able to land a knight later (although f5 can be covered with e6, unlike the h5 square).

A) 13 ♘xg5 hxg5 (13...♘f4 14 ♕f3 hxg5 15 ♗xg5 ♘g6∓) 14 ♕xh5 gxh4 15 ♘f3 ♕d6∓;

B) 13 ♗xg5 hxg5 14 ♘xg5 ♘f4;

C) 13 ♗g3 13...♘xg3 14 hxg3 e6 15 ♘f1 (15 g4 ♕f4; 15 e5!? g4 16 ♘h2 h5) 15...g4 16 ♘3h2 h5;

12...♘e5?! is inaccurate; 13 ♘xe5 ♗xe5 14 g3! and White is ready to expand in the centre with f4, etc.

12...b6; 12...e6; and 12...a6 are all of roughly similar value, although in each of these cases White may well consider 13 e5!? as 13...g5 hands White a big advantage – after 14 ♗xg5! hxg5 15 ♘xg5 ♘f4 (with the white pawn still on e4 this move would be strong...) 16 ♕e4 (...but now White is winning) – so Inarkiev decides to play forcefully, concretely, as all young players seem to do these days.

13 ♗b5

13 ♗d3? ♘f4 would not be part of White's plans – of course, the light squared bishop should not be given up so easily.

13...a6 14 ♗a4 b5

Now we get a position that is in some ways similar to the Ruy Lopez – with Black gaining space on the queenside and White hoping to develop active operations in the centre.

15 ♗c2

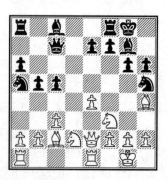

15...e5!?

Very consistent, nipping in the bud any ideas White may have had of playing e5 himself. However we always have to be aware of what drawbacks each move might have, and in this case it is clear – the d5 square suddenly becomes a target for White and if he can land a knight there, unmolested, he will enjoy a healthy initiative. Also Black's long term plan is not clear – he can't very well play on the kingside, as any ...f5 break will surely be too risky; but then again neither has White any weaknesses that he can exploit on the queenside.

16 ♘f1

Magnus now heads his knight towards the attractive outpost on d5.

16...♘f4! 17 ♕d1

17 ♕e3 ♘c4 18 ♕c1 ♗g4 19 b3 ♗xf3 20 gxf3 ♘d6 and White's pawn structure has lost much of its potential.

17...♘c4

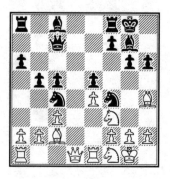

18 ♕b1!

An ugly looking place for the queen, but Magnus wants to expel the marauding knights gradually, since an immediate 18 b3? ♘a3! extinguishes one of the white bishops. Also 18 ♖b1 g5 (18...♗g4) 19 ♗g3 ♖d8 20 ♕c1 ♗g4 would allow Black some initiative.

18...♗g4 19 ♗d1!

Magnus, with acute positional sense, avoids any disruption to his pawn structure.

19...g5 20 ♗g3

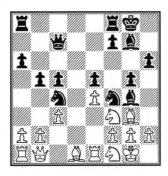

Now it may appear as if White's play resembles something akin to a drunken 1400 Elo rated player – but though his pieces are all clumsily placed along the first few ranks, things are not so simple. In fact at this point the game is fairly balanced and if White is given the chance, he will gradually push back the black forces. So Inarkiev has to act quickly...

20...♖ad8

Threatening ... ♘d3.

21 h3 ♗h5

The humble retreat 21...♗c8 gives White a choice – to continue as in the game with ♗xf4 – or find some other idea. In fact 22 b3! ♘b6 23 ♘e3 seems to pose real problems, e.g. 23...c4 24 b4.

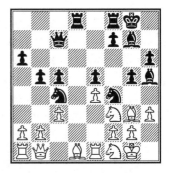

22 ♗xf4

22 b3 ♘d3 23 bxc4 (23 ♖e2 ♘a3! is an amusing queen trap) 23...♘xe1 is the reason why Inarkiev played the bishop to h5 – the bishop drops off after 24 ♘xe1 ♖xd1.

22...exf4 23 ♗e2!

Now, as well as the simple ♗xc4, White intends a4 generating an easy initiative on the queenside – moves such as b3, axb5 and ♖a6 spring to mind.

23...♗xf3

23...♘b6 24 ♘3d2 ♗g6 25 ♗g4!?

24 ♗xf3

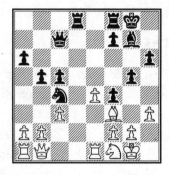

24...♘d2?!

A slightly risky move from the positional point of view. If Inarkiev had been more alert to the attacking potential of opposite colour bishop middlegames, he might have chosen to blunt the light-squared bishop with 24...♘e5! when White has a much harder task opening up the light squares to get at the black king. In the game Inarkiev can still defend, but it will be a much more difficult practical task.

25 ♘xd2 ♖xd2 26 e5!

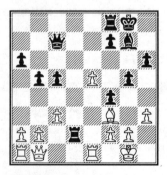

Magnus knows that this position isn't about pawns, but more about how to reach the black king. He sacrifices the e5 pawn so as to open up the b1-h7 diagonal and thereby

free the white bishop. It would be interesting to see if this would also be the choice of a strong computer here.

26...♗xe5?

After this further mistake it is extremely difficult, maybe impossible, to defend the black position! White's initiative becomes too strong. 26...♖e8! looks obvious doesn't it? What would Magnus rustle up then? 27 ♖d1!? (If 27 a4 ♖xe5 28 axb5 axb5 29 ♖a8+ ♗f8; or 27 ♕f5 ♖xe5 28 ♖xe5 ♕xe5.) 27...♖xd1+ 28 ♕xd1

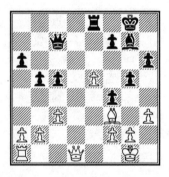

...and in general White will always have very good play. For example after 28...♕xe5 he has 29 ♕d7 or 29 a4!?, but it is questionable whether he has anything more than very good compensation. Nevertheless it is clear that the white king is very much safer than his counterpart – so from a practical point of view I would always prefer to be White here. I'm sure Magnus agrees!

27 ♕f5

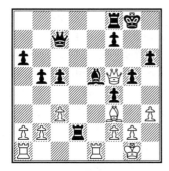

Now Black runs into big problems.

27...f6

From here on the light squares are weakened to the point of danger level. 27...♗g7 allows the scary looking 28 ♖ad1! ♖xb2 (28...♖fd8 29 ♖xd2 ♖xd2 30 ♖e8+ ♗f8 31 ♗e4 is terminal, e.g. 31...f6 32 ♗d5+ ♔g7 33 ♕e6!) 29 ♖d7. Only a computer would allow such a move – any grandmaster would get this far and look no further, dismissing the line as untenable for Black on account of White's raging initiative and the fact that Black has no counterplay at all against the white king. The end would be 29...♕b6 30 ♖xf7!! ♖xf7 31 ♖e8+ with the silicon beast delivering mate in five moves after 31...♗f8 32 ♗d5.

28 ♖ad1 ♖fd8 29 ♕e6+ ♔g7 30 ♕xa6 b4 31 ♖xd2 ♖xd2 32 ♖d1 bxc3 33 bxc3 ♖xd1+ 34 ♗xd1

It seems that with the rooks exchanged White's attacking chances are greatly reduced; but Magnus has shown great insight in realising that his attacking potential

on the light squares, in the face of so little counterplay, leaves Black with an uphill struggle to save the game.

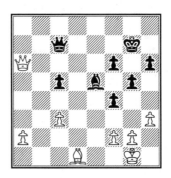

34...c4?

34...♗xc3 was a better chance. Then, after 35 ♗b3 (35 ♕d3 ♗d4 36 ♗c2 ♔f8 doesn't achieve anything), despite the pawn deficit White has much the better chances as the black queen will be tied down to defence, thereby allowing White to push the a-pawn at his leisure.

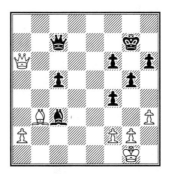

A) 35...♗e5 36 ♕e6 h5 (36...♕d8 37 f3) 37 ♕g8+ ♔h6 38 ♗f7!;

B) 35...♔f8 36 ♕e6 (36 f3 ♕e5 37 ♔h2 ♕e1) 36...♗d4 37 a4±;

C) 35...♕e7? 36 ♕c4! ♕e1+ 37 ♔h2 ♕e8 38 ♕xc3.

35 ♗e2 ♗xc3 36 ♗xc4

Now the position is lost – defending against the light-squared bishop and the a-pawn is too much.

36...♗e5 37 ♕e6 ♕d8 38 ♕f7+ ♔h8 39 f3 ♗d6 40 a4 ♗b4 41 ♔h2 ♕f8 42 ♕g6 ♗e1 43 ♗d3 f5

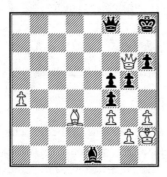

Magnus has made inexorable progress so in desperation Inarkiev sacrifices another pawn.

44 a5 ♗g3+ 45 ♔h1 ♕g7 46 ♕e8+ ♕g8 47 ♕e5+ ♕g7 48 ♕b8+ ♕g8 49 ♕b6 ♕d5 50 ♕xh6+ ♔g8 51 ♕xg5+ ♔f7 52 ♕xf5+ ♕xf5 53 ♗xf5 ♗f2 54 g4! fxg3 55 f4 ♔f6 56 ♗e4 ♗e3 57 a6

The three pawns can't be stopped.

It was amusing that after Magnus sacrificed a pawn with 26 e5!, Inarkiev felt obliged on a number of occasions to try to sacrifice one back, simply to blunt White's initiative. Strong grandmasters often use a single idea to win a game – in this case Magnus focused on the attack on the light squares.

1-0

In the following game Magnus faces a fellow *enfant terrible*, Teimour Radjabov, from Baku in Azerbaijan (also the home town of Garry Kasparov). Though Radjabov has been overshadowed by the meteoric rise of the younger Carlsen, he remains a world class grandmaster in his own right.

34

M.Carlsen – T.Radjabov

Biel 2007

1 e4 d6

Not Radjabov's principal choice – against 1 e4 he generally favours the Sicilian or defending against the Ruy Lopez.

2 d4 ♘f6 3 ♘c3 e5 4 ♘ge2!?

Magnus takes advantage of the fact that he has not committed his knight to f3. White intends to fianchetto the bishop. 4 dxe5 dxe5 5 ♕xd8+ ♔xd8 6 ♗c4 ♔e8

(6...♗e6!?) 7 ♘f3 ♗d6 8 ♗g5± may appeal to the likes of a super grinder such as English grandmaster Mark Hebden, but playing for a slightly better endgame at such an early stage is not to everyone's taste.

4...♘bd7 5 g3 c6 6 ♗g2 b5 7 a3! ♗e7

Alternatives are 7...♗b7 and 7...a5.

8 0-0

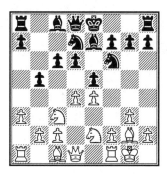

8...0-0

Perhaps the immediate 8...a5!? was more accurate. If White continues as he did in the game, then he runs into

A) 9 h3 ♗a6

A1) 10 b4 ♘b6 or 10...axb4 11 axb4 ♘b6 makes the c4 square a constant problem for White;

A2) 10 g4 b4! Small differences in move order can be crucial. Why be in a rush to castle when your king is not in any danger? And here Radjabov had a chance to gain time on the game. Weaker players (well, Radjabov obviously isn't included)

often tend to make the mistake of thinking they need to get the king to safety as quickly as possible, and miss more promising options along the way. This may be a lazy reaction or possibly an overestimation of the dangers posed to their king.

B) 9 d5 is an alternative. Then might follow 9...cxd5 (9...♗b7) 10 ♘xd5 ♗b7 11 ♘xe7 ♕xe7.

9 h3! a5

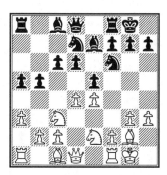

10 g4

Less patient players may be inclined to lash out with the aggressive 10 f4 here, but in fact this does little to combat Black's plan, which is to put the bishop on a6 and then play b4. As we have already seen, it is always useful to take into account the opponent's plans, and think in prophylactic terms of how best to deal with them. In fact in a book by Mark Dvoretsky and Arthur Yusupov on positional chess, there is an exemplary game with a similar opening in which Karpov denies Timman any counterplay by means of masterly prophylaxis. There g4 had also been played before f4. As Black is not threatening anything, why not gradually improve the position before embarking on an aggressive operation? Karpov was in fact one of the most effective attacking players since his style, based on the gradual restriction of his opponent's counterplay and slow build-up of forces before launching an attack, meant that he nearly always conducted an offensive from a position of great strength.

10...♗a6 11 ♘g3 b4

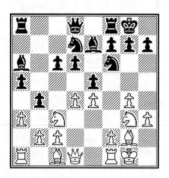

12 ♘ce2

Now we see the drawback of not playing ...♗a6 earlier. The knight can retreat to the much more useful square e2! Already threats of ♘f5 are in the air. On the other hand 12 axb4 axb4 13 ♘ce2 can be met by 13...♕b6 rather than 13...♗xe2 14 ♖xa8 ♗xd1 15 ♖xd8 ♗xd8 16 ♖xd1 ♗b6 17 c3±

12...bxa3

Radjabov tries to mix it up, but in fact it doesn't work out very well.

12...exd4 gives up the centre and after 13 ♕xd4 White intends ♔h2, f4 etc.

12...c5 13 dxe5 dxe5 14 ♘f5 ♘b6 15 ♗g5! provides nagging pressure.

12...g6 weakens the king. Then although the immediate attempt to attack with 13 ♗h6 is unlikely to achieve anything, however simply strengthening the centre with 13 c3! – to be followed by the easy moves ♗e3, ♔h2 and eventually f4 – should ensure a comfortable advantage for White.

13 ♖xa3 d5 14 ♖e3

The critical position. The rook is not ideally situated on e3, but in some lines it may be able to contribute to the attack. Necessity is the mother of invention!

14...dxe4

14...exd4 looks like it wins material, but in fact runs into 15 ♘xd4! ♗xf1 (15...♕b6 16 ♖b3!; or 15...♖c8 16 ♖fe1 dxe4 17 ♘xe4 with a pleasant positional edge for White) 16 ♘xc6 ♕e8 17 exd5.

Alternatively 14...g6 15 dxe5 ♘xe5 (15...♘xe4 16 ♘xe4 dxe4 17 ♖xe4 wins a safe pawn;) 16 exd5 ♘c4 17 dxc6 ♘xe3 18 ♗xe3 looks very risky for Black.

15 ♖e1!

Very calm, just stepping out of the pin and continuing his mobilisation of forces. Once White regains the e-pawn he will have a much better pawn structure – Black's a- and c-pawns are horrendously weak. However when you are playing Magnus you must first watch out for any danger of getting checkmated!

15...♕c7?

Radjabov intends a quick ...♖d8 with counterplay along the d-file, but is never given the opportunity for this. 15...g6! would at least prevent one of White's ideas – the knight coming to f5. You should try to stop your opponent's plans whenever possible! Though 16 ♘xe4 (16 dxe5 ♘xe5 17 ♘xe4 ♘d5 and Black is not without counterplay) 16...♘d5 17 ♖g3 ♗h4 18 ♖f3 leaves White with the superior pawn structure and the better chances – even if the rook is a bit clumsy – this would still have been better than what occurs in the game!

16 ♘f5

16 ♘xe4 ♖fd8.

16...♗d8

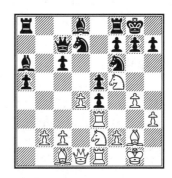

17 g5!

Now the rook can come to e4, where it constantly threatens to swing over to h4 and trigger a decisive attack.

17...♘d5 18 ♖xe4

18...f6

Is this weakening move really forced? Of course removing the knight on f5 – which is casting its pernicious glare over Black's kingside – should be the top priority, but that is easier said than done.

18...g6 19 ♘h6+! ♔g7 20 dxe5 ♘xe5 21 ♕d4+-;

18...exd4 19 ♘exd4;

18...♗c8 espies the knight from afar, but there is the simple 19 dxe5 ♘xe5 20 ♘eg3!

19 ♘eg3!

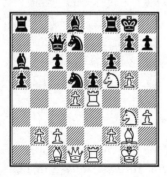

Every one of White's pieces has the potential to participate in the attack.

19...g6

19...exd4 (19...fxg5 20 dxe5) 20 ♘h5!? (the simple 20 ♕xd4 is strong as well) 20...g6 (20...♖f7 21 ♖e8+ ♘f8 22 ♘hxg7! ♖xg7 23 ♘h6+ ♔h8 24 ♖xf8+) 21 ♘h6+ ♔h8 22 ♖e8 gxh5 23 ♕xh5! ♗e7 24 ♖8xe7.

20 ♘h6+ ♔g7 21 dxe5

Of course, with such a knight on h6 there are many attacking possibilities, e.g. 21 gxf6+ ♗xf6 (21...♘5xf6 22 ♖h4 ♘d5) 22 ♘g4.

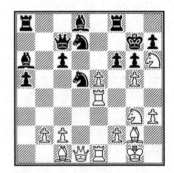

21...fxg5

Radjabov understandably has no appetite to allow the knight to remain on h6, so seeks to remove it as quickly as possible. In any case after 21...fxe5 White has the instantly destructive 22 c4! (22 f4?! has the idea of blasting a way through to the d4 square as quickly as possible, but unfortunately Black can cover it with 22...♕a7+! 23 ♔h1 exf4) 22...♘b4 (22...♘f4? 23 ♗xf4 ♖xf4 24 ♖xf4 exf4 25 ♕d4+) 23 f4 ♘c5 24 ♖xe5 ♘cd3 25 ♗e3!

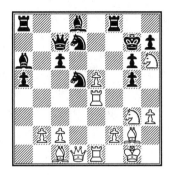

22 e6!

Magnus doesn't know the meaning of the words 'going backwards'!

22...♔xh6

22...♘7f6 23 e7 ♗xe7 24 ♖xe7+ ♘xe7 25 ♖xe7+! and the queen is lost.

22...♘7b6 23 ♘g4 and White enjoys a raging initiative. ♕d4 is threatened, for starters, and the e-pawn is a monster. Play might continue 23...h5 24 ♘e5 h4 25 ♘f1±

23 e7!

Despite being temporarily a pawn down, 23 exd7 is surely better for White as well – but why bother to calculate this when 23 e7 just wins?

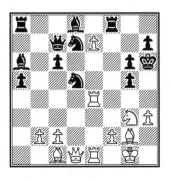

23...♕b6

Capitulation, but the position was gone in any case;

23...♘xe7 24 ♖xe7 ♗xe7 25 ♖xe7 ♕b6 (25...♖ad8 26 h4; 25...♖ae8 26 ♖xd7 ♖e1+ 27 ♕xe1 ♕xd7 28 h4 gives a huge advantage) 26 ♕xd7 ♕xf2+ 27 ♔h2 ♖h8 28 h4;

23...♖e8 gives White a pleasant choice of wins – not surprising with the king on h6 and the pawn on e7 – 24 exd8, 24 ♕d4 24 ♖e6 just to name a few. 24 ♕d4 (24 exd8=♕ ♖exd8 25 ♕d4 is similar) 24...♘7f6 (24...♗xe7 25 ♖h4 mate) 25 ♗xg5+ ♔g7 (25...♔xg5 26 ♕d2+ ♘f4 27 ♖xf4!) 26 exd8=♕ ♖exd8 27 ♗xf6+ ♘xf6 28 ♖e7+

24 exf8=♕+ ♘xf8

The curtain can be drawn here. Not only is White the exchange to the good but his attack rages on.

25 c4 ♘f4 26 ♕d6 ♔g7 27 ♗xf4 gxf4 28 ♖e7+ 1-0

As in Alekhine's best games, Magnus's attack here came out of a clear blue sky – even if Radjabov did have an off-day and failed to do anything to counter White's plans. So how soon will Magnus be world champion? Well, I predict it will happen within the next two years. A possible future challenger to Magnus is the Ukrainian former prodigy Sergey Karjakin – and there's an even younger Ukrainian, only 12 years old, who recently scored a 2600 performance in their national championship. The future is in the hands of the kids! I think it's only a matter of time before we see a 16 year old, or even younger, become world champion. Indeed chess has always been a fertile ground for prodigious talents. Personally, I have a terrible record against junior players – it's intimidating having to play someone so young and so strong. Still you have to remember that they too are human – well almost.

Chapter 8

My own experience

So you want to know about the author – right? After all this talk can he actually play chess himself? Well, yes… In fact I've always considered myself an attacking player. Somehow the idea of playing a dashing attack and unleashing a brilliant combination has always seemed more appealing to me than grinding someone down in a boring endgame. I first realised that I had some talent for the game in the final years of primary school. The teacher there, a Mr Keane, (no relation to the 'penguin' grandmaster Raymond Keene, nor indeed the rabid footballer Roy Keane) was indeed very keen (excuse the pun) on chess, and we had a particularly bright class, so it was always very competitive. One time we were on a school journey and everyone was eager to go to the disco – but, typical of me, I wanted to stay behind and play the teacher at chess. However he didn't want to play and I burst into tears… so he finally relented. I managed to get the better of him for the first time ever, and what stuck in my mind was playing this brilliant combination at the end – with the result that my appetite for the game was enhanced still further.

Sometimes you just want to take the shackles off … all those boring rules about pawn structure, opening theory and so on … and just play like you did when you first discovered this great game … when you used to chuck the pieces around the classroom and shout at the teacher (or maybe I'm getting confused with my days as a chess coach.) … i.e. to play with a total lack of restraint and throw caution to the winds. And the following game was one of those…

35

D.Gormally – A.Norris

Manchester Open 1997

Bogoljubow-Indian Defence

1 d4 e6 2 c4 ♘f6 3 ♘f3 ♗b4+ 4 ♘bd2 0-0 5 a3 ♗e7?!

5...♗xd2+ is considered more normal.

6 e3 b6 7 ♗d3 ♗b7 8 e4!

I wasn't sure what Black was doing, so I thought I should occupy the centre.

8...d5?! 9 cxd5 exd5 10 e5 ♘fd7

Black has given up the centre and the kingside. The useless bishop on b7 would be better back on its original square. The alternative 10...♞e4 would have been met by 11 ♕c2!

11 h4!?

Right, let's get on with it then. Patience was never my strongest point... White creates the threat of ♗xh7 followed by ♞g5 – a motif that is only possible with the rook still on h1 and another example of how it can pay to delay castling!

11...h6

On 11...f5 follows 12 g4! cleaving open the kingside (12 ♕c2!? g6 13 h5) 12...fxg4 13 ♞g5! ♗xg5 14 hxg5±;

11...c5? leads to an amusing king hunt; 12 ♗xh7+ ♚xh7 13 ♞g5+ ♚g6 14 h5+ ♚xg5 (14...♚h6 15 ♞de4! dxe4 16 ♞xf7+ +-) 15 ♞e4+ ♚f5 16 ♞g3+ (or 16 ♕f3+ ♚e6 17 ♕g4+ f5 18 exf6+ ♚f7 19 ♕g6+) 16...♚e6 17 ♕g4+ f5 18 exf6+ ♚f7 19 ♕g6+ with a massacre.

Of course, 11...g6? only provokes White into 12 h5.

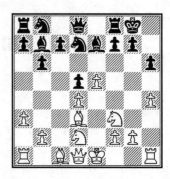

12 g4!?

Less Neanderthal types may have been tempted into a more sedate continuation such as 12 ♞f1 or 12 ♗b1!? – an interesting idea, envisaging ♕c2 and an attack on the king – but it was far too late for such conventional schemes. I think this was an old weakness of mine – whenever my opponent had a vulnerable point in his castled position (in this case the pawn on h6) I always felt I had to attack it directly, whereas in most cases it would have been better to rely on the general weaknesses created by a move like ...h6 to promote my attack in the future.

12...c5!

Of course, classical play – Black meets a wing attack with a counter-thrust in the centre!

13 g5

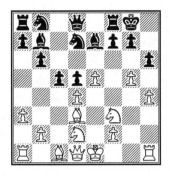

13...cxd4

13...h5 occurred to me during the game as a possible defence, whereupon my intention was to play 14 g6 opening up the light squares. But Black gets reasonable counterplay due to White's unwillingness to continue with normal development and can play 14...♕e8! (14...fxg6 15 ♗xg6) 15 ♕e2 f5

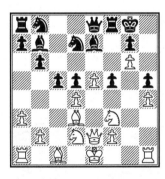

A) 16 e6 ♘f6 17 ♗xf5 ♘c6 18 ♘b3?! ♘e4! and Black's counterplay in the centre is much more relevant than White's vague ideas of mating the black king. Seeing variations like this in the game worried me greatly – had I been too bold? After all, if the attack doesn't break through I've

effectively burnt my bridges – my position will just be left with holes which his pieces can flood into.

B) 16 ♖g1!, supporting the g-pawn, is of course much more effective than 16 e6?, handing Black the f6 square. Now White has the threat of ♘h2 and ♕xh5. How does Black stop this? 16...cxd4 17 ♘h2! (17 ♘xd4 ♗c5!; 17 b4!? should also give leave White well on top) 17...♘xe5 18 ♕xh5 ♘xg6 19 ♖xg6 and White has a great advantage.

14 gxh6 ♘c5

Now however, I was happy. The attack is crashing through, isn't it? 14...gxh6 is clearly bad because of 15 ♘b3 with the threat of ♕d2, amongst others.

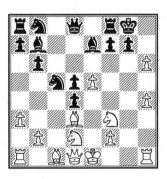

15 ♘b3

Today I might be more inclined to preserve the bishop with 15 ♗b1. Then after 15...g6 (15...♖e8 16 ♘xd4 ♗xh4 17 ♕g4! ♖xe5+ 18 ♔f1 ♗g5 19 ♘2f3 and Black is in big trouble 19...♗c8 20 ♕g3) 16 h5 I clearly have a very dangerous attack.

15...g6

15...♘xd3+ 16 ♕xd3 g6 17 h5 gives White a very straightforward and simple attack that even I probably wouldn't struggle to understand. (17 e6!?; 17 ♖g1!?) And after 17...g5 comes 18 ♖g1.

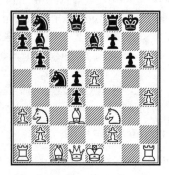

16 ♘xc5!?

Black's game is on the verge of total collapse but, as I said, I lacked patience and in making this capture strengthened his centre. Doubtless Karpov would have instantly played the simple 16 ♘bxd4 – although he would probably only get this position in a simul – after all, no variations are really necessary since White has an overwhelming positional advantage.

16...bxc5

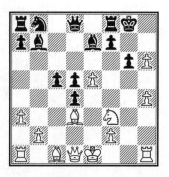

17 e6

Why did I refrain from 17 h5 ? – which is the obvious continuation of the attack! 17...c4 may have been the move I feared, but then there is 18 hxg6 cxd3 19 ♕xd3 – which during the game I probably underestimated. Playing this position today, I would make this move without hesitation as it doesn't really need variations to see that the two pawns are too strong: 19...♗a6 20 ♕f5 ♕d7 21 gxf7+ ♖xf7 22 ♖g1+ ♔f8 23 h7 ♗b4+ 24 axb4 ♕xf5 25 h8=♕+ ♔e7 26 ♗g5+ is just one winning line of many.

17...♘c6!?

17...♕d6!? 18 exf7+ ♖xf7 19 ♖g1 ♖f6 20 h5 and White keeps coming; or 17...f5 18 h5 gxh5; while 17...fxe6 18 h5 gxh5 19 ♘e5 (or 19 ♖g1+ ♔h8 20 ♖g7) and the black king is far too exposed to survive for much longer.

18 ♖g1 ♔h8 19 h5

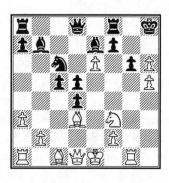

19...g5

What was my intention after 19...gxh5 ? Is this a more reliable defence? No! With the direct 20 ♖g7! White maintains considerable pressure: 20...♗f6 (20...fxe6 21 ♖h7+ ♔g8 22 ♔e2! is similar.) 21 ♖h7+ ♔g8 22 ♔e2! would have been a pleasing finish.

20 ♘xg5 fxe6 21 ♘xe6 ♕d7 22 ♕g4

22 ♘f4 also wins.

22...♖g8

23 ♕f5!

Consumed by a fever, a desire to produce a masterpiece that would supersede any of the great attacking games of yesteryear, I decided to produce a 'brilliant' double rook sacrifice. Nevertheless, unlike the 'Pearl of Wijk aan Zee', the 'Pearl of Manchester' doesn't have quite the same ring to it. The amusing thing was that I had seen the trivially winning 23 ♘g5! ♕e8 24 ♕f5 ♗xg5+ 25 ♔f1 ♕e7 26 ♗xg5 and Black is not long for this world – but decided that was too boring and made up my mind to sacrifice efficiency for beauty. Fortunately, even after this White still has a huge

attack, so my ego and intuition didn't let me down on this occasion.

23...♖xg1+ 24 ♔e2 ♗h4

24...♗f8? 25 ♕f6+ ♔g8 26 h7+ wins.

25 ♗f4!?

25 ♗g5!? was another forceful way to continue the attack: 25...♗xg5 (25...♖xa1? 26 ♕f6+ ♔g8 27 h7+) 26 ♖xg1 ♖e8 (26...♕e7 27 ♖xg5 ♗c8 28 ♖g6 and the attack is overwhelming) 27 ♔d1!

25...♖g5?

Under pressure to prevent ♗e5, Norris forgets about the attack coming from a different direction, but the game could not be saved in any case: 25...♖g2 26 ♗e5+ ♘xe5 27 ♕xe5+ ♔g8 28 h7+ ♕xh7 (28...♔f7 29 ♗g6+ is a quick mate) 29 ♗xh7+ ♔xh7 30 ♕c7+ ♔h8 31 ♕xb7+– mops up in trivial fashion. 25...♖xa1 26 ♗e5+ ♘xe5 27 ♕xe5+ ♔g8 28 h7+ is also mating, while 25...♖e8 26 ♗e5+ ♘xe5 27 ♕xe5+ is sufficient.

26 ♕f6+

A nice game which even a child could understand very well! Incidentally, during the tournament a large gay festival was going on in Manchester and I remember returning to my room to rest during one of the rounds and receiving a phone call. At the other end of the line a rather camp voice enquired: "Hello, is that David?" to which I replied, "No, this is Danny" "This is room 212?" he persisted. "Yes, but there's no David here, my name's Danny" "Oh," he replied. "So we didn't meet in love muscle last night then?" It probably didn't occur to me at the time that I could have been acting out some barely restrained latent homosexual desire while sleepwalking through Manchester – which I suppose is just as well.

1-0

In the following game I was up against the top seed in the Isle of Man chess tournament, which took place in Port Erin. Sadly, the tournament has now come to and end, which is a great pity. I will miss the windswept view of Port Erin harbour and the long and winding walk up to the tower at the top of the hill – from where you can gaze upon the breathtaking panorama of the surrounding area, including the Calf of Man. Incidentally, Port Erin was home to German civilians living in England at the outbreak of the Second World War. They were shipped there against their will and kept in seclusion as many were suspected, erroneously, of being spies.

36

D.Gormally – M.Ulibin

Monarch Assurance,
Port Erin 2001

French Defence

1 e4 e6 2 d4 d5 3 ♘d2 ♘f6 4 e5 ♘fd7 5 ♗d3 c5 6 c3 ♘c6 7 ♘gf3

Kasparov has championed this line for White. Possible replies are 7...g6, 7...f6, and 7...cxd4.

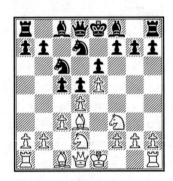

7...♗e7

7...cxd4 8 cxd4

A) 8...f6 9 exf6 ♕xf6 (9...♘xf6) 10 0-0 ♗d6 11 ♖e1 0-0 12 ♗xh7+!? is an interesting trap – the idea being 12...♔xh7 13 ♖xe6! ♕f4 14 ♘e4 (14 ♘f1);

B) 8...g6!? 9 0-0 ♗g7 10 ♖e1 0-0 11 ♘f1 f6;

C) 8...♕b6 9 0-0 ♘xd4 10 ♘xd4 ♕xd4 11 ♘f3 ♕b6 12 ♕a4 is a promising pawn sacrifice. When I beat my first ever international master, Bob Wade, the doyen of British chess, he essayed this line against me, got a very promising position but later blundered. What was peculiar about this game was that it was played at Bob's house! At this time Bob was already in his seventies, and was too tired to keep travelling to and from the venue. Fortunately for me Bob lived only a short distance from my house in Lewisham, and it was only a brisk walk across Blackheath Common to his flat, which was overflowing with chess material. Sadly, during the writing of this book Bob passed away, but I will always remember how – as was the case with so many other English players before me – he was always happy to help me with my game, allowing me access to his huge library and so on. He believed that a player shouldn't simply learn theory by rote, but should build up his own theory and ideas about the openings, unique to himself. Bob will be sadly missed by so many in the British chess community.

8 0-0 a5 9 ♖e1 cxd4

9...g5!? is another radical attempt to dismantle the white centre. Then could follow 10 dxc5 g4 11 ♘d4.

10 cxd4 ♕b6 11 ♘b1!

As the knight does little on d2, it is re-routed to greener pastures, heading for the weak square on b5.

11...♘xd4   12   ♘xd4   ♕xd4 13 ♘c3 ♕b6

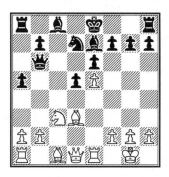

14 ♕g4

14 ♗e3!? d4 (14...♕d8?! turned out poorly for Black in Oratovsky – B.Lalic, Salou Open 2004; 15 ♕g4 0-0 16 ♗h6 g6 17 ♗xf8 ♗xf8 18 ♗b5 ♗g7 19 ♕d4! f6 20 ♘xd5! fxe5 21 ♕c4 exd5 22 ♕xd5+ ♔h8 23 ♖ad1 ♕b6 24 ♗xd7 and White made the extra exchange count) 15 ♘a4 ♕a7 is fairly unclear.

14...g6

14...0-0 15 ♗h6 g6 16 ♘b5 ♘c5 17 ♕d4 ♗d7! 18 ♗xf8 ♖xf8 19 a4 f6 20 exf6 ♗xf6 left the Armenian player Smbat Lputian with plenty of compensation for the exchange in the form of activity and control over the dark squares, in his encounter with Rublevsky at the FIDE World Championship knockout, 2000. The game ended in a draw.

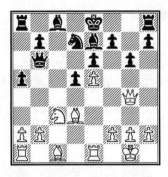

15 ♗g5?!

Clearly I wasn't familiar with an earlier game Ulibin had in this line where he got into trouble after 15 ♘b5 0-0 16 ♗h6 ♘c5 17 ♕d4 ♖d8? (17...♗d7! would transpose into the Lputian game and presumably is what Ulibin would have done if I had repeated this line. Black never fears the loss of the exchange as he obtains the dark squares in return.) 18 ♖ac1 ♖a6 19 ♗e3 ♘xd3 20 ♕xd3 d4 21 ♗xd4 ♗c5 22 ♗xc5 ♖xd3 23 ♗xb6 ♗d7 24 ♗d8! ♗xb5 25 ♖c8 ♔g7 26 ♗f6+ ♔h6 and the king was caught in a net and didn't last much longer in Smirin – Ulibin, Croatian team championship, Pula 2000.

15...♗xg5 16 ♕xg5 0-0 17 ♕h6

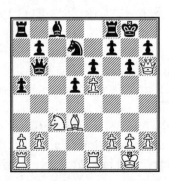

However I still felt I had good attacking chances, as my plan seemed obvious – push the h-pawn up the board to soften the kingside, perhaps combined with latent threats of swinging the rook via e3 to h3, or try to bring the knight round to d6. Sometimes it can be easier to play when you are material down since from a psychological point of view you are freed from the shackles of the fear of defeat and can simply attack without caution. (After all, here I am two pawns down to a much higher rated player so it can hardly get any worse.)

17...♕xb2!

The attempt to break out with 17...f6? is of course bad because of 18 ♗xg6 hxg6 19 ♕xg6+ ♔h8 20 ♖e3.

17...♘c5?! springs to mind but then White can at least utilise one of his ideas: 18 ♖e3! and if the greedy 18...♕c7 (18...♕xb2 fails to 19 ♖h3! ♕xa1+ 20 ♗b1 ♖d8 21 ♕xh7+ ♔f8 22 ♖f3! ♖d7 23 ♕h8+ ♔e7 24 ♕g8 f5 25 ♖h3 and mate will follow shortly)

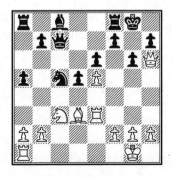

…what attacking moves spring to mind now? How does my opponent intend to defend? Once we see that 19 ♖h3 is met by the lateral defence 19...f5! (19...f6? 20 ♗xg6) that should give us some clue to the idea – put a piece on that square!

But Fritz wants to play the surprising 19 ♗f5.

Without the system of looking for as many candidate moves as possible it would be difficult to identify this idea, which is actually what I would call a prophylactic attacking move! i.e. one designed to block Black's main defence of ...f5.

For example:

A) 19...f6 20 exf6! ♖xf6 (20...♕f7 21 ♗xg6) 21 ♘xd5! unleashes a ferocious attack!;

B) 19...exf5? 20 ♘xd5;

C) 19...gxf5? 20 ♖g3+;

D) 19...♖d8 20 ♖h3 ♕xe5 21 ♕xh7+ ♔f8 22 ♗xg6 with a big initiative.

18 ♖ac1

It would be rather embarrassing to overlook the tactic 18 ♘b5? ♘xe5

19 ♖ab1 ♕xf2+!

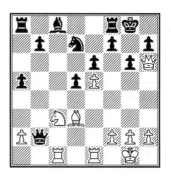

18...♕a3

Pinning the knight. There's a theory in chess that keeping your queen in an advanced position often slows down your opponent's attack – indeed, the irritation value should not be underestimated.

However 18...♘c5 does now come into consideration as there is no ♖e3.

Possibly he feared 19 ♘xd5!? (although 19 ♗b1 would have probably been the reluctant reply). Objectively White should not part with this knight so easily as it clarifies matters, but the attack with h2-h4 is still obvious and dangerous: 19...exd5 20 ♖xc5 ♕xa2 21 h4 ♕a3?! (21...♗e6 22 h5 still gives an attack) 22 ♖xd5 ♗e6 23 ♖d6 ♖ad8 (23...♖fd8 24 ♗xg6 hxg6 25 ♖xe6 fxe6 26 ♕xg6+ ♔h8 27 ♕h6+ ♔g8 28 ♖e3 is similar) 24 ♗xg6! hxg6 25 ♖xe6 and Black is forced to give up his queen after 25...fxe6 26 ♕xg6+ ♔h8 27 ♕h6+ ♔g8 28 ♖e3.

19 h4!

Onwards and upwards!

19...♕e7

19...b6!? 20 h5 ♕e7.

20 ♘b5

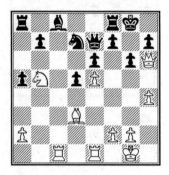

20...♘c5!?

Although objectively Black may still be winning after this move, I was more worried by 20...b6!? (20...f6 21 ♘c7 ♖b8 22 ♘xe6 ♕xe6 23 ♗xg6 is a draw), keeping an eye on the e5 pawn. I felt the d7 knight would come in handy for any future defence.

Then 21 ♘d6

A) 21...f5 22 ♖c7 ♗a6 23 ♗xa6 ♖xa6 24 h5;

B) 21...f6 22 ♖c7! and the following line should give some

clues to White's attacking chances; 22...fxe5 23 ♗xg6 hxg6 24 ♕xg6+ ♔h8 (24...♕g7 25 ♕xe6+ ♔h8 26 ♘xc8 ♖axc8 27 ♖xd7);

C) 21...♘c5 22 ♖xc5!? bxc5 23 ♖e3 c4 24 ♗c2 ♖b8 25 h5 ♖b6!? aiming to eliminate the strong knight on d6 (25...♖b2 26 ♘xc8 ♖xc8 27 hxg6 fxg6 28 ♗xg6 ♔h8 29 ♖h3 ♕g7 30 ♕g5)

C1) 26 hxg6 fxg6 27 ♗xg6 (27 ♖g3 ♕g7) 27...hxg6 28 ♖g3 ♖b1+ 29 ♔h2 ♕h7 pours a cold shower on the white attack;

C2) 26 ♖g3! ♔h8 (26...♖xd6? 27 hxg6 and the attack blasts through after 27...fxg6 28 ♗xg6 ♔h8 29 ♗xh7) 27 ♖f3 ♔g8 28 ♖g3 with a repetition.

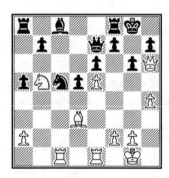

21 ♖xc5!

I was relieved to be given the chance to remove this strong knight and deposit my own on d6, where it will wait patiently to deliver a hammer blow to the black king. On the other hand after 21 ♗b1 ♗d7 22 ♘d6 b6 23 ♖e3 there is the strong rejoinder 23...f5! and it is not clear how White can meet the threat of ...♕g7.

21...♕xc5 22 ♘d6

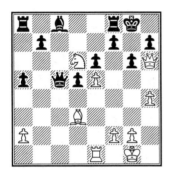

22...♗d7

A sensible idea, to bring more pieces into the defence. At the moment Black is only playing with his queen! But perhaps in any case this move is too slow? After all, the bishop does little to help the defence and in some lines the idea ...b6 and ...♖a7! might help to defend the black king. 22...♕c3!? would be an obvious attempt to refute the attack. I intended to meet this with 23 ♖e3! whereas the computer wants to respond with 23 ♕e3 – but of course this is ridiculous.

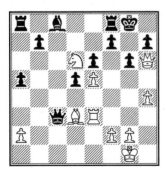

A) 23...♕c1+?! 24 ♔h2 d4 25 ♘e4 f5 26 exf6 ♖f7 27 h5 dxe3 28 hxg6 ♕c7+ 29 g3;

B) 23...♕a1+?! 24 ♔h2 ♕xa2 25 h5 ♕xf2 (25...♕a4 26 ♖h3 ♕d7 27 hxg6 fxg6 28 ♗xg6 and the attack is too strong) 26 ♖g3! and Black will be forced to give up queen for rook to stop the waves of attack.

C) 23...♕d2! pinning the rook

C1) 24 h5 b6 with the idea of defending laterally with ...♖a7 when it is not clear how White should continue the attack – ...♕d2 is a strong idea.

C1a) The imaginative 25 ♘e8!? may be the best try: 25...♖xe8 (25...♕d1+ 26 ♔h2 ♕xh5+ 27 ♕xh5 gxh5 28 ♘f6+ ♔h8 29 ♖h3 won't be enough after 29...h6 30 ♖xh5 ♔g7) 26 hxg6 fxg6 27 ♗xg6 ♕c1+ 28 ♔h2 is dangerous;

C1b) 25 hxg6 fxg6 26 ♗xg6 ♕xf2+;

C2) 24 ♔h2! b6 (24...♕xf2 25 h5) 25 h5 ♖a7! seems to be the best play, but what now for White? 26 ♕f4!?

(26 ♘xc8 ♖xc8 27 hxg6 fxg6 28 ♗xg6 ♕xf2 29 ♖h3 is likely to lead to equality) 26...f5! 27 exf6 ♕b4 28 ♕g3 with a real mess.

23 h5

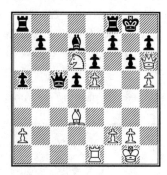

23...♗a4

With the clever idea of meeting ♖e3 with ....♗c2!, taking the sting out of any sac on g6. How can I proceed? I have to introduce a new idea – bring the pawn to h6 and set up a mating net.

There is also 23...♕c3!? 24 ♖e3 (24 ♕e3 is an admission of defeat) 24...♕d2 – a defensive idea which I think I saw during the game, although in fact White's attacking chances are still very good: 25 ♔h2 ♕xf2 26 ♖h3 and it is not easy to deal with the threat of capturing on g6.

24 ♕g5!

24 hxg6 fxg6! and of course there is no perpetual with 25 ♗xg6, because of 25...♕xf2+ 26 ♔h2 ♕f4+.

24...♕c3

24...f6 can be met by the simple 25 exf6.

25 ♖e3

25...f6?

25...♕d2 26 h6! (26 ♕f6 ♕d1+ 27 ♗f1 ♕xh5) 26...♕d1+ (26...f6 27 exf6 ♗e8 28 f7+ with a nasty attack;) 27 ♔h2

A) 27...f6 28 exf6 ♗e8 (28...♕h5+ 29 ♕xh5 gxh5 30 ♖g3+ ♔h8 31 f7 with a huge advantage) 29 f7+;

B) 27...♕h5+ 28 ♕xh5 gxh5 29 ♖g3+ ♔h8 30 ♖g7 looks like a draw.

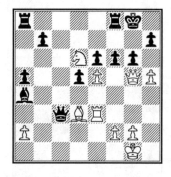

26 ♕h6!

"From whence I came, I shall soon return" is a line from a poem by the little known 19th century writer Danny Gormallius.

26...♛c1+

26...fxe5 27 hxg6 ♛c1+ 28 ♚h2 ♛c7 29 ♖g3 is crushing.

27 ♚h2

27 ♗f1 ♗c2!

27...♛c7 28 hxg6 ♛g7

Now he was also desperately short of time and I was sure I had him. If 28...fxe5 29 ♖g3.

29 ♛h4!?

29 gxh7+ ♚h8 is another way to continue the attack; then 30 ♛h4 fxe5 (30...♛g5; 30...♗c6 31 ♖g3 ♛e7 32 ♖g6) 31 ♖g3 ♖f4.

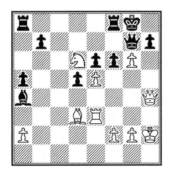

29...f5

A final mistake, but understandable given the huge pressure both on the board and also on the clock – in fact he was down to his final seconds.

29...♚h8 30 ♛xa4;

29...fxe5 30 gxh7+ ♚h8 31 ♖g3 ♖f4 32 ♛h5 ♗d1 33 f3! and Black is

in big trouble.

29...♗c6 was probably a more resilient defence. 30 gxh7+ ♚h8 31 ♖g3 ♛e7 and White still has a winning attack with 32 ♖g6! ♖ad8 33 exf6 ♛xd6+ 34 ♖g3

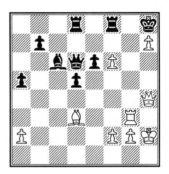

and the dangerous placing of the h- and f-pawns makes it incredibly difficult for Black to survive; White threatens ♛g5 and after 34...♖f7 comes 35 ♛g5 ♛xg3+ 36 ♛xg3+ – still, this line would have been more difficult to find than the one in the game.

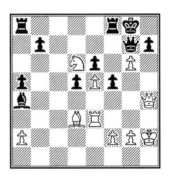

30 ♘f7

With his flag hanging I couldn't resist the temptation to complicate the situation even further! This is an old weakness of mine, I tend to 'lose my head' in my opponent's time trouble and, rejecting simple continuations, get too easily distracted by their own battle with the clock. Effectively I get drawn into their tension. White had a couple of very promising lines: 30 ♕xa4!? hxg6 31 f4± and 30 gxh7+! ♕xh7 31 ♖g3+ ♔h8 32 ♖h3 ♕xh4 33 ♖xh4+ ♔g7 34 ♖xa4 when White enjoys a large positional advantage in the endgame. However I have very rarely gone for an exchange of queens when my opponent was in time trouble!

30...hxg6?

A losing blunder, but understandable given the huge pressure from both the board and the clock; 30...♗d1! was still a draw after 31 ♖g3 (31 gxh7+ ♔xf7; 31 ♖h3 ♕xg6 32 ♖g3 ♖xf7) 31...hxg6 (31...h5 32 f3) 32 ♘h6+ ♔h8 33 ♘f7+

31 ♘h6+ ♔h8

32 ♕xa4?

Giving him another chance! But my nerves had obviously gone at this point (as had his) and I was playing far too quickly. It was a good time to sit on my hands! If I had done so, I would have seen 32 ♖h3!, with the threat of ♘xf5, is a very simple kill.

32...f4?

Now it really is all over. After 32...♕e7 Black is more than back in the game! I would have been disgusted if he had found this. After 33 ♖h3 ♔g7 34 g4 comes 34...♖h8 35 g5 and White has been forced to block his own attack to save his knight!

33 ♖h3 ♕c7

34 ♕d1!

34 ♗xg6! is also destructive.

34...♔g7

34...f3 35 ♕d2 ♕xe5+ 36 g3 ♔g7 37 ♘g4+−

35 ♕g4 ♖f5 36 ♗xf5

A game that I was terribly proud of at the time, but it is easy to see in the cold light of analysis that a horrific number of mistakes were made by both players! Even so, I enjoyed the fact that my sacrificial and attacking ideas gave him practical problems that he wasn't able to solve.

1-0

Postscript: as so often happens when I beat someone, this gave my opponent such motivation that he went on to win the tournament anyway!

37

P.Wells – D.Gormally

London Agency 1998

Sicilian Defence

Though the following game was also deeply flawed, at the same time it was rather an amusing battle.

1 e4 c5 2 ♘c3!

A good move order against Najdorf players, who loathe to commit their queen's knight to c6.

2...d6

Calling his bluff. He won't play the Grand Prix Attack, surely? 2...♘c6 3 ♘f3 and the Najdorf player is forced to play ...e5 if he wants to avoid transposing into another main line Sicilian. Of course today's universal players should know all Sicilians equally well!

3 f4!

Oops!

3...a6!? 4 ♘f3 ♘c6?!

Showing my lack of knowledge in this line, I soon run into trouble. More logical is 4...b5 5 g3 ♗b7 6 d3 and the knight can be more flexibly placed with 6...♘d7!

5 g3 e6 6 ♗g2 ♘f6 7 0-0 ♗e7 8 d3 0-0 9 h3!

Preparing an advance on the kingside.

9...d5 10 g4

10...dxe4?

At this stage of my career (and still now) under pressure I often resorted to panic measures. Here, this move is simply positionally bad. After a subsequent e5, the e4 square will become a useful reference point for the white pieces. 10...b5 11 e5 ♘d7 12 ♘e2 (12 g5!?) 12...f6!

11 dxe4 b5 12 e5 ♘d7

If 12...♛xd1 13 ♖xd1 ♘d7 14 ♘e4 (14 ♘g5!? ♘db8 15 ♘ge4 ♘d4 16 ♘f6+) 14...♘b6 15 c3± ;

while 12...♞d5 13 ♞xd5 exd5 14 f5! looks highly unpleasant.

13 ♞e4 ♞b6 14 ♕e2! ♕c7

Feeling very unhappy with the outcome of the opening, I was forced to make these passive moves. The attempt to break free from White's grip with 14...f6 15 ♖d1 ♕c7 16 exf6 gxf6 17 ♕f2! (Hitting the weak spot c5.) 17...♞d5 18 ♞xc5 ♞cb4 19 ♞d3 ♞xc2 20 ♖b1 f5 21 g5 also runs into trouble.

15 g5!

Looks a bit crude doesn't it? At the time I felt this way, though it soon became clear that this was the prelude to a direct kingside assault. Now it becomes almost impossible to break out with ...f6, so Black is forced to hustle around on the queenside for counterplay.

15...♞d5

15...♗b7 16 c3; 15...♞d4 16 ♞xd4 cxd4 17 ♞f6+±

16 c3 ♗b7

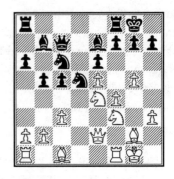

17 ♞h2!

A very powerful re-routing. White simply wants to swamp Black on the kingside.

17...♖fd8 18 ♞g4 ♗f8

18...♖d7!? 19 ♞gf6+

19 ♞gf6+ ♔h8

Of course the computer would always snap the knight off with 19...gxf6, but any flesh and blood player would fear opening up the g-file and giving the knight a square on g5. Indeed after 20 gxf6 c4 21 ♕h5 ♖d7 22 ♖f3 ♔h8 23 ♖g3 Black is in big trouble.

20 ♕h5!

20 ♞xh7 fails after 20...♔xh7 21 ♕h5+ ♔g8 22 ♞f6+ ♞xf6 23 gxf6 g6.

20...♞xf6!

At the time this seemed like the only chance to get out of the vice.

20...gxf6 21 gxf6 ♖d7 22 ♖f3 ♖ad8 23 ♖g3;

20...h6!? 21 ♖f3 (21 ♞g4 g6 22 ♕h4 h5 23 ♞gf6) 21...♞ce7

22 ♘d6!

21 gxf6 g6 22 ♕h4 ♖d3!

Forced, to prevent White's plan of ♖f3 followed by ♖g3.

23 ♘g5 h6

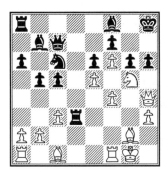

24 ♗e4?

At this point, with White's army eagerly swarming around the black king like hornets around a wasp's nest, I greatly feared the thrust 24 f5! which would have been a fitting conclusion to White's attack. A useful point to remember – when it is not possible to break through with pieces, sometimes an imaginative pawn break can push your opponent over the edge... The key idea behind this move is to release the latent power of the bishop on c1 – which at this stage is not contributing to the attack.

A) 24...exf5! is actually not as crazy as it looks, but whether I would have had the guts to play it in the game is doubtful. 25 e6! ♕g3! (It looks insane to give White two connected passed pawns on f6 and e6, but Black is very active here. On

the other hand 25...fxe6 is met by 26 ♘xe6 ♕h7 27 ♘xf8 ♖xf8 28 ♗xh6) 26 ♘xf7+ ♔h7 27 ♘g5+ ♔g8 28 ♕xg3 ♖xg3 29 ♘f3 ♘e5 30 ♘h4 ♗xg2 31 ♘xg2 ♖xh3 32 a4!? and White has the better chances in a wild endgame. Certainly a computer might try this line but it still looks very risky to allow such strong pawns.

B) 24...♘xe5 25 fxe6;

C) 24...gxf5 25 ♕h5 (25 ♘f3 ♔h7 26 ♕h5 ♖xf3!; 25 ♘xe6)

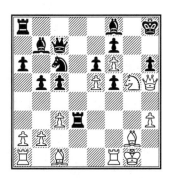

C1) 25...♘xe5 26 ♗f4;

C2) 25...♔g8 may be the toughest defence.

C2a) 26 ♘f3 ♘xe5 (26...♖xf3 27 ♖xf3; 26...♔h7) 27 ♘xe5 ♕xe5 (27...♗xg2 28 ♘xd3 ♗xf1 29 ♗f4) 28 ♗xb7 ♖a7 29 ♗f4 ♕xf6 30 ♗g2 may take some winning;

C2b) 26 ♗f4!

C2b1) 26...♖ad8 27 ♘f3! (27 ♔h2 ♘xe5) 27...c4 and now by means of the quiet move 28 ♔h2! (28 ♗xh6? is too early: 28...♘xe5 29 ♘xe5 ♕xe5 30 ♗xb7 ♕g3+ 31 ♗g2 ♗xh6

32 ♕xh6 ♖d2 33 ♕g7+ ♕xg7 34 fxg7 ♖xb2 35 ♖f2 ♖xf2 36 ♔xf2 ♖d2+ leads to an endgame where Black is at least not worse) White will carry out a decisive raid along the g-file: 28...♘xe5 29 ♘xe5 (29 ♗xe5 ♗xf3) 29...♖d2 30 ♖g1 which looks winning.

C2b2) 26...hxg5 27 ♕xg5+ ♔h8 28 ♔h2! and the threat of the rook coming to the g-file is decisive;

C3) 25...♖g3 Perhaps Pete feared this move? However after 26 ♗f4 ♖xg2+ 27 ♔xg2 ♘xe5+ 28 ♔g3 White still has powerful attacking trumps.

24...♖ad8!

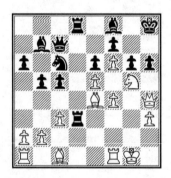

Not fearing the loss of the exchange – although there was no choice anyway!

25 ♘f3

Here 25 f5 is nothing like as strong – as the e4 bishop is en prise: 25...exf5 26 ♘xf7+ (26 e6 ♕g3+; 26 ♗xf5 gxf5 27 e6 ♕g3+) 26...♕xf7 27 ♗xh6 ♕h7; 25 ♗xd3 ♖xd3 and there is a strong possibility that the weaknesses that

are now apparent on the light squares will prove decisive.

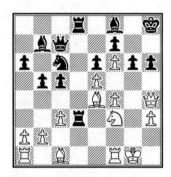

25...h5?

I wanted to prevent for ever any ideas of taking on h6, as continually watching out for this tactic was scaring me to death. A more cold-blooded calculator might have played 25...♘d4, but through sheer laziness I couldn't be bothered to calculate it – 25...h5 looked a lot simpler and there is also 25...♖d1!?

But it is in sharp positions like this that the willingness to calculate variations is most important!

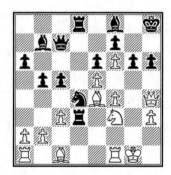

In fact 25...♘d4! would have taken advantage of White's hesitancy in the prosecution of his own attack as he has given Black time to take active measures of his own. In attacking play every move counts!

A) 26 cxd4 ♗xe4 27 f5 ♗xf3 28 ♖xf3 (also 28 ♗xh6) 28...♖8xd4! (28...♖xf3? 29 ♗xh6 ♔g8 30 ♗xf8) 29 ♕g3 ♖xf3 30 ♕xf3 ♕xe5;

B) 26 ♗xd3 ♘xf3+ 27 ♖xf3 ♗xf3 28 f5 h5 (28...♖xd3 29 ♗xh6 ♗h5 30 ♗xf8 ♕xe5 triggers a very powerful counterattack, similar to that which occurred in the game);

C) 26 ♗xb7 ♘f5! kills the white attack completely after 27 ♕f2 ♕xb7∓. It would then be very hard to switch to defensive play.

26 ♘g5

26 f5 exf5 27 ♗xd3 ♖xd3 and I'd rather be Black.

26...♔g8

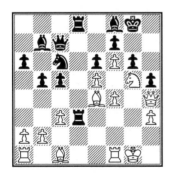

27 ♘xe6!

Pete, already in desperate time trouble, lashes out with a bold sacrifice but fails to follow it up correctly. However this is not surprising when you consider he had

barely seconds left! In fact I once asked Pete why he got into time trouble so often, as it has been a recurring problem for him and a reason why he'd thrown away so many promising positions over the years. He claimed it was because of a chronic lack of self-confidence, which may seem a strange answer from such a talented grandmaster but it shows that even strong players can suffer from real self-doubt. It may also go back to what I was saying earlier about self-handicapping, since a player who continually finds himself in time trouble may subconsciously be looking for an excuse for any defeat. 27 f5!? is a real mess. Both kings are under threat! Play might continue 27...exf5 (27...♘xe5 28 fxe6) 28 ♗xd3 ♖xd3 29 e6 fxe6 30 ♘xe6 ♕e5.

27...fxe6

28 ♗xg6?!

The calm 28 ♕g5! would have put me under all sorts of pressure – and I'm not sure I would have coped. But his flag was hanging so any result was possible. The sequel might have been 28...♖xh3 (28...♕h7 29 ♗xg6 ♕h6 30 f7+ ♔h8 31 ♕xh6+ ♗xh6 32 ♗xd3 ♖xd3 33 f5! ♘xe5 34 fxe6 and the pawns are likely to be decisive) 29 ♕xg6+ ♗g7 30 ♔g2 ♖h4 31 ♕h7+ ♔f8 32 ♗e3 ♖g4+ 33 ♔h3.

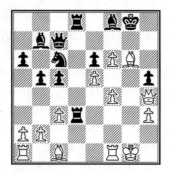

28...♘xe5!

The kind of move that's impossible to deal with when you are about to lose on time!

29 fxe5?

29 ♗xd3! ♘xd3 30 ♕g5+ ♔h7 31 f5 is another crazy mess, but White is always likely to bail out with a perpetual if he needs to.

29...♕xe5

Now White will regret pushing all those pawns after all. The black pieces flood in with an irresistible surge. As so often happens in such situations, the player who has staked everything on an all out assault is hit with a deadly counterattack when his own attack fails. "You've shot your bolt Stromberg, now it's my turn" – from *The Spy Who Loved Me*.

30 ♗xd3 ♖xd3 31 ♗f4 ♕d5

And White lost on time, but it's gone in any case. However my opponent got his revenge later in the tournament… When I innocently enquired what was needed to become a GM (at this point I was still searching for my first grandmaster norm) Pete instantly replied "Talent!"

0-1

Test yourself against the best

I am often asked the question, who is the best player I've ever played? I remember being slightly gutted when I was paired against Dreev in Gibraltar, not because Dreev himself isn't top class, but because I was very close to being paired against Shirov, who was on the next board. Playing against such a living legend would have been a great experience. That's why I play chess, to get the opportunity to cross swords with such players – it would be wonderful to test myself against the likes of Anand and Kramnik and see with my own eyes what makes them so strong. My ultimate dream would have been to play Kasparov, though now that looks highly unlikely. Probably the best player I've ever played is English grandmaster Michael Adams. He's also the strongest player that I've seen the most as we often play for the same team. Watching Mickey play is always a learning experience – at times he's almost boringly consistent, and he makes the game look easy. That's the key thing – people who compete at the highest level in any sport or activity have the ability to make the difficult look deceptively simple. I'll look at one of Mickey's games, and he's grinding down someone in a Nimzo or Ruy Lopez and think, "There he goes again, why can't I do this?" It's also a question of psychology. When Mickey gets into trouble (which isn't that often) he never panics, but just keeps playing in the same unerring way. When I get into difficulties I have a tendency to panic, to feel down on myself and get depressed with my position. David Bronstein once said to me that chess was an easy game. It may be easy for a genius like he was, but for the rest of us mere mortals it can be a real struggle. Still I think that if the potential is there then there is really no limit to how much a player can improve – chess is a game of knowledge after all, and the more work and study you put in, the more your knowledge will increase, and the stronger you will become.

See Gibraltar and die

Gibraltar 2005 was a watershed tournament for me. It was the first tournament where I played many players of a world class level – and indeed I didn't come off worse. I drew with Nakamura, Sasikiran, Aronian and Sargissian, beat Rogers and Dreev, and lost to Sutovsky. My rating performance was close to 2700. Perhaps I would put down this sudden improvement to the fact that it was my first tournament abroad for four years. For a while I had a fear of flying and had to overcome a huge mental barrier to get on that plane. It gave me a massive boost for the tournament and removed much of the fear factor. Of course the surroundings in Gibraltar were awe-inspiring as well, with the huge rock dominating the landscape. In round two I came up against the Internet whiz-kid Nakamura, who is one of the brightest exponents of speed chess in the world. Having been defending for much of the game I came close to winning when he over-stretched, which he is wont to do, and boldly sent his king up the board in an effort to avoid perpetual check. In the next round I was up against Sasikiran, a young Indian star. The fact that I managed to survive a probably losing position for much of the game, which lasted over 100 moves, gave me a huge psychological kick for the rest of the tournament. It felt like one of those key moments that you get in tournaments, where you start to feel that things might turn out alright after all. A win against a lower rated opponent and in round five I was paired against the imaginative Israeli sacrifice specialist, Emil Sutovsky.

The following game was in fact the most spectacular of the tournament.

38

D.Gormally – E.Sutovsky

Gibraltar Masters 2005

Sicilian Defence

1 e4 c5 2 ♘f3 d6 3 d4 cxd4 4 ♘xd4 ♘f6 5 ♘c3 a6 6 ♗c4

Fischer's favourite move when playing the white side of the Najdorf. This line was analysed to death in the Kasparov v Short match in 1993. White goes for a direct attack but Short was unable to prove any real theoretical advantage for White in that match. Indeed the bishop often turns out to be blunted by the pawn on e6.

6...e6 7 ♗b3 b5

7...♘bd7, intending ...♘c5, is the main alternative.

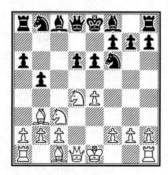

8 0-0

8 ♗g5!? is a line that is proving to be increasingly popular these days. I have often met it on the Internet playing blitz, perhaps due to the game where Ivanchuk unleashed a startling queen sacrifice against Karjakin. Everyone wants a chance to sac their queen! 8...♗e7 9 ♕f3 ♕c7 (9...♕b6! 10 0-0-0 ♘bd7 scores well for Black on the database) 10 e5 ♗b7 11 exd6 ♗xd6 12 ♕e3 ♗c5 13 0-0-0 ♘c6 14 ♕xe6+!?, with unclear play, was Ivanchuk's novelty, which no doubt he analysed with a computer, although it is extremely doubtful that the computer would suggest this sacrifice in the first place.

8...♗e7

8...b4!? has been essayed by Anand and Gormally, though not necessarily in that order :-) Unclear play erupts after 9 ♘a4 ♗d7.

9 ♕f3 ♕c7

9...♕b6!? 10 ♗e3 ♗b7 was not adopted by Kasparov in the match, though he did score an impressive win with it against Short in the rapidplay afterwards. 11 ♕g3 b4 12 ♘a4 0-0 13 f3 ♘bd7 and the black knight will head for e5.

10 ♕g3 ♘c6 11 ♘xc6 ♕xc6 12 ♖e1 ♗b7 13 a3

13 ♘d5 exd5 14 exd5 ♘xd5 15 ♕xg7 0-0-0.

13...♖d8!

This novelty was introduced by Kasparov in the above-mentioned rapidplay match against Short. The idea being that the g7 pawn is essentially poisoned.

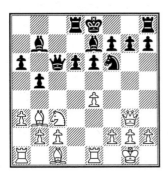

14 a4

14 ♕xg7 ♖g8 15 ♕h6 d5! 16 exd5 ♘xd5 17 ♘xd5 ♖xd5 18 ♗xd5 ♕xd5 and Black has a winning attack against the white king. Against Richard Palliser in the Hereford international 2006, I improved with 14 f3! 0-0 15 ♗h6 ♘e8 16 ♖ad1 ♔h8 17 ♗g5 ♗xg5?! (17...♗f6 was preferable) 18 ♕xg5 ♘f6 19 ♕e3 ♖d7 20 ♖d3 ♖fd8 21 ♖ed1 ♕c5 22 ♘e2 ♕xe3+ 23 ♖xe3 (Now White is better in the endgame.) 23...♔g8 24 a4! (Remarkably, this was still part of my preparation – well, remarkable for someone so lazy.) 24...b4 25 a5 ♖c8 26 ♖ed3 e5 27 ♖xd6 ♖cd8 28 ♖xd7 ♖xd7 29 ♖xd7 ♘xd7 30 ♘c1 ♘c5 31 ♗c4 and as my opponent was losing another pawn, he chose to resign. The game lasted less than 40 minutes!

14...0-0 15 axb5 axb5 16 ♗h6 ♘e8 17 ♖a7?!

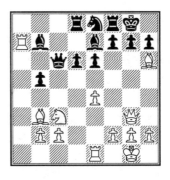

Due to a terrible lack of professionalism, I didn't have Chessbase with me in Gibraltar and so had to make the journey each day from my luxury suite on the top floor of the Caleta Hotel to the less salubrious surroundings of my friends Alan Walton and Simon Williams, two floors below, in order to get some help. Though Simon later went into an apoplectic fit when I spilled coffee all over his laptop, forcing it to short circuit, fortunately I did manage to do some preparation and was here following the game Morozevich – Rowson, 4NCL 2001.

17...♖a8!

Rowson played the seemingly less accurate 17...♔h8?! to which I had prepared Fritz's suggestion (don't worry, I don't have any novelties of my own : -)) 18 ♘d5! (Morozevich played the less critical 18 ♗e3.) 18...gxh6 (18...exd5 19 ♗xd5±) 19 ♘xe7 ♕d7 20 ♕h4 with good attacking chances for White. However all this seemed fairly irrelevant as Sutovsky played the excellent 17...♖a8! Interestingly, in the post mortem he felt 17 ♖a7 was a mistake, as it allowed him to exchange his inactive rook.

18 ♖xa8 ♗xa8

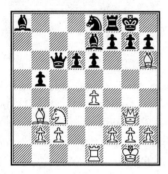

How should White continue now? What is Black intending to play?

19 ♗f4?!

This 'headless chicken' move shows a lack of consideration for my opponent's ideas. 19 ♗d2! is a much more solid prophylactic measure, intended to cover the b4 square in case of a subsequent ...b4 by Black.

19...♘f6 20 ♗h6 ♘e8 21 ♗f4?!

"Can I have a draw please, mister?"

21...b4!

"No you can't, young Oliver Gorm!"

22 ♘a2

Played with a miserable hangdog expression on my face, which was only partially enlivened by admiring the gorgeous view across the Gibraltar bay which all the players could see from the tournament hall. I now realised that the opening had gone rather wrong, and without any real targets in Black's position I was forced into grovel mode. Black has a superbly compact position – with tremendous potential – and his king is under no threat whatsoever. By contrast, White's pieces on the queenside in particular are a sorry sight – the bishop on b3 is doing nothing, and the knight on a2 is out of play.

22...♘f6 23 ♗h6

23 ♘xb4 ♕b5 24 ♘d3 ♘xe4 hangs the key e4 pawn.

23...♘h5! 24 ♕g4 ♕b5 25 f3 ♗f6! 26 ♖b1

At least I managed to spot that 26 ♗c1 ♗d4+ 27 ♔h1 ♗f2 28 ♖d1 ♕e2! is rather embarrassing. But unfortunately Black can now pick up a pawn with a clever tactic.

26...♗d4+ 27 ♔h1 ♗xb2! 28 ♗d2 ♘f6 29 ♕g3

How far can you calculate? My opponent saw all the way to checkmate here. Not bad! With his next move he explodes a seemingly innocuous looking position into a tactical melee. But Sutovsky didn't calculate everything! In fact it was impossible to do so at this stage.

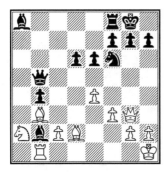

29 ♕h4!? was a real possibility but I was determined to continue my fruitless crusade against the d6 pawn.

29...d5!?

Played with feeling! Objectively, if we are all only looking for the truth in chess, then this move deserves a '?!' as now with best play Black should get into trouble. Still, for the idea that Sutovsky conceived in the game – and which with my help he was able to carry out – it deserves a '!!' 29...♗e5 30 ♕h4 ♖b8 with a comfortable edge for Black, was objectively safer but much less entertaining!

30 ♗xb4 dxe4

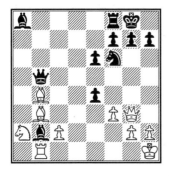

The crucial moment of the game.

31 c4?

I played this move intuitively – but this is not an intuitive position! To really compete with my opponent here I needed to get down to the nitty gritty and really calculate, but being nervous I fell into my old weakness of playing too quickly in my opponent's time trouble (Sutovsky had less than five minutes here after spending most of his time calculating 29...d5, while I had over half an hour) and almost immediately played 31 c4 after some rudimentary calculation of the main move 31 ♗xf8! This overly quick play may be a result of a desire to escape the tension of the situation and to shed the uncomfortable burden of having to look at difficult variations when under competitive pressure. It also shows a lack of awareness of a critical moment. As we can see, the main variations are mind-bogglingly complicated! 31 ♗xf8! was of course the first move I looked at, and in fact it does win! However the variations are horribly complicated – and everything hangs by a thread after 31...♘h5! 32 ♕d6 exf3.

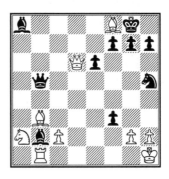

A) 33 ♕d8? ♕e8! was the move that scared me during the game, and the reason I rejected 31 ♗xf8, but of course I should have looked for alternatives! Black is winning after 33...♕e8 34 ♕d6 (34 ♕xe8 fxg2+ 35 ♔g1 ♗d4#) 34...fxg2+ 35 ♔g1 ♕b8! 36 ♖xb2 (36 ♕d2 ♕a7+ 37 ♕f2 ♗d4; 36 c3 ♘f4!) 36...♕a7+ 37 ♕c5 ♘f4! and in all variations the g2 pawn is the decisive factor;

B) 33 ♗e7! fxg2+ 34 ♔g1 g5! The only try, controlling the f4 square for the knight; (34...h6 35 ♕d8+ ♔h7 36 ♕xa8 ♗d4+ 37 ♔xg2 ♘f4+ 38 ♔h1+-) 35 ♕d8+ ♔g7

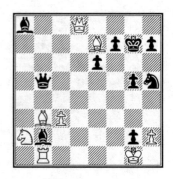

B3a) 36...♗f3 37 ♗xe6! (Of course, this crushing blow was suggested by the computer.) 37...fxe6 38 ♕f8+ ♔g6 39 ♕xf3+-;

B3b) 36...♕xb3 37 ♕f8+ ♔g6 38 ♕xa8 ♕c2 39 ♖e1;

B3c) 36...♗e4! is a good try. 37 ♕d4+ (37 ♖e1 ♕xb3) 37...f6 38 ♕xe4 ♕xb3 39 ♕a8! (39 ♘b4 ♘f4 40 ♗d6 e5! reinforcing the knight 41 ♗c5 ♕xc3 42 ♗e3 ♕xe3+ 43 ♕xe3 ♗d4 44 ♘c2 ♗xe3+ 45 ♘xe3 h5 46 ♘xg2 is about the best that Black can manage, with a resulting peculiar ending that will still take some winning – if indeed it is even winning) 39...♕c2 40 ♕f8+ ♔g6 41 ♕e8+ ♔f5 (41...♔h6 42 ♗f8+ ♘g7 43 ♖e1 ♗xc3 44 ♘xc3 ♕xc3 45 ♕xe6) 42 ♕b5+ e5 43 ♕xb2 and Black's attack has run out of steam;

B1) 36 ♗f8+ ♔g6;

B2) 36 ♕xa8 ♘f4 (36...♗d4+ 37 ♔xg2 ♕e2+ 38 ♔h1 ♘g3+ 39 hxg3 ♕h5+ is a perpetual) 37 ♕f8+ ♔g6 is winning for Black after 38 ♕g8+ ♗g7 39 c4 ♕f5!;

B3) 36 c3!

The key move, immolating the bishop on b2, which was perpetually threatening to deliver a crushing check on d4. Now Black has four candidate moves but it would seem that White's counterattack is decisive in each case:

B3d) 36...♘f4 is the critical test, but still insufficient: 37 ♕f8+ ♔g6 38 ♗c2+ ♔h5 (38...f5 39 ♕f6+ ♔h5 40 ♕xg5 mate) 39 ♗d1+! (The bishop tiptoes the black king into a mating net.) 39...♘e2+ (39...g4 40 ♕xf7+ leads to mate as does

39...♔h4 40 ♕h6+ ♘h5 41 ♕xh5 mate) 40 ♗xe2+ ♕xe2 41 ♕xa8.

31...♕f5!

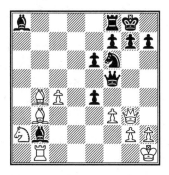

32 ♗xf8?

This final mistake seals my fate but as I had still failed to see what was coming, I continued blithely on my merry way. Necessary was 32 f4! which with best play seems to result in an unclear endgame: 32...♘h5 33 ♕e3 ♕f6 (33...♖d8!? 34 ♖xb2 ♘xf4 leads to a complete mess – Black is a piece down but this is more than compensated by the menacing stance of his remaining forces) 34 ♗xf8 ♗d4 35 ♗e7 ♗xe3 36 ♗xf6 ♘xf6 37 ♖d1 ♗c6 38 ♘b4 ♗d7 39 g3 ♔f8∞.

32...♘h5!

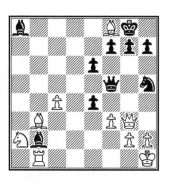

33 ♕g4

Unfortunately by this stage I had finally woken up and realised what was coming and that my 'bail out' option 33 ♕b8 didn't work either: 33...♘g3+! 34 ♕xg3 (34 hxg3 leads to forced mate after 34...♕h5+ 35 ♔g1 ♗d4+ 36 ♔f1 ♕h1+ 37 ♔e2 ♕xg2+ 38 ♔d1 ♕f1+ 39 ♔d2 e3+ 40 ♔c2 ♕e2+ 41 ♔c1 ♕d2 mate) 34...exf3 and White will have to give up his queen to prevent mate.

33...exf3!

The coup de grace!

34 ♕xf5 fxg2+ 35 ♔g1 ♗d4+ 36 ♕f2

36...♘f4!

I resigned, as White will have to give back a queen and a rook to prevent mate; for example, 37 h4 ♘e2+ 38 ♔h2 ♗xf2 after which he is left with a hopeless endgame, three pawns down. A staggering conception by Sutovsky, which was rendered even more impressive to my eyes by the fact that he claimed to have seen the final position when he played 29...d5. In fact it scared me that he had seen so much further into the position than I had, and made me realise what playing at the highest level was all about. Besides, if a 2650 could calculate this well, what could a Kasparov do?! In fact this was a game that I was just glad to be a part of, and further lustre was added when in a *New In Chess Magazine* interview, Vishy Anand was asked what was the best game of chess he had ever seen... Amazingly he replied "Gormally – Sutovsky was a lot of fun" !

0-1

After losing to Sutovsky I managed to bounce back at once with a sacrificial attack against Gary Quillan. It seemed a lot easier to play against players of a lower level – indeed I think I won pretty much every game I played against lower rated players than myself around about this period. Playing 2600+ players was raising my game, forcing me to think at their level – at times it was exhausting, but going down a level seemed so much easier by comparison. In round 7 I was paired against the Australian grandmaster Ian Rogers. I was able to score a somewhat fortuitous win when he blundered horribly in a probably drawn endgame. What did I learn against Sutovsky? It taught me that I wasn't taking enough time in critical situations, and against

players of this level, you can't simply play moves on intuition in complicated positions and expect to get away with it. Because they calculate so well, you have to try and compete with them in this same area. Against Dreev I was determined that I wouldn't make the same mistake. I said to myself before the game – don't beat yourself, make him beat you. So when the game heated up, when it became critical, and he was short of time – I kept reminding myself to sit on my hands, to calculate the position with a degree of discipline, not just play the first move that comes into my head because I feel anxious...

39

D.Gormally – A.Dreev

Gibraltar Masters 2005

Semi-Slav Defence

1 d4 d5 2 c4 c6 3 ♘f3 ♘f6 4 ♘c3 e6 5 ♗g5 h6 6 ♗h4

Dreev is an expert in this variation, but I realised I had no choice but to face him head on. My only real chance was to mix it up, and if I chickened out with the dull (well, relatively speaking) 6 ♗xf6 ♛xf6 he'd surely grind me down in the long run with his superior technique.

6...dxc4 7 e4 g5 8 ♗g3 b5

The *tabiya* of one of the hottest variations in modern day theory, debated by most of the top grandmasters in the world, including Anand, Kramnik, Topalov and Carlsen, to name but a few. Black is a pawn to the good but White always has good compensation due to his strong centre and the fact that Black has weakened his kingside.

9 ♗e2

I've tried 9 e5!? a few times; it's an interesting alternative to the much more heavily analysed main line. Then 9...♘d5 (9...♘h5!?) 10 ♘d2! ♘d7 11 ♗e2 ♗b7 12 0-0 ♕b6 13 a4 a6 14 ♘de4 c5?! 15 ♘xd5 ♗xd5 16 ♘c3! cxd4 17 ♘xd5 exd5 18 axb5, with advantage to White, is one line for Black to be wary of.

9...♗b7 10 h4 g4 11 ♘e5 h5

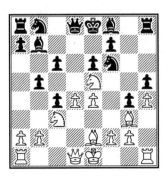

12 0-0

12 f3!? was Kasparov's choice when he played Dreev in the Russian championship in 2004; Dreev found an interesting sacrifice of a rook after 12...♘bd7 (12...gxf3? led to a quick finish in D.Gormally – N.McDonald, Hampstead 1998: 13 ♗xf3 c5 14 0-0 ♕xd4+ 15 ♕xd4 cxd4 16 ♘xb5 ♘a6 17 ♘xc4 ♖g8 18 ♗e5 ♘d7 19 ♗xd4 ♗c6 20 ♘xa7) 13 fxg4 hxg4 14 0-0 ♘xe5 15 ♗xe5 ♘d7!? 16 ♗xh8 ♕xh4 17 ♗xg4 (Forced, otherwise ...g3 is coming.) 17...♕xh8 and the game was relatively unclear, though Kasparov went on to grind Dreev down in a study-like endgame. Knowing that Dreev was happy to take on probably the greatest opening expert of all time of course made me rather nervous; on the other hand I had a positive experience of this opening and, as the old cliche goes, 'if it ain't broke why fix it?' Besides this variation favours tactical players and sharp calculators and that's always been the strong part of my game. Once more into the breach dear friends!

12...♘bd7 13 ♕c2 ♘xe5 14 ♗xe5

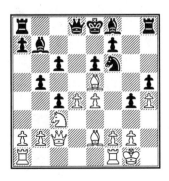

14...♗h6!?

I was taken aback when he confidently played this novelty. But the idea is to avoid the almost forced draw that results after the main move 14...♗g7 15 ♖ad1 0-0 16 f3 (16 ♗g3 is an attempt to keep the game going, when after 16...♘d7 17 f3 c5 18 dxc5 ♕e7 things are rather unclear) 16...♘h7!? 17 ♗xg7 ♔xg7 18 fxg4 ♕xh4 19 gxh5 ♘g5 20 ♕d2 and Black has practically nothing better than 20...♘h3+ which forces a draw by perpetual check after 21 gxh3 ♕g3+.

15 b3!?

Having made a frantic study of this line in the Williams/Walton boudoir that very morning, I realised that in a number of variations it was useful to play this move to undermine the imposing cluster of black queenside pawns which control some useful squares. Besides, any plan with f3 seemed less useful now that he could just slip in ...♗e3 with check.

15...cxb3 16 axb3 0-0 17 ♗d3 ♖e8 18 ♘e2!?

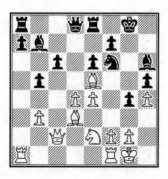

I remember at the time being quite proud of this re-organisation of my pieces. Rowson would be quite impressed ("Talking to your pieces again, Danny, I've always wondered about you."). The knight controls some useful squares on the kingside. But now I'm not quite so sure. What exactly is White's threat? ♘g3 won't do because of the reply ... ♘d7. When you win a game it's all too easy to get carried away by your joy with the result that you take an uncritical view of your own play. But that's a mistake. You can learn just as much from looking for improvements in the games you win as much as you can in your losses. Now Dreev sank into a fairly long think and managed to find a fairly logical continuation, though I'm not sure it was the best.

18...♘d7!?

Possible was 18...♕e7!? (18...g3? 19 ♗xg3) as it may be useful to have ...♘g4 in reserve in case of f3, ...gxf3 and ♖xf3. And if 19 f3 gxf3 20 gxf3 ♗e3+ 21 ♔h1 ♘d7 22 ♗g3 e5! the white monarch is arguably even more exposed than the black one.

19 ♗g3 e5!

Grabbing some much needed dark squares in the centre.

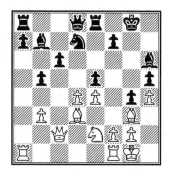

20 f3

Perhaps this is premature and 20 ♖ad1! was more to the point. Improve your position before taking active measures! Then, for example, 20...♕b6 (also there is 20...♕e7 or 20...♕f6 21 f4 gxf3 22 ♖xf3 ♕g6 23 dxe5 ♖e7) 21 ♔h2 (21 f3 ♗e3+) 21...♖ad8 22 f3 exd4 23 fxg4 hxg4 24 ♖f5 c5 25 ♖df1 ♖e7 26 ♘f4 ♘e5 27 ♘h5 ♘xd3 28 ♘f6+ and White develops a dangerous initiative against the exposed black king.

20 ♔h2 is met by exd4 21 f3 ♘e5!

20...♗e3+! 21 ♔h2

As soon as I played this move my heart sank. I thought "I've just blundered, I should have put the king on h1, now he can just play ...♗f4 and I can't take, so I must be lost". But then I realised it wasn't so simple: 21 ♔h1 exd4 22 fxg4.

21...exd4

21...♗f4!? was indeed what I feared: but then 22 ♗xf4 ♕xh4+ 23 ♔g1 exf4 24 fxg4! and 24...hxg4 is met by 25 ♖xf4 – so it turns out that 21 ♔h2 wasn't a blunder after all.

22 fxg4

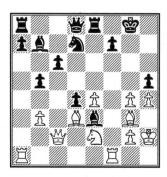

Now what should Black play?

22...♘e5!

This allows White to close up the kingside, after which – for the time being at least – only the black king is really vulnerable. More dynamic but by no means better was 22...hxg4!?

A) The natural looking 23 ♘f4 leads to a similar mess: 23...♘e5 (23...♕e7 24 ♘h5) 24 ♘h5 ♖e6 25 ♖f5 ♘xd3 26 ♕xd3 c5 27 ♕e2!;

B) 23 ♖f5 ♖e5! Of course I completely missed this idea during the game – but sometimes ignorance really is bliss because it would have scared me to death! Nevertheless there are still good attacking chances after 24 ♖af1 ♖xf5 25 ♖xf5 and I would undoubtedly prefer to be White here. My king is relatively safe (so long as I don't play ♗d6) compared to its counterpart and White has easy-to-find attacking moves – everything is forced – ♘f4, followed by ♕e2, e5 etc.

If Black replies 25...♕e7 then not 26 e5?! ♔g7! 27 ♘f4 ♖h8 (27...♗xf4) 28 ♘h5+ ♔f8 29 ♕d1 ♘c5 30 ♕xg4 ♖g8 31 ♕d1 ♗c8, but 26 ♘f4! ♗xf4 27 ♖xf4 ♘e5 28 ♖f5 ♘xd3 29 ♕xd3±

23 g5!

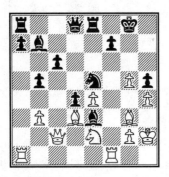

Now I felt in my bones that at least I wasn't going to lose this game. White's kingside play is very obvious – whereas for Black the correct defence is far less clear.

23...♘xd3

After 23...♕d7 24 ♗xe5 ♖xe5 comes 25 g3!? with the simple plan of doubling rooks on the f-file, perhaps combined with ♘f4 etc.

24 ♕xd3

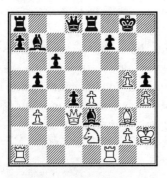

24...c5!?

Now White is able to exchange the irritating bishop on e3, and what's more – to create a middlegame attack with opposite coloured bishops!

24...♕d7?! with the idea of posting the queen on g4 (we have already discussed how having the queen in an advanced position can be a source of irritation for the attacking player) but in this case White is too well co-ordinated: 25 ♖f3! (25 ♗f4? ♕g4; 25 ♘f4) 25...♖e7 (25...♕g4 26 ♘xd4 ♗xd4 27 ♕xd4±) 26 ♗f4! (26 ♘f4 ♕g4!) 26...c5 27 ♘g3 ♕g4 (27...c4 28 bxc4 bxc4 29 ♕xc4 ♕g4 30 ♗xe3 dxe3 31 ♘f5 and the knight thrust leaves Black in trouble) 28 ♗xe3 dxe3 29 ♘f5!

25 ♘f4! ♗xe4

25...c4 26 bxc4 ♗xe4 27 ♕b3 bxc4 28 ♕xc4.

26 ♕xb5 ♗xf4 27 ♖xf4 ♕d5

"Doesn't that drop the pawn on a7?"

28 ♖xa7

28...♗f5?

Dreev played this instantly so I was pretty sure that he had overlooked the capture on a7. Grandmasters often reply quickly in such situations so as not to give the impression that they have blundered. However in this case Dreev's ego got the better of him! It would have been better to steer the game towards a draw: 28...♖eb8! (28...♗g6 29 ♖d7) 29 ♖xa8 ♖xa8 30 ♖f6 d3 31 ♖d6 ♕f5 32 ♖f6 ♕d5 and neither player can realistically avoid the repetition of moves.

29 b4

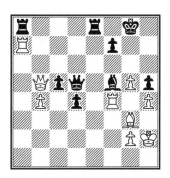

29...♖ac8

After this White's initiative reaches unmanageable proportions, but also after 29...d3 White should be technically winning: 30 ♖xa8 ♖xa8 31 ♕xc5 ♕xc5 32 bxc5 ♖d8 (32...♗d7 33 ♖d4 ♗b5±) 33 ♖xf5! (33 ♗e1 ♗e6 34 ♗d2 ♖c8 35 ♗e3 ♖d8 36 ♖f2±) 33...d2 34 ♖f1 d1=♕ 35 ♖xd1 ♖xd1 36 c6 ♖c1 37 c7 ♖c4 (37...♔f8 38 ♗f4 ♖c4 39 g4 hxg4 40 ♔g3 ♔e7 41 h5 ♔d7 42 h6+-)

38 ♗f4 ♔f8 39 g4 hxg4 40 ♔g3 f6 41 g6 f5 42 h5 and the pawns are overwhelming.

30 ♕f1!

30...♗g6?!

Not surprisingly, 30...♖e5! is a cold-blooded computer-generated defence; but Dreev was already very short of time and defending this precarious position would have been difficult enough even under normal circumstances.

A) 31 ♖f3 is still quite messy: 31...cxb4!? (31...d3 32 ♗xe5 ♕xe5+ 33 g3 d2 34 ♖xf5 d1=♕ 35 ♕xd1 ♕xf5 36 bxc5 ♕f2+ 37 ♔h3) 32 ♗xe5 ♕xe5+;

B) However 31 ♖a5 should, with accurate play, give White a big advantage as Black's dark squares are too weak. 31...♗g6 (31...d3!? 32 ♖f2 ♗g4 33 ♗xe5 ♕xe5+ 34 g3)

B1) 32 bxc5 ♖xc5 33 ♖xd4 (33 ♖a4 ♖f5 34 ♖xf5 ♕xf5) 33...♖xa5 (33...♕xd4 34 ♖a8+) 34 ♖xd5 ♖exd5 35 ♕f6 ♖a4 and Black is defending;

B2) 32 ♖f6! d3 (32...♖ee8 33 ♖d6) 33 ♖xc5 ♖xc5 34 bxc5 d2 35 ♕d1 ♗c2 36 ♕xc2 d1=♕ 37 ♕xd1 ♕xd1 38 ♗xe5 leads to an easy technical win for White as the c-pawn can't be stopped in the long run.

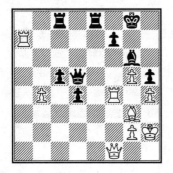

31 ♖f6!

Creating the crushing threat of ♖xf6 followed by ♕f6. I was sure I was going to win now as he was not only looking increasingly nervous but was also very close to losing on time. My only concern was holding my crumbling nerves together.

31...♖c6

31...♖a8 32 ♖xa8 ♖xa8 33 ♖d6 ♕f5 34 ♕xf5 ♗xf5 35 bxc5 should be a technical win.

32 ♕b5!

Back again!

32...♖ec8?

A final blunder but his position is more than likely gone anyway. If 32...♖ce6 33 ♖d7 ♗d3 34 ♕a4+–

33 ♕b7!

Ouch! ♖xg6 is again a threat.

33...♕e4 34 ♖xf7

…and he resigned, but I struggled to sign the score sheets because I was shaking so much!

1-0

A monumental victory, as not only did I beat my first 2700+ player at my first attempt, but also at long last got the grandmaster title. I had scored a 10 round grandmaster norm with two rounds to spare, which made me realise that I should have gained the title much sooner than I did. However a history of missing grandmaster norms by half a point held back my progress. After this breakthrough, my rating went from strength to strength, and within a year I had gained about 100 points. But really this tournament was a great learning experience for me. It comes back to the point that only by playing against, and spending time with stronger players than yourself, can a player really improve. Books and computer programs cannot substitute for the actual skills you can pick up from the thoughts of grandmasters in post mortems, for example. Reading an article by someone like Kramnik isn't the same as hearing it from him in real life. If I was a billionaire I might hire Kasparov for coaching sessions, but my advice would be – spend as much time as you can in the company of stronger players. Stronger players think in a different way, but if you have the raw ability you can soon bring yourself to think on their level. Before this tournament I always had a fear of elite players, but then I realised that all they could do was make one move at a time, and if you kept your discipline, you could score points against them.

Getting the rhythm right

Finding the right tempo at which to play is very important. Play too quickly and you are likely to overlook many things. Play too slowly and you will continually run into time trouble. Only by accumulating a good wealth of experience will you be more easily able to recognise the situations where it is important to take your time, and when it is important to move more quickly. That is why the Sutovsky game was so important to me – it gave me an idea of the right rhythm at which to play against Dreev – and not to play too quickly

in his time trouble. When you are in great form, then the right playing tempo comes easily – but when you are not playing so well it's important not to panic, not to change too radically. I tend to play quite quickly anyway, but when I've suffered a crisis of confidence I've been inclined almost to give up and play incredibly quickly – and leave myself wide open for an accident waiting to happen. The best players in the world tend to play pretty quickly – Anand being a good example. I remember the former world junior champion Tal Shaked being asked a very pertinent question right after his baptism of fire in the Tilburg super-tournament, where he was crushed by the likes of Kasparov. "What is the major difference between players of that class and grandmasters of a lower level?" He replied that they simply play much quicker – they see the right move almost immediately, and of course calculate much faster. When playing opponents who play very quickly it's important not to panic. For example, I had (or rather have) a bad record against international master Jack Rudd, who has a reputation for playing incredibly quickly – although moving at such a breakneck speed means that he inevitably makes a lot of inaccuracies. It's very hard to get into the right rhythm against someone that fast – I am used to thinking in my opponent's time but against Jack that's impossible. So, with my huge ego, I often get drawn into playing at his speed – and with disastrous results. Still, sometimes you can exploit this kind of situation to your own advantage. A few years back I played Sasikiran and had noticed that he generally intimidated his opponents by playing very quickly – so I decided to play even quicker. This clearly made him very uncomfortable, knocked him out of his natural playing rhythm and I won quite easily.

Preparing for tournaments

I think the correct approach is to try to do as much preparation for a tournament beforehand, as preparing during a tournament can be tiring. Working 2-3 hours before the game on Chessbase or Fritz can be tiring. Moreover, staring at a computer screen for hours at a time not only saps your energy and is likely to give you a headache, it is also likely to kill your appetite for the game. Nowadays there tend not to be many rest days during a tournament – so it is important to conserve as much energy as possible. On the other hand if you come into a tournament cold, without having looked at any chess, you might find that it takes a while to shake off the rust and get into the right rhythm. You might also experience extreme difficulty in calculating complicated variations.

So, prior to the game, say 2 hours beforehand, I recommend that you try to switch off from chess completely – go for a walk, as doing some exercise will help to relieve the build up of nervous tension and take your mind off the forthcoming game. Then, during play, try to store up energy by eating at regular intervals. I've lost track of the number of games that I've thrown away through being too tired and hungry at the board. This becomes particularly important after the time control, where your energy levels are dropping and you are more prone to blunders. Also drinking alcohol during a tournament is a very bad idea – not only will this dull your senses but it has a negative accumulative effect. I find that when I've been drinking (sometimes quite heavily) I'm completely exhausted and lethargic by the end of the tournament. You may or may not be a professional, but you surely do want to give of your best – so there's no excuse not to adopt a correct approach.

Blundersville

The following game is a good example of what happens if you lose discipline in the opponent's time trouble. Having achieved a winning position, I nearly threw it all away with a stupid blunder.

40

D.Gormally – I.Gourlay

Hereford International 2006

28 ♖d5??

My opponent had only 20 seconds left and so, instead of proceeding 28 ♗xf5, I figured "just play any move and he'll resign". But not this one!! True he now used up most of his remaining seconds and not seeing anything, resigned. But, amongst other moves, he could have won comfortably with the stunning yet simple…**28…♖xe4!!** A stinging blow! How red my face would have become then. **29 ♕xe4 ♖e8!** and the back rank is the decisive factor after **30 ♕b1** as Black has the killing **30…♘h4!!** when White has no choice but to resign.

This is a good example of a blunder caused by being too relaxed and thinking that it's all too easy and then losing concentration. In Rowson's excellent book *The Seven Deadly Chess Sins*, he talks about the danger of ego. Certainly in this game I was guilty of allowing my ego to take over, but I would also like to introduce another similar concept, 'denial.' – in the sense that sometimes we are in denial of our opponent's counterplay … that we don't look for his chances … that we don't look for his ideas. This is a common problem because it's all too easy to get stuck in the rut of only looking at our own ideas and plans. We don't look for candidate moves like 28…♖xe4, because we simply don't want to admit that the game might not yet be over. In my mind I had already chalked up the point – a huge mistake. In the following game between two super-grandmasters, Black, by contrast, blunders when under extreme pressure.

41

E.Bacrot – P.Leko

Elista 2008

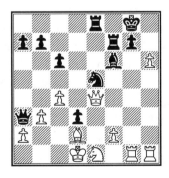

30…♕xa2??

What candidate move for his opponent did Leko miss when making this losing blunder? Also 30…♖d7 31 hxg7 ♖xg7 32 ♕h7+

♔f7 33 ♖xg7+ ♗xg7 34 ♖g1 ♖g8
loses a large amount of material after
35 ♕f5+.

31 ♕h7+!!

Of course. Perhaps we can
speculate why Leko overlooked this
move – perhaps because he was
under pressure here? After all, most
mistakes occur in a similar scenario
to this one, i.e. when a player is
under extreme pressure and the
game is very complicated. But of
course if White doesn't have ♕h7
then he has nothing! Let me think of
an answer – that in fact Leko saw
31 ♕h7 – but gambled that he was
lost in any case – and decided to risk
that Bacrot might not see it. By the
way, 31 hxg7 would have lost on the
spot – 31...♕b1+ 32 ♗c1 ♕xb3+
33 ♔d2 ♘xc4+ 34 ♕xc4 ♖e2 mate.

1-0

The end of the story

We've come to the end of the
book. I hope the reader has enjoyed
this journey. Anyway I'd like to
leave you with another good
example of strange candidate moves
– and how looking for them can
expand your chess imagination and
improve your calculating ability.

In the next position, so far, nothing
peculiar, just another boring Slav.
But when I put the position on Fritz
after the game, I found it came up
with a remarkable suggestion…

42

D.Gormally – S.Collins

Le Touquet 2008

15...♖g8!!

Could any human identify this as a
candidate move?! I couldn't!! The
idea, as with most computers, has a
tactical basis – if White takes on f6,
the black rook is in some variations
lined up against the g2 pawn. In the
game he played the much less
imaginative 15...♘xd5 16 ♗xd5
♖c8 and I had slight pressure with
little risk – although the game ended
in a draw anyway.

16 ♘xf6+ 16 ♗d2 ♗e6! 17 ♘xf6+
gxf6. **16...gxf6 17 h3** 17 ♖g1??
♗xf3+ **17...♗e6!** Black's pawn
structure won't be shattered for
long… **18 ♗xe6 fxe6**

And Black is more than okay. A
good example of how computers
play concrete moves – they are
changing the way that we think
because all the old rules are being
torn up.